the
AMERICAN
JURISPRUDENCE
reader

Edited by

THOMAS A. COWAN

Professor of Law
Rutgers, The State University of New Jersey

DOCKET SERIES
Volume 8

Oceana Publications
New York City
1956

Library of Congress Catalog Card Number: 56-12585

Printed in the U. S. A.

TABLE OF CONTENTS

THIS BOOK IS AFFECTIONATELY DEDICATED TO
LEHAN KENT TUNKS

PREFACE

Jurisprudence is the sum total of organized reflections on the nature of law and its relation to other learned disciplines. A Jurisprudence Reader should therefore aim to give at least a bird's-eye view of this vast territory. This volume does not deal with the history of Jurisprudence. It attempts to show a cross-section of the work presently being done in Jurisprudence by American scholars.

It may come as a surprise to many readers both in America and abroad that science and philosophy in their relation of law are receiving such widespread attention from American students of law. The phenomenon is of recent origin. Fifty years ago, a survey of Jurisprudence would have been much more restricted to European sources. But the tide has turned strongly. Jurisprudence in America has come of age.

It is my hope that the present collection of jurisprudential materials will appeal to a wide reading public: laymen and lawyers in this country and elsewhere. I should like to think that it may serve as a do-it-yourself kit for students and young instructors in philosophy and in political and social theory, and for practitioners of the law who desire to engage in theory-building in the higher reaches of their craft. In brief, it should be an aid to all those who are interested in the law as an intellectual pursuit.

Since this Reader is to serve as an introduction to the subject of Jurisprudence, I have tried to keep the materials as brief and the presentation as elementary as the subject will permit. For convenience in reading, the footnotes have been re-numbered and collected at the end of each section. I hope that an Advanced American Reader on Jurisprudence will follow this one some time in the near future.

It will be noted that no excerpt from the work of Justice Oliver Wendell Holmes, Jr., is contained in this book. Another volume of the Docket Series is wholly devoted to this subject.

I desire to take this opportunity to thank my colleague Vincent E. Fiordalisi, Librarian and Professor of Law at Rutgers University for his interest and aid in the preparation of this work. I should like also to thank Mrs. Florence Wotherspoon and Mr. Richard A. Maguire for their painstaking efforts in seeing this volume through the press.

THOMAS A. COWAN

Rutgers University School of Law
    Newark, New Jersey

ACKNOWLEDGMENTS

The editor expresses appreciation to the following authors, publishers and periodicals for granting special permission to reprint passages from their books and articles. Specific acknowledgment is made where the passage appears in this Reader.

The Columbia Law Review; The Estate of Morris R. Cohen; Mrs. Felix S. Cohen; The Julius Rosenthal Foundation of Northwestern University and Boston Law Book Company; The Bobbs-Merrill Company, Inc.; The New York University Press; Foundation Press; Edwin W. Patterson; Harvard University Press; Yale University Press; Fallon Book Company; Fordham Law Review; Ohio State Law Journal; The Oxford University Press, Inc.; University of Wisconsin Press; Harvard Law Review; University of North Carolina Press; Coward-McCann, Inc.; Columbia University Press; Journal of Legal Education and Rutgers Law Review.

INTRODUCTION

Law is a craft. Its craftsmen have selected out and reserved to themselves over the millenia an area of human behavior. While the boundaries of this area are not sharply defined and while what goes on inside of it is subject to much dispute, yet its existence can be sensed even by a small child.

Those who study the nature of this area of human behavior are engaged in the study of Jurisprudence. They may work inside the law itself, studying the relation of its parts to one another, and the relation of the parts to the whole. Or they may be interested primarily in the interactions of law and the other learned disciplines.

Those who work within the structure of the law itself, examining it bit by bit, section by section, or in the overall, are engaged in what is called *analytical jurisprudence*. This is an English and American specialty and its *development* calls for formal training in law. Of course one does not have to be learned in the Common Law or in any other system of law to benefit greatly from the *results* of the labors of the analytical jurists.

Outside of law lies the rest of the vast domain of human learning. Many of its disciplines are closely related to law, have always exerted pressure on it and occasionally have tried to swallow it up. One such is *philosophy*. Philosophy purports to rationalize the whole sum of human experience. It concerns itself with general theories of human thought and action. It studies the *practice of theory* and on this score has much to say of interest to law since law is a highly theoretical practice. But more important, philosophy also studies the *theory of practice*: ethics or morality or action that is appropriate to the human species. This last is so critical for law that there have been periods in human history when morality (or its next door neighbor, religion) has treatened to engulf law and wash it away from its ancient moorings.

It is customary in this country to call all attempts

to bring the light of philosophy and particularly that of ethics or morality to the workings of the law *philosophical jurisprudence*. Since in the study of law it is proper to call in question the rightness or wrongness, goodness or badness, of every legal disposition we could say that the whole of law is a study in philosophical jurisprudence: This is true, of course. But experience has shown that philosophical inspiration for law works in the main from the outside and not from within the body of the law. The philosophers, not the lawyers, have developed philosophical jurisprudence. Indeed from the time of the ancient Greek philosophers to the beginning of the last century, every major philosophical thinker has taken law as one of the most important sectors of human behavior to be philosophized about. In the last century or so, philosophy has largely abandoned law to its own devices. This is to be regretted. Nevertheless, the balance seems at present to be slowly righting itself. Perhaps the importance of the philosophical investigation of the nature of justice will once again become apparent to the students of philosophy, and law, rather than physical science, may again step to the forefront of philosophical concern.

Another cluster of disciplines akin to law is known under the collective name of *science*. All sciences are related to law since law is a body of knowledge. In addition, the fruits of all the sciences are of consequence to law. How to fit means to ends is the work of science and how law may most efficiently achieve its ends is therefore a scientific problem. The subject matter of law is human behavior and the behavioral sciences are law's nearest neighbors. History, anthropology, ethnology, psychology, social psychology and sociology beckon to us whenever we stray beyond the bounds of the law.

There is an activity, now almost quiescent, known as *historical jurisprudence*. Its practitioners were mainly Europeans and its chief influence was felt by us in the nineteenth century. Its interest of course was the relation of history and law. We shall not include in this Reader any contribution from this school, since contemporary English and American scholars have almost entirely neglected it.

The other disciplines, the social sciences, are of lively contemporary interest to the law. In this country, largely due to the influence of the greatest living jurist, Roscoe Pound, this study is known as *sociological jurisprudence.*

The present Reader will therefore be divided into three parts: philosophical, analytical, and sociological jurisprudence. This comports with the usual practice in the study of jurisprudence in this country.

Part I

PHILOSOPHICAL JURISPRUDENCE

Philosophical Jurisprudence is nothing other than the application of philosophical ideas to the study of law. Hence it is at once philosophy and law. From the earliest Greek times until comparatively recently, these two subjects were very closely related in the minds of both philosophers and lawyers. For example, the life-work of Plato culminates in two great treatises on the law: the famous dialogues known as The Republic and The Laws.

Among common law lawyers an anti-metaphysical bias ruptured this traditional connection, so that for a century and a half (roughly from about 1750 to 1900) the English and American lawyers and philosophers went their separate ways. The past fifty years have witnessed a reversal of the trend first in this country and then in England. Led by Roscoe Pound, American jurists began to import into this country continental ideas concerning the nature of law. This movement progressed very rapidly and soon gave rise to a body of native literature on the subject of the philosophy of law. In the following section we shall deal mainly with the work of these American legal philosophers.

If we consider for a moment the ancient division of the field of philosophy into science, morality and art, we find philosophical jurisprudence unevenly interested in the three. Science (or theories of knowledge) are of some concern to law and morality is of overwhelming importance. The function of art in law or legal aesthetics is virtually unknown. Following this heavy preponderance of interest in morality, it is often said that philosophical jurisprudence concentrates on the ideal element in law, the law as it *ought to be* rather than as it is. This means that philosophical jurisprudence is concerned very little with the sanctions that law imposes and very much with the moral foundations of legal rules and doctrines. The nature of justice is its abiding concern, and the ways in which this conception takes concrete form in the living law is its constant study.

To understand philosophical jurisprudence it is necessary to have some acquaintance with the major philosophical systems, all of which are represented in some degree or other in the various schools of jurisprudence. A knowledge of law is not a requisite, as is the case for anything more than a very general understanding of analytical jurisprudence.

A. Introductory

Thomas A. Cowan, A Report on the Status of Philosophy of Law in the United States, 50 Columbia Law Review pp. 1086-1100 (1950); reprinted by permission of the Columbia Law Review.

I. *Introduction**

The most striking observation which occurs to one reporting on recent trends in philosophy of law in the United States is that at first the subject matter of the report seems not to exist. Since the decline of natural law, no received philosophical tradition appears to have guided and influenced legal thinkers in the United States in the way in which, for example, scholasticism, Kantian idealism, positivism, logical positivism and existentialism have provided philosophical orientation for Latin-American legal philosophers, as well as for their European prototypes.

This state of affairs reflects the tenuousness of the connection between the study of general philosophy and the study of law in this country. Theorists trained in both disciplines are few. In the main, those students of jurisprudence who do direct serious attention to philosophical speculation generally come to it only after their legal training is well under way. In the American universities, the faculties of philosophy and law are as far apart as are the faculties of medicine and law.

The situation has moved a prominent American legal theorist, Professor Jerome Hall, to call for a closer integration of legal and philosophical studies to the end that the members of the legal and the philosophical communities might enrich each other's work by cooperative enterprise. That there is great interest in such possibilities was dramatically evidenced at the annual meeting of law school teachers held three years ago, where a conference on the subject of legal philosophy and the teaching of jurisprudence originally scheduled for a small room had to adjourn to a large auditorium because of an extremely heavy attendance. But the great crowd of law teachers who came to hear something suggestive of

* This Article was prepared for the Third International Congress of Comparative Law, held in London, July 31 to August 5, 1950. The author desires to acknowledge with gratitude the courtesy and assistance given him by the Director and Staff of the Legal Research Library of the University of Michigan in the preparation of this report. (Minor changes have been made in this article.)

the way philosophy might illumine the teaching of law listened silently to the different speakers and then quietly melted away. Apparently they felt that in some mysterious way philosophy is important for law but that, since the mystery had so successfully been preserved, humble teachers of law must simply wait until its secrets should be disclosed.

The difficulty which American legal and philosophical thinkers experience when they do attempt to effect rapport is illustrated in a strikingly dramatic way in Professor Hessel E. Yntema's recent article, *Jurisprudence and Metaphysics—A Triangular Correspondence*.[1] The article sets forth a three-way correspondence between two students of jurisprudence and a professional philosopher. The argument concerns the philosophical implications of the movement known as legal realism. A major difficulty, never resolved, besets the correspondents: inability to agree upon the meaning of terms in the philosophical vocabulary. This results not from the lawyer's intransigence, but because the philosophical vocabulary is still in a state of flux among its professional users. The outcome of the correspondence is a steady resolution on the part of the legal theorist that jurisprudence must attend its concerns free from the trammels of metaphysics. The metaphysician concludes that while jurisprudence may develop its theories in isolation from metaphysics, it must be prepared to submit its conclusions to metaphysics for approval or disapproval. Thus the "queen of the sciences" accords colonial status to jurisprudence, with a large measure of autonomy in local affairs but subject to disallowance of its laws if not in accord with imperial policy.

II. *Philosophy in the United States*

Any discussion of the status of legal philosophy in the United States must first take account of the status of general philosophy.[2] In this country, more than anywhere else in the world, philosophical speculation appears still to be an individual enterprise. Each professional philosopher seems charged with the obligation to prepare an *apologia pro sua vita* in the form of a distinctive philosophical position. Each is sensitive to the charge that he subscribes to this or that philosophical "ism." To the foreigner, American philosophers, apparently spurning all philosophical traditions, seem to be characterizable under only one all-inclusive "ism," namely, anarchism.

For the past twenty-five years, the chief type of concerted activity American philosophers have been willing to engage in is the very loose confederation of symposia wherein groups associate themselves very briefly under terms rich in philosophical tradition but quite worn out by current loose usage. These terms are idealism, naturalism, realism, materialism, value, and the like.[3] It has frequently been remarked that such symposia serve mainly the purpose of showing the participants how very little they have in common.

More striking even than the divergences evident among the philosophers willing to associate themselves under any philosophical rubric is the complete lack of any central trend or pattern of thought. Thus, in a very important collection of the philosophical creeds of many prominent thinkers, *Contemporary American Philosophy*,[4] it was quite evident that American philosophers are so committed to individualism that no two of them accept the same fundamental philosophical doctrines. Philosophy for the professionals apparently has the same connotation it has for the man on the street. It seems to mean a personal *Weltanschauung;* something which he prizes as a part of his own individual personality, the more nearly unique the better.

American philosophy is said to be characterized by pluralism, but there is not even a well thought out pluralistic philosophy. A Catholic philosopher might well see a parallel between the present situation in American philosophy and the disintegration of the Protestant sects as a historical process. However, American philosophy has not disintegrated. It was never truly integrated. While there were early integral movements in philosophy in this country, they were strictly European imports, and when speculative activity in the United States began to emerge along with intellectual activity generally, the European philosophical movements quickly melted into the general cultural stream. A recent example of a European import which suffered the same fate is Phenomenology which has had no development in this country comparable to its reception in, for instance, Latin America. American followers of this movement are rapidly yielding to the processes of disintegration typical of American philosophical speculation. As in the Roman Pantheon, there is room in the United States for any number of foreign philosophic gods however exotic so long as no newcomer proclaims himself the one and only true god.

It is evident that such philosophical pluralism is quite compatible with an enormous activity in philosophical speculation. And there never was a time in this country when so many people devoted themselves so assiduously to philosophical speculation. Is any pattern discernible in this welter of doctrine? What are the chief marks, if any, of American philosophy? American philosophers recognize one another. Most of them write at least one book, sooner or later. What authentic characteristics do they possess? The solution of the mystery is contained in the response to the question: How does a pluralism remain a unity?

The answer to these questions is that in each case the activity, however professionalized, is in fact closely bound up with the complex and multifarious stream of the general culture. American philosophy partakes of the aspects of American intellectual life in general. This is characterized by an immense personalized activity of an exploratory character which produces extensive excursions over the whole field of ideas rather than intensive penetration into and careful working out of the implications of any central notion. Intellectual undertakings are democratic, that is, open to all with a minimum of intellectual equipment, and the outcomes too are generally democratic, that is, optimistic, public, exoteric, and well within the accepted political and economic framework. By the same token, the philosophic temper is still strongly pragmatic. Even though avowed adherents to traditional pragmatism are hard to find, there remains a strong tendency to subject every philosophical proposal to the pragmatic test: its workability within the accepted way of American life. This is accompanied by an insistence that the moral implications of philosophical theories be quickly drawn. Any philosophical system which either postpones moral inquiry too long, as pragmatism continually finds itself doing, or disavows it altogether, as logical positivism and symbolic logic do, either is under constant running attack to handle the moral question or else is at once set down as a mere adjunct to the technical arts.

Despite its pluralism, therefore, American philosophy is of a piece with the general intellectual culture. But this does not distinguish the activity as philosophy. It remains to be seen whether specifically philosophical trends can be discerned.

As has been indicated, the philosophical tenets of pragmatism still dominate American thought. Pragmatism is the traditional American philosophical bias, and almost all contemporary American philosophers begin their inquiries against this background, just as the generation past began against that of German idealism. Thus, the most prominent characteristic of any present-day American philosophical speculation is its reaction to pragmatism. It may be said that American philosophers are divided into those who accept the pragmatic tradition and those who oppose it, or more precisely, since from the point of view of European philosophy the vast majority of American philosophers are pragmatic, into those who devote themselves to *continuing* the pragmatic tradition and those whose activities are in the main *directed against* this tradition.

The continuators of the pragmatic tradition are at present directing their efforts to widening the base of pragmatism in philosophy of science, in value theory in its relation to science, in the study of language and sign theory in general, and in the problem of the relation of philosophy to the social sciences. The pragmatists are facing up to the demands for unity in philosophical speculation and the most important tenet of pragmatism—pluralism—is at present most heavily under attack.

Of those who oppose pragmatism the first to be mentioned are the idealists. These are the conservatives in the American scene. They were here before the pragmatists came and they hope to outlive them. The idealists attack pragmatism at two points: first, its lack of coherence, unity, consistency; and second, its failure to handle value theory. Their slogan is *integration*. After suffering very severely at the hands of pragmatism, idealism seems to be renewing the fight in pragmatism's favored field, education. Here the progressivism of our leading pragmatic philosopher, John Dewey, has been dominant for a long generation, but *integration* is the war-cry now. It remains to be seen what effect this new though ancient movement will have on American legal education.

It is to be noted of the American idealistic philosophers that they are heavily indebted to the pragmatic tradition. So great is this debt indeed that our idealists are regarded as pragmatists by Europeans. There are, for example, no absolute idealists of prominence in American philosophy today.

Next in opposition to pragmatism are the logical positivists, the representatives of the Vienna Circle who settled in America between the Wars. It is at once apparent that logical positivism has certain very close affinities with pragmatism. To begin with, pragmatism is in the general positivist or empirical tradition. Another respect in which the two movements resemble each other is that both exhibit the same weakness in handling value theory. The differences between the two, though bitterly stressed, are less fundamental. Logical positivists characterize true value judgments as meaningless; pragmatism attempts to assimilate them to the other objects of scientific inquiry. Logical positivism is dualistic and develops logical theory as separate and distinct from investigation of fact. Consequently, logic is for it autonomous, subject only to the laws of formal science. Pragmatism is pluralistic,[5] and considers logic a branch of inquiry. Scientific inquiry is just as applicable to logic

as to experience. While theoretically pragmatic pluralism is as much opposed to logical-positivistic dualism as it is to philosophic monism, practically the
dualism offers hope for negotiation, and there are
signs that logical positivists and pragmatists are getting together.

A third philosophical movement opposed to pragmatism, at least in name, is called *naturalism.* A large
group of prominent American philosophers associate
themselves under this rubric. They are almost all in
the pragmatic tradition and unite, apparently, only on
the single issue of their opposition to supernaturalism;
not a very daring program for secular philosophers,
one might say. And yet the future may make the
point of agreement more than one of a simple and
single article of faith or agnosticism. The naturalists
incline more to process philosophy under the influence
of Whitehead than do the genuine pragmatists. So
the movement is a combination of emphases on empirical, pragmatic and organicistic or process philosophy.
The influence of Hegel is apparent here.

The last group in opposition to pragmatism to be
mentioned is very definitely opposed to it: the neo-
scholastics. Americans are not outstanding in the
movement. Nevertheless, the neo-scholastic opposition to pragmatism in this country as elsewhere is
sustained and principled. It is of course to be noted
that neo-scholasticism is equally opposed to all other
philosophical movements and spends much time dis-
avowing its would-be adherents, especially those of
idealistic bent who seem to feel that because scholasticism uses against positivism and pragmatism arguments to which idealism can subscribe, scholasticism's
objections to idealism must be somewhat blunted.
Scholasticism has to labor to reject these and other
offers of philosophical collaboration. In its own right,
neo-scholastic philosophy exerts little influence in this
country outside of Catholic circles.

To sum up, the American philosophical scene is still
predominantly pragmatic and its continuators are
many. Opposition from phenomenologists is negli-
gible. Logical positivism and naturalism have effected

a strong rapprochement with it. Idealism is the strongest opponent and gains strength daily. Only neo-scholasticism remains completely outside the fold.[6]

Foreign students of philosophy coming to this country are apt to view the American scene with amazement. Lulled into a false sense of security by the American use of the traditional philosophical vocabulary they are led to assume with much justification that these terms denote activities which have their reasonable counterparts in contemporary European philosophy. This assumption is strengthened by an examination of the curriculum of graduate studies in America. One learns with satisfaction that the neophyte is apparently steeped in the classical tradition through courses in the Greek philosophical texts and through seminars in medieval philosophy. The student reads the moderns from Descartes to the contemporaries with special emphasis on Kant and Hegel. But when the visitor comes to examine the works of modern American professors of philosophy he discovers that his task has become immensely complicated. Instead of being able merely to direct his attention to relatively familiar theories of philosophy our foreign expert must contend with a whole complex culture. In brief, American philosophical theories are merged in the general culture and nothing less than a knowledge of this culture suffices to appraise them.

III. *Legal Philosophy in the United States*[7]

In this country the term philosophy of law often serves as a synonym for jurisprudence or legal philosophy which includes the broad field of thoughtful speculation on legal problems, but this Article is concerned with the subject matter referred to when the term is used in its more literal meaning. Despite the fact that there is little direct intercourse between law and philosophy in the United States, present legal theories bear a marked resemblance to philosophical ones. This is not surprising since American legal and philosophical theories arise out of the same social milieu. Thus it will be interesting to see how far the analogy between law and philosophy holds. Some cutting and fitting must be done and the writer must be indulged somewhat if the parallel is to be drawn. Nevertheless, striking similarities do exist.

The fundamental legal philosophy in America today is still pragmatism. Its best known instance is of course sociological jurisprudence as developed by Roscoe Pound. In a revolt against nineteenth century idealism Pound imported European ideas of the nature of law, fitted them to current pragmatic theories of philosophy, and with their aid gradually reworked the whole structure of American legal thought.

The pragmatic tradition also includes widely influential legal theorists who have worked independently of Pound. The late Walter Wheeler Cook was a pragmatist with training in and inclination toward scientific method. The work of Hessel E. Yntema in Jurisprudence, Conflict of Laws and Comparative Law is likewise well within the pragmatic tradition though developed independently both of the dominant sociological jurisprudence of Pound and of traditional theories of legal philosophy. These men are often called "realists," but actually cannot be classified as part of the realist revolt from sociological jurisprudence. Substantially the same things may be said for Edwin W. Patterson[8] of Columbia and the late Max Radin of California.[9]

No American legal theorist claims that he is not as concerned as Pound is with the social nature of law and the actual social effects of legal doctrines. Substantially all accept the basic shift in viewpoint for which he has battled so valiantly during half a century. Therefore, the fundamental question in American jurisprudence today is what to do with sociological jurisprudence. With the exception of those who share the pragmatic viewpoint but work and have worked independently of Pound's influence, notably Yntema and the late W. W. Cook, American theorists can be classified roughly into those who *continue* sociological jurisprudence and those who *oppose* it. A warning is in order, however, that the opposition is never more than partial.

Of the continuators of Pound, Julius Stone and the late Sydney P. Simpson are easily the most direct. Although Stone is an Englishman now teaching in Australia, we may claim him as an American jurist. His book, *The Province and Function of Law*,[10] is the most important work on sociological jurisprudence in a decade. It represents a thorough re-working and systematic criticism of sociological theories and of all other important juristic theories in their relation to sociological jurisprudence. He and Simpson have also completed a massive survey of readings entitled *Law and Society*.[11] Nothing exists in our jurisprudential literature comparable to this heroic empirical labor of love. It answers a need for a collection of materials which will permit, it is hoped, the teaching of jurisprudence in a throughly pragmatic fashion.

In addition, it must be noted that the founder of sociological jurisprudence himself continues his work with unabated zeal. In the last decade, Pound has produced many important books and articles.[12] Some of these latest productions are in a pessimistic vein and are extremely critical of the realist position. Nevertheless the opposition is not fundamental because the basic philosophical orientation is the same.

Also in the sociological tradition, and most important for its attempt to effectuate a rapport between social science and law on the basis of scientific methodology, is the work of Huntington Cairns.[13] His efforts to create a new pragmatic legal science on an adequate foundation in general philosophy of science are unique in their sustained search for fruitful hypotheses to serve as fundamental bases for scientific legal investigation. The success of the work must await, in the present author's opinion, an experimental social science, but in the meantime it should serve as a stimulus to the creation of an adequate social scientific apparatus.[14] The present author has likewise attempted to formulate postulates for experimental jurisprudence[15] and may thus be classified as one of the continuators of sociological jurisprudence on its scientific side.

The work of Levi of Chicago, which is pragmatic,

also studies in this vein the important problem of the relation of social science to law.[16] Among the younger men who should be mentioned in this connection are Miller of Florida and Murphy[17] of Alabama.

To be counted as continuations in the pragmatic tradition are the very numerous writings of American legal theorists on specialized subjects in the law. Although these are not to be regarded as essays in legal philosophy they serve as witnesses to the pervasive influence of sociological jurisprudence and pragmatic philosophy. Indeed, it is precisely this great mass of American legal writing, pragmatic in spirit and directed to specialized if not minute examination of legal problems, that is the despair of the foreign legal theorist attempting to gain an understanding of American law.

In considering the opposition to sociological jurisprudence, it is necessary to remember that just as American professional philosophers seem to be united only in their resistance to classification, American legal theorists appear to glory in radical independence of thought. This is made to appear in a recent collection of the philosophical creeds of a number of prominent American legal theorists,[18] wherein no two admitted to sharing even remotely the same philosophical outlook. The accent is on the personal pronoun and, indeed, most disclaim any pretension to a well worked out philosophical position. This avowed independence is more apparent than real, however, since most of the contributors are staunch supporters of the pragmatic position.

So, as we turn to those who oppose sociological jurisprudence in revolt against Pound's dominant influence, we come first to the legal realists, who are nevertheless continuators of the pragmatic tradition. Elsewhere, the present writer had an opportunity to examine the relation of the legal realists to pragmatism.[19] He came to the conclusion that even the sceptics among them are still pragmatists. Thus, their opposition to sociological jurisprudence has always been loyal opposition. They opposed, the better to attain pragmatism's avowed aims. Where a good deal of Pound's work on the relation of law to society is theoretical, the realists have steadfastly insisted that the actual social setting is the beginning of legal theorizing. It is necessary to report that most of the intransigence of the legal realists has disappeared. Although they began in opposition to Pound, they remained to turn their attention to constructive work after the period of sharp critical attack was over.[20]

Llewellyn of Columbia is at work on codification of Commercial Law,[21] Judge Jerome Frank continues to write with vigor on the importance of fact in law.[22] However, his radical empiricism is being tempered by practical application to pedagogy, the philosopher's testing ground for theories from time immemorial. Judge Frank has become increasingly interested in the clinical method of teaching law.[23]

The influence of idealism in American juristic writings represents a very definite break with, or at least clear opposition to, sociological jurisprudence. This break, however, is only a contemporary reemergence of an influence always existing at least in an inarticulate condition in American legal thought for, although classical natural law doctrines faced growing hostility in this country from the adoption of the federal Constitution, it cannot be said that natural law influence ever suffered extinction. As a source of inspiration for "higher law" theories, for exaltation of received traditions, for principles of unity and coherence over the body of the law, and for emphasis upon the necessity of converting moral obligations into legal ones, the "ideal" element in the law has been the constant concern of able jurists since the beginning of the American legal system. Pound has never ceased to teach the importance of this tradition and in recent years seems to be stressing it.

Three American jurists in particular are at present working out an approach to a recognizably idealistic position in legal philosophy. They are Lon L. Fuller[24] of Harvard, Jerome Hall[25] of Indiana and Edmond N. Cahn[26] of New York University. While stressing at all times the social nature of all legal phenomena, these men have nevertheless opposed the pragmatic philosophical position in two main respects. They attack its pluralism as leading to cultural determinism and scepticism and they attack its alleged amoralism. For them, the ideal element in law needs conscious elaboration in order (1) that competing ideals may be examined and evaluated and the fundamental purposes of law be given unified direction ;(2) that value judgments themselves may be put on a rational basis so that the gap between morality and law be closed; and (3) that the effects of legal scepticism may be overcome by a reaffirmance of faith in American legal and political ideals, that is, ideals of justice and democracy. All this is directed to the end that the law may be placed upon a firm support in ethics and value theory.

Fuller's book, *The Law in Quest of Itself*,[27] most nearly approaches the temper of idealism. The claims of idealism are opposed to positivism, and while that movement rather than pragmatism is most severely scored, it is apparent that the author is more concerned with pragmatism than with the generally discredited positivism. Fuller shows in this book quite clearly the links of modern legal idealism with natural law. In fact, he just barely misses calling for a revival of natural law. It is too bad for the idealists that the tempting phrase "natural law" is still a little too hot to touch. Its free use would at least put the present-day idealists in a rich historical tradition, a tradition which they feel unable to accept but for which a nostalgic longing pervades their writings.

Jerome Hall's recent book on *Living Law in a Democratic Society*[28] is less clearly in the idealistic tradition. His concern like Fuller's is with the harmful effects of "positivistic" separation of law and morals, with ideals of jural purpose, such as democracy and justice, and with the preservation of ancient wisdom in the classical philosophical and legal texts.

Philosophy for the idealists traditionally has been more concerned with wisdom than with science. Wisdom is conservative, subtle, classical, moral and self-conscious. Wisdom protects itself from excess and asks youth to bring its aims to the level of self-consciousness and at the same time suggests what these self-conscious aims ought to be. The idealistic philosophy especially prizes consistency or coherence. Among our legal idealists these demands apparently call for a leap backward beyond Hegel whose dialectical system actually rendered infinitely more difficult the idealists' task of making nature coherent and consistent. My own personal distress with idealistic legal philosophers stems from their tendency to sound a retreat to Plato. Their failure to face up to Hegelian idealism deprives them of an opportunity to make their idealism modern.

It is common knowledge that Hegel really made it impossible for idealists to escape the dilemma of absolutism. After him all idealistic systems must either arrest progress and stagnate in some species of absolutism; or, foreswearing the absolute, come to grips with the relativism of modern science. For better or for worse, knowledge has become dialectical and the ancient dilemmas—is and ought, freedom and necessity, idealism and realism—are dissolving away. Not alone Marx and Freud, but Kierkegaard, Husserl, the phenomenologists and existentialists owe their existence to Hegel, as do the modern pragmatists. It will be recalled that the greatest of them, John Dewey, began as a Hegelian, and that all pragmatists are or ought to be grateful to Hegel for relativizing "fact," and for the notion of interpenetration of "fact" and "law." [29]

Edmond N. Cahn in his recent book, *The Sense of Injustice*,[30] seems to have escaped the dangers of regression to Ancient Greece. He does not regard the old positivistic-idealistic contradictions as fruitful sources of inquiry. In his work recognition of the influence of Hegel appears through the German romantics, and the secular ethics of humanism rather than an appeal to a revived natural law is looked upon as the source of the "ideal" element of law. *The Sense of Injustice* is an attempt to lay a foundation for the scientific study of man as an emotional animal whose feelings find expression over the range of an enormous number of law situations. It is suggested that in the moment of crisis men make known their preference for justice over injustice, and that a thorough working out of these "critical" reactions anthropologically will reveal the foundations of law and order. Cahn feels that such a science of law can raise no fundamental question of ethics in opposition to itself since the emotions, which are the source of all values, are the very stuff out of which this legal science must be made. It is apparent that modern psychoanalytic theory lends much support to the above ideas. The work is in the tradition of Spinoza, for whom the emotions are not irrational despite the sense of uncontrolled or capricious freedom which often accompanies instances of choice. For Spinoza, scientific investigation would disclose the grounds of moral and emotional decision. It is thus obvious that Cahn's work is more important for the philosophy of science than as an example of diffuse idealistic wisdom.

Professor Cahn's style in the *Sense of Injustice* is in the traditional spirit of idealism. The book is balanced, quietly optimistic, conserving. Its content, however, reveals that he is much closer to the group of philosophers in this country who range themselves under the rubric "naturalism."

Logical positivism though important for general philosophy in America has had little or no influence on legal speculation despite the presence of Hans Kelsen in this country. Although attacks on the pure theory of law have been many, they are in the main abstract.[31] Kelsen himself continues to write[32] and has had an able follower in the legal field in Ebenstein.[33] But pure theories of law are of small consequence here. Nothing corresponding to the contributions of logical positivists to symbolic logic exists in our law. Legal logic and indeed analytical jurisprudence generally are quite neglected in the present period.[34] Little interest in basic legal terminology is in evidence.[35] However, an analytical study of the nature of American government has been published by Burke Shartel of Michigan.[36]

In concluding this brief notice of logical positivism

and the law it is safe to say that the rapport between logical positivism and pragmatism is even closer in legal speculation than it is in general philosophy.

Legal neo-scholasticism stands fundamentally opposed to all other legal philosophical positions.[37] Nevertheless much of sociological jurisprudence is grist for its mill.[38] It might be suggested that in sociological jurisprudence the scholastics find much more empirical comfort and assurance than they do in any of the systems of jurisprudence opposed to it. The essentially secular character of sociological jurisprudence permits the scholastics to follow up to the point where sociological jurisprudence is felt to lose itself in the problem of the nature of law, and here the scholastics find it fairly easy to substitute scholastic legal philosophy, predominantly that of St. Thomas Aquinas.

IV. *Conclusion*

The foregoing review of legal theories indicates that the present search is the perennial one for unity in diversity. This demand succeeds the nineteenth and early twentieth century emphasis upon relativism. The responses to the demand for unification are various for the differently oriented philosophical and legal groups but each is typical of its kind.

Legal idealists seek fundamental intuitions to serve as bases for legal inquiries. The activity is reminiscent of eighteenth century legal rationalism which developed after seventeenth century deductive systems had been abandoned as impractical for sciences involving life.

"Naturalistic" legal thinkers, more interested in legal speculation as a basis for social and legal science, strive to develop postulates or postulational systems. F. S. C. Northrop[39] of Yale and, very particularly, Huntington Cairns fit this description. As was previously noted,[40] the present writer has formulated a postulate set for an experimental philosophy of law which emphasizes scientific methodology. Its spirit is in consonance with that of the pioneer in experimental jurisprudence, Frederick K. Beutel of Nebraska.[41]

Pound still seeks to express basic legal postulates in the form of empirical or pragmatic summaries of the individual and social claims that demand legal recognition. Yntema increasingly stresses the importance of codification in American law.[42]

Described in the widest possible terms, speculative activities whose end is a postulational foundation for legal science are the modern continuation of the *rationalistic* tradition as it has come down to us through Kant and Hegel. On the other hand, attempts at generalization on the basis of fact for the purpose of detecting or constructing patterns,[43] policies,[44] norms, inductive rules, codifications are in the *empirical* tradition. The perennial task of philosophy of law is of course to get both movements together.

It seems safe to say that legal philosophy in the United States will continue for some time its present tendency to develop in isolation from philosophy; that in consequence legal philosophy will retain its present non-professional and pluralistic character; and that pressure from the social disciplines will continue to be exerted on the legal experts to the end that rapport between the social sciences and law be more firmly established.[45] On all sides it is said that the present era is one of crisis and confusion in law but this may be saying no more than that it is the present era. Posterity may see it as a relatively stable period whose problems of choice were rather narrowly confined.

B. Legal Idealism

As a philosophical movement, idealism has two main interests: idea-ism and ideal-ism. It emphasizes the importance of *ideas* in man's knowledge of the world, and of *ideals* in human *action*. It brings such leading notions as unity, coherence, rationality and the power of reflection to the task of understanding the world, and formulates ideals of justice, the value of the good, and the worth of reason and human dignity in the study of law and morals. In the common parlance of jurists, it is said to be concerned with the law as it ought to be rather than with the law as it is. This last point is shared with the doctrine of "natural law."

In America, all idealistic systems of philosophy are formed

in a setting of empirical science. Absolute idealism is virtually extinct in this country.

Morris R. Cohen, Law and the Social Order (1933) pp. 195-196; reprinted by permission of the Estate of Morris R. Cohen.

Law without concepts or rational ideas, law that is not logical, is like pre-scientific medicine—a hodge-podge of sense and superstition, as has indeed been most of the world's common sense as distinguished from science.

To urge that judges, for instance, should rely on their experience or intuition in disregard of logically formulated principles is to urge sentimental anarchy. Men will generalize in spite of themselves. If they do it consciously in accordance with logical principles, they will do it more carefully and will be liberally tolerant to other possible generalizations. But those who distrust all logic think that they deal with facts when they are occupied with the product of their own grotesque theories.

Science, to be sure, is abstract. It tends to emphasize abstract considerations and deals with the definable classes rather than with the particular cases. But in doing so it forces us to see things from a wider point of view, and this tends to make us more just to the diversity of human interests. The air of unreality that science presents to the uninitiated is like the unreality which modern machinery presents to the old-fashioned artisan or to those who cultivate the soil by hand.

Nor can we respect the metaphysical objection that life is changing but concepts are fixed. It is precisely because concepts are fixed in meaning that we can measure or determine the rate of change. Should the rules of arithmetic be changed whenever the volume of our business transactions is changed? Will even the change of our system of weights and measures require us to discard the multiplication table?

The real objection to conceptually mechanical jurisprudence is one against all human activity that is unintelligent. So-called strong judges, who decide to follow principles regardless of consequences, are simply too lazy to examine countervailing considerations and special circumstances which are relevant to the application of these principles. At best they are guilty of the fallacy of simplism, of supposing that the law always consists of theoretically simple cases, whereas the concrete cases actually before us are more complex because they generally involve many principles. This is the root of what is sound in the distinction between "law in books" and "law in action," and in the warning that the needs of life should not be sacrificed to the needs of the study.

Felix S. Cohen, Ethical Systems and Legal Ideals (Falcon Press, 1933) pp. 1-8; 93-101; 291-292 (footnotes omitted); reprinted by permission of Mrs. Felix S. Cohen.

THE ETHICAL BASIS OF LEGAL CRITICISM

1. *The Problems of Legal Criticism*

At the heart of man's ancient quest for justice is the search for some measure of good and bad in the most powerful and flexible instrument of social control, the law. This problem of the ethical appraisal of law is no pseudo-question invented by philosophers. It is inescapably presented by the most fundamental of man's social institutions, and no philosopher of the first rank has been able to overlook it. Indeed, historically, most of the distinctive problems of metaphysics and epistemology have arisen in the attempt to clarify discussion of social ideals. The nature of ideas or essences, the relation of reason to life and to the cosmos, the status of "natural laws," the meaning of possibility and necessity, the validity of knowledge, the reality of the individual will and mind, the relation of universal laws to particular facts—each of these cardinal problems of philosophy has roots deep in legal-ethical controversy. Without the vision of these connections, philosophy tends to become simply the noblest of games and social reform the most pathetic of humanity's aspirations.

Shifting terminologies cannot obscure the continuity with which the Western world has faced the problem of the ethical valuation of law. Whether treated by Greek philosophers analyzing the nature of "justice," by Roman and medieval jurists under the rubric of "natural law and equity," by scholars of modern Europe speaking in the language of "natural rights," or by social scientists of our own day who are concerned with "social interests," the problem has remained essentially the same. Fundamental to all adequate thought on politics and society lies the question of what law ought to do, the search for valid standards of legal criticism.

The problem is, in the first place, an ethical one, since legal criticism is a passing of judgments of good and bad, right and wrong, upon human acts and works. This has led to a tendency apparent in most modern "scientific" studies of law to disclaim responsibility for its solution, to pass the buck to the ethical philosopher. But in the second place, the problem involves a calculation of the nature, effects, and potentialities of legal machinery which only the jurist or social scientist as such can attempt, and this has led most ethical philosophers to ignore crucial legal problems, throwing responsibility back to the jurist. This game of battledore and shuttlecock, or, to put the analogy in modern terms, volley ball, is carried on through most of the social sciences today. The historian, the economist, the political scientist, the sociologist, all argue that science is non-moral, and that their task is done when they have portrayed the facts. Ethical philosophers, on the other hand, are seldom anxious to descend from the ethereal realm of abstract duties and intrinsic goods to the mud of social statistics. Indeed, a Platonic reluctance to recognize that there is any essence or idea of mud has persisted through the most diverse currents of philosophical thought. But it is of mud that human edifices are built, and no dainty philosophy can pass adequate judgment upon the buildings of men, their weakness and their strength. Only when freed from the last vestiges of professional snobbery can philosophy offer to an unphilosophical world tributes worthy of her dignity.

Shunned alike by scientists and philosophers, most social-ethical questions are left today in a No Man's Land where only those with strong practical and emotional interests will make a stand. This arbitrary and inadequate division of intellectual labor would be pitiable enough if the limitations it imposes upon social thought were regularly recognized. But the moral philosopher who disdains the data sheets of social science as irrelevant to questions of value continues to assume human desires and human abilities which those data refute; and the social scientist (not least of all the jurist) continues to assume ethical norms which have not withstood the test of philosophical analysis.

An ethics, like a metaphysics, is no more certain and no less dangerous because it is unconsciously held. There are few judges, psychoanalysts, or economists today who do not begin a consideration of their typical problems with some formula designed to cause all moral ideals to disappear and to produce an issue purified for the procedure of positive empirical science. But the ideals have generally retired to hats from which later wonders will magically arise. A historical school of law disclaims concern with ethics and repeatedly invokes a *Zeitgeist* or a *Volksgeist* to decide what the law ought to be. An analytical school of jurisprudence again dismisses questions of morality, and again decides what the law ought to be by reference to a so-called logical ideal, which is not an ideal of logic at all, but an aesthetic ideal of symmetrical analogical development. Those who derive the law from the will of the sovereign usually introduce without further justification the premise that it is good to obey that will. And those who define the law in terms of actually prevailing social demands or interests make frequent use of the undisclosed principle that these demands *ought* to be satisfied.

The objection, then, is not that jurists have renounced ethical judgment but that they have renounced ethical science. Ethical science involves an analysis of ethical judgments, a clarification of ethical premises. Among the current legal crypto-idealisms there can be no edifying controversy, since there is no recognition of the moral issues to which their differences reduce. One looks in vain in legal treatises and law-review articles for legal criticism conscious of its moral presuppositions. The vocabularies of logic and aesthetics are freely drawn upon in the attempt to avoid the disagreeable assertion that something or other is intrinsically better than something else. Particular decisions or legal rules are "anomalous" or "illogical," "incorrect" or "impractical," "reactionary" or "liberal," and unarguable ethical innuendo takes the place of critical analysis. Little wonder then that on a more abstract plane of thought the classification of ideas has taken the place of legal philosophy, while Hegelian pictures of inevitable trends are offered as substitutes for the delineation of the desirable.

But the relevance of ethics to the philosophy of law would be clear even if it were not unconsciously assumed by those who appear to deny or to ignore the connection. For ethics is the study of the meaning and application of judgments of *good, bad, right, wrong,* etc., and every final valuation of law involves an ethical judgment. When we say, for instance, that a given law is bad, that one judicial decision is better than another, that the American constitution ought to be revised, or that laws ought to be obeyed, we are passing judgments whose truth or falsity cannot be established without a consideration of ethics. That portion of jurisprudence which is not concerned merely with the positive nature of law or with its technical relation to assumed ends is, accordingly, a part of the domain of ethics.

There is no way of avoiding this ultimate responsibility of law to ethics. Every final determination of the general end of law, the standard of legal criticism, (whether this be labeled "justice," "natural law," "the protection of natural rights," or "the organization of social interests"), must reduce to the general form, "The law ought to bring about as much good as it can."

Our problem is to give content to this formal principle by defining the nature of the good and indicating the extent of the law's actual powers over that realm. In attacking this problem our first concern will be to formulate precisely the relation between ethics and legal criticism. Having established the dependence of critical thought in law upon the ethical concept of the good life, we shall turn in our second chapter to an examination of certain more specific legal ideals in the light of this general conception, paying particular attention to the significance of the good life and rival ideals for positive legal science. To fill in the abstract conception of the good life with the content which a scientific ethics can support will be the purpose of the third chapter. Finally an attempt will be made to sketch the lines of positive scientific inquiry which legal criticism must undertake in the application of its ethical ideal.

✿   ✿   ✿   ✿   ✿

JUSTICE AS THE STANDARD OF
LEGAL VALUATION

Of all the standards by which law has been measured, none has been more widely urged than the ideal of justice. But while most jurists will agree that law is good in so far as it is just, this agreement is to a large extent merely verbal, so various are the meanings with which the word *justice* is currently endowed. We shall attempt to show that when this meaning it not simply identical with *the good which law is able to achieve,* justice, although a useful and important concept, cannot furnish a final standard for the evaluation of law. In order to proceed to this point, we must distinguish as carefully as may be, the various ideas which the word *justice* has been used to symbolize.

In its narrowest sense, justice is simply the fulfillment of the positive law. We speak of courts of justice in this sense, and we frequently mean by just obligations, rights, demands, etc. simply those that are guaranteed by law. But in this sense of the term, justice cannot be significantly put forward as a standard for the valuation of law itself. It is therefore inadequate for our present purposes, and if conceived as a supreme standard of legal criticism must lead to error.

At the opposite extreme from this narrow meaning is the identification of justice with human goodness. Unlike the former positive definition, this is one from which the imperative or ideal character of justice can be analytically derived. The distinction is an important one. If we define justice in terms of goodness, either as identical with goodness in general or as a limited portion of the realm of goodness (*e.g.* goodness in external action), then our task is to find, by a positive examination of legal elements and an ethical evaluation of them, what things are just (*i.e.* what things in this realm are good) and, if possible, what further secondary criteria are available for the determination of this question. That is essentially the task which we have laid down on the constructive side of the present essay, which may, in this sense of the word, be considered an inquiry into the nature of justice. But on the other hand we may start off with a purely positive definition of justice such as the strictly legal concept first mentioned, and then our task must be to determine how far the attainment of justice is a good. These procedures cannot be confused without serious error, although their purpose is the same, namely to discover what the law ought to do. To return to our definition of just law as the law that ought to be, we may say that in this sense justice provides a valid ethical standard, but one which is identical with the standard we have already insisted upon, a standard which demands the complete calculation of legal activities in terms of the good life. And this fact is not altered if we restrict the term *justice* to that realm of goods which applies to conduct in society, to outward conduct, or to conduct which affects other people than the agent, since the immediate effects of law fall under all of these categories. Further consequences of legal activity upon other realms of conduct will not be ignored in this way, since they receive treatment under the head of instrumental values involved in the conduct primarily affected by law. We have seen, similarly, that if the law can effect goods outside of human life, these goods may nevertheless be considered as endowing the good life with instrumental values. Thus with each of these normative definitions of justice, our essential problem and our general formulation of its solution remain unaltered.

But there are alternative conceptions of justice, primarily positive in their nature, whose ethical validity cannot be analytically deduced from their definition. They present us with material formulae for the just solution of legal problems, and leave us with the significant task of deciding to what extent *justice* is a desirable end. Thus when people say that in certain cases justice should be sacrificed to mercy or to expediency, they cannot mean by *justice* "that which ought to be (in the realms under consideration)," although they may think that justice is one of the desiderata that should be taken into account. That is to say, if I define *justice* as equality, or distribution of goods in proportion to moral excellence, or distribution according to the principle of need, I must be prepared to consider the logical possibility that just activities will not be good. With such definitions, our primary problem is not to work out their positive content (as is the case with normative definitions), for this is already given, at least in outline. It is rather to determine the adequacy, from an ultimate ethical standpoint, of these principles. And when we find that any of these conceptions of justice is in some respect inadequate for ethical criticism, we may conclude that its content does not provide the ultimate standard for which we are searching.

The classical formula of justice, "to give every man his due", is frequently interpreted in a non-ethical sense, although the ease with which this meaning can be shifted to one that is analytically normative perhaps accounts for its great convenience and popularity. The nub of the problem lies in the word *due*.

Are we told to give every man what ought to be given to him, or, on the other hand, what, by law or custom, he is protected in demanding? The two principles are distinct in meaning, although in most cases they may point to identical conclusions. The first principle being analytically normative does not give any definite content to our ethical standard. We have always to ask what it is that is due to each man. And since every legal action may be phrased in terms of giving something (a right, privilege, power, or immunity, if not a more material entity) to somebody, we are still left with the general formal principle that the law ought to do as much good as it can, which is only expressed in a new language under the terms of this theory. But if the second interpretation is given to our present formula, its ethical inadequacy is obvious. Certainly it is not always good to protect or to fulfill the demands that have been traditionally protected. In many cases such protection or observance achieves, immediately, certain elements of human well-being. In other cases, although no such benefit is conferred upon the parties most directly concerned, a certain amount of social security or personal discipline is produced by the observance of socially accepted obligations. But only a mystical and unscientific deification of the state or society can lead us to believe that such observance constitutes a legal norm of universal validity. And if this is not such a norm, then it remains a limited ideal, coordinate with other limited ideals already examined, and demanding for its application a final court of appeals in which all such standards may be weighed, one against the other, in the light of some more fundamental ethical principle.

There is another conception of justice, which sets up as its supreme principle the maxim, "to each according to his merit." The distribution of rewards and punishments in "proportion" to merit and demerit has a philosophical pedigree dating back to Aristotle. In criminal law it is the basis of the retributive theory of punishment, and in civil law it serves in one way or another to provide a philosophical basis for the general theories of liability (*i.e.* tort and contract) and property.

We may ask two questions of this theory of justice. In the first place, what is meant by *proportion* between merit and reward? In the second place why should such a proportion be realized?

It appears that in no rigorous sense of the term can a proportion or ratio be said to exist between merit and reward. For such a relation to exist it would be necessary that both entities should be capable of a quantitative expression in terms of each other or in terms of some common denominator. That this is not the case is possibly a rash assertion, but it is certainly true that there is no known reduction in this case. What is meant, then, by the principle, "to each according to his merit", must be simply that in any two instances the greater merit should be recognized by the greater reward, and, negatively, the greater demerit by the greater punishment.

This principle, however, appears to be both inadequate and fallacious. It is inadequate because it offers no determination of the extent of reward or punishment appropriate to a given merit or fault. All we are told is that this should be greater or less than in certain other cases, and we have a set of variables with no constant, which is clearly indeterminate. But even this inadequate formula seems to involve error. To repay evil with good, is certainly not, as this theory would imply, the blackest of sins. Nor is it true that equally grave offenses merit equally severe punishment. Some offenses, such as stupidity, are generally incapable of cure by punishment. Punishment can then be justified only as an intrinsic good, and we must make the further assumption that the value of punishment is in no way dependent upon the human welfare or happiness which it achieves, if we are to hold the theory that equal offenses merit equal punishments.

Such a doctrine we cannot, of course, disprove. But it appears to be repugnant alike to civilized common sense and to all philosophical thought that is not based upon logical fallacies. Its limited application in law, in the form of the *lex talionis*, is generally regarded as a mark of barbarism. While the fundamental and almost universal aesthetic appeal in the "eye for an eye" doctrine may be great enough to justify certain concessions to the principle for the sake of legal economy, certainty, and popular support, no plausible reason can be given for the doctrine except on the basis of this immediate aesthetic appeal. It must therefore be considered as coordinate with other limited and equally immediate interests, such as the interest of the wrong-doer in his own happiness, and it remains the task of ethics to formulate some wider principle by which these various intuitive value judgments may be weighed together and unified.

There are various other conceptions of justice which it will not be necessary for us to examine. Such are those which, on the basis of the Kantian morality or some other system of pure ethics, give a content to the normative definition of justice. These we shall examine in our analysis of ethical systems. There are other theories of justice which we treat in other parts of the present chapter, under such headings as "natural law" and "liberty". There are still other theories which we are unable to understand and shall not, therefore, attempt to criticize.

But we must turn, at parting, to a final conception of justice which is perhaps the most popular of all, a conception which refuses to be bound by any formula and which finds its roots in a peculiar sentiment or instinct. As Gény says, "It is a kind of instinct which, without appealing to the reasoning mind, goes of its own accord straight to the best solution, the one most conformable to the aim of all juridical organization."

Clearly there is some such sentiment in the human soul, but is there any ground for supposing that it always or generally provides a correct solution for social problems? It does not seem to us that this question can possibly receive an affirmative answer. For even assuming that this instinct begins to work only when all the positive data of our problem have been collected (or are statistics also gathered by an inner feeling?), the sentiment of justice, working upon such materials, is, like all moral sentiments, largely a composite of accepted moral doctrines. It is thus as variable as the theories from which it springs, and this fact alone would show that it cannot serve as an ultimate standard of valuation. Furthermore, if this sentiment is a complex of implicit moral beliefs, it is no more impregnable to intellectual criticism than the beliefs upon which it is based. To refine this sentiment of justice by a critical examination of its foundations is as much the task of legal philosophy as the refinement of common sense, in general, is the task of philosophy and science. To make such a sentiment the supreme arbiter of our legal-ethical problems is simply to assign ultimate authority to our moral ignorance.

❋   ❋   ❋   ❋   ❋

The life of legal philosophy is the search for the ethical constant in the ideal of "natural law with changing content." That this constant in natural law is simply its goodness is the recurrent burden of the present essay. What is constant in ideal law is not a body of material commands, but a highly abstract ethical framework. What is variable is not an ultimate form but a set of social conditions.

From another point of view, this fundamental polarity appears in the relation of existence and value. We have tried to show that the valuation of law involves mutually relevant poles of idealism and positivism, and that no juristic approach that neglects ethics and no philosophical approach that neglects positive science can give us an adequate philosophy of law. The crypto-idealism of Duguit, Savigny, *et al.*, is as inadequate as the crypto-positivism of the Kantians, Hegelians, and other formalists in legal philosophy. Each current represents the development of an illicit abstraction made workable only by the unrecognized and therefore uncritical acceptance of complementary factors.

Legal philosophy, when it is sundered from a wider intellectual world, either to be caged in the narrow realm of the existent or to be exiled into an ethereal region of irresponsible desires, cannot live. For in the human world of which philosophy is a part the choice of ideals, which is love, and their understanding must co-exist. That understanding without love is empty, that love without understanding is blind, that the good life is found only in the intimate union of these ideals,—the wedding of reason and faith, as the phrase of another age ran,—these are the most important truths to which men have attained.

John Dickinson, My Philosophy of Law (1941) pp. 97-102; reprinted by permission of Julius Rosenthal Foundation of Northwestern University and Boston Law Book Co.

For government to act through rules and established procedures rather than sporadically has two consequences which have hitherto been regarded as socially desirable. The first is that in important respects it enables individuals to plan their conduct by foreseeing the consequences of certain of their own acts as well as of the acts of others. "If the decision of one case were not to be ruled by or depend upon former determinations in other cases of a like nature, I should be glad to know what person would venture to purchase an estate."[1] At the same time men are stimulated to supposedly desirable conduct by being given some assurance that they will be able to enjoy the fruits of effort and industry, while they are deterred from at least some anti-social acts by like assurance that such acts will be followed by punishment or civil liability.

The second supposed consequence of requiring government to act through law is to subject its action in some degree to control and direction by rational processes. Where a government follows the practice of taking in each individual case any possible action that it pleases on any possible ground, now enforcing a contract for one individual which it refuses to enforce for another, now imposing liability upon one for some act which is held not to establish liability against someone else, its acts are neither controlled by, noi subject to the test of, rational principles, since inevitably the employment of rational principles of decision will in and of itself result in the evolution of like decisions for like cases, and thus tacitly in the formulation of decisional rules. The purely arbitrary and sporadic cannot avoid being the irrational.

In recent years a school of so-called 'realistic jurisprudence' has challenged what has always been understood as law in the past by contending, first, that decisional rules are impossible in point of actual fact, and certainty a mere deceptive illusion; and, secondly, that decision in conformity with rules would be undesirable even if possible, as representing an immature psychology of escape from reality. On this theory, law is simply whatever government does; it, therefore, necessarily ceases to be a guide for or limitation upon governmental action and becomes only another name for what has hitherto been called government without law.

The basis for this nihilistic theory appears to be failure to recognize that like other human institutions law is approximate and relative—a more or less imperfect effort toward a goal rather than a perfected attainment. It is entirely true that decisional rules do not provide in advance complete and conclusive solutions for all doubtful cases; that no two cases are ever absolutely alike, and there is, therefore, always the possibility that cases which are similar in certain respects may be decided on the ground of their differences rather than of their likeness; and that for these and other reasons discretion and choice play an important part in the process of decision. All this has always been understood by lawyers, except possibly a minute academic minority; but it has at the same time also been understood that where an organ of government with the power and duty to decide, recognizes that in its decision it must take certain rules into account, its discretion is guided and controlled in a way that it would not be, and the resulting decision is a different decision from what it would be, if those rules were not recognized as authoritative and as, therefore, essential ingredients in the decisional process. In other words, legal rules are not inert mechanical instruments; they grow, expand, contract, and from time to time alter their direction. As a result the certainty which law produces is never more than a relative certainty,—indeed, some statutory rules are so vaguely expressed as to give little or no assurance how they will be applied. Where this is done deliberately it may reflect an effort on the part of officials to govern without law. Even, however, the most carefully drafted rules or the most thoroughly considered precedents will inevitably leave loopholes for unforeseen cases. Certainty, however, like other human values need not regarded as valueless merely because it is imperfectly achieved.

The view that such relative certainty as law can provide is undesirable and caters only to human immaturity is of a piece with the social philosophy which sees the highest good in 'living dangerously', prefers adventure to order, and 'transvaluates values'. The degree of order and peace which men have been able to achieve in their societies has seldom been so excessive, even with the aid of law, that constructive spirits who seek to build have not felt the need of still further certainties; while it has generally been the immature, the adolescent, and the irresponsible who have aimed to make of life primarily an adventure.

From what has been said, the close relationship between law and government is manifest. Government, while required to act through law, is at the same time the agency through which law is constructed and moulded and formulated. In this sense, government is legally the 'sovereign' source of law; but since it is sovereign *legally* and not by virtue of mere brute force, a lawful government, although there may be no way of enforcing law against it, maintains its character only insofar as it acts through law and within the framework of the requirements which are implicit in the idea of government by law. To this self-restraint it is subject by no external compulsion but simply by the principle of its own being. Machinery may be provided in the form of an independent judiciary and the institution of judicial review to make this self-restraint more probable; but if a government refuses to observe it, the only corrective, if corrective is desired, is in the last analysis the extra-legal 'right' of revolution.

Law in the sense of the rules which are formulated through government for the guidance and control of governmental decisions necessarily derives its content from a source or sources external to itself. This source may be custom,—government may, and in its more primitive stages usually does, simply lend its force to compel compliance with established social usage. On the other hand, it may deliberately formulate a rule to defeat a custom under the influence of some progressive ideal. Men, since they have begun to speculate about law at all, have always been fascinated by the conception of a system of ideal law, to which the actual law applied in decisions ought to, but never quite does, conform. Under the name, 'law of nature', this ideal law, derived from currently active moral aspirations by philosophers, divines, and judges, has supplied not merely a pattern and model, but a powerful stimulus for changes in and additions to the law of a given time and place. Of course, such ideal law can only influence the actual insofar as portions of it are from time to time adopted by judges and legislators. Naturally the ideal has varied, and not merely from period to period, but from individual thinker to individual thinker; yet, in the large, the pursuit of it has usually represented an effort to discover and give effect to fundamental underlying human values, and the judge who has been influenced by the concept in his decisions has for the most part been doing what he could to build the law according to the better lights of his own age.

In a fully developed state, law grows through two processes—the direct process of legislation and the older indirect process of judicial decision. Of course, an existing rule may be changed or a new one brought into existence for a hitherto unprovided state of facts by legislative enactment. Even, however, in the presence of an active organ of legislation judges will inevitably, in the exercise of their jurisdiction, have cases brought before them for which no statutory mandate or clear judicial precedent exists. A court cannot refuse to decide such a case; and necessarily in doing so, it provides for the novel situation what amounts to a new rule which by force of precedent will govern in like cases for the future. These rules of so-called 'judge-made' law are being constantly evolved by courts on the basis of reasoning from, and analogy to, pre-existing rules. While in this process progressive ideals of what the law ought to be have a larger or smaller part, they can operate only within the limits fixed by the principles which underlie the already existing precedents. In this sense changes in the direction of law which are brought about by judicial decision are, in Holmes' phrase, always merely "interstitial" or "molecular". Legislation, on the other hand, is free to effect broad changes suddenly—its action is 'molar' in contrast to 'molecular'.

Jerome Hall, Living Law of Democratic Society (1949) pp. 56-58; 94-100; reprinted by permission of the author and Bobbs-Merrill Co., Inc.

LAW AS VALUATION

Even the theory that law represents merely the impact of the dominant forces in the society concedes that there is reason in the process. For unless the rulers are insane, their edicts represent deliberate end-seeking and the use of generalizations to attain their goals.

That sort of rationality, however, is hardly a sufficient foundation for a defensible philosophy of law. More significant in that regard is Aristotle's observation that certain laws are found in all societies whereas others are not. The former, he declared universal and natural, the latter, particular and conventional. As was pointed out above, the Stoics took the decisive step in the development of this theory by insisting that justice ("virtue," "Natural Law") is an essential attribute of positive law. Though it was subjected to continuous attack and was modified and restated in various ways, the Stoic theory of law prevailed for over a millenium and a half.

This perennial perspective rests ultimately on the position that human beings are rational and social. What do these words mean, and how can that position be defended in view of man's evident passion and aggressiveness? "Reason" is a term pregnant with endless ambiguity. It has been restricted to the recognition of logical implication, correct reasoning. It has, on the other hand, been taken to mean no less than the apprehension of universals, "the one in the many." It may designate only scientific thought or it may mean practical judgment exhibited in the efficient attainment of desired ends. It means merely the recognition of self-interest and it means wisdom, including knowledge of moral as well as factual truth. "Reason" has been defined to include all of these and, no doubt, other meanings. The common thread running through most of these meanings is that human beings manifest certain, probably distinctive functionings in generalizing and in the invention and use of symbols to communicate their ideas and ideals.

The other ultimate component of human nature, sociability, stems from the Greek view that man is a "political animal" and it has been stressed in secular Natural Law theory beginning, in modern times, with Grotius. Reason, alone, being regarded as insufficient for the discovery of what is right or good, the "social nature of man" became an essential complement. This sort of sociability must be distinguished from the gregarious instinct. For example, no one has ever recorded any Thoreau-like behavior among bees or ants.[2] On the other hand, there is ample evidence to support the insight that man's intelligence permeates his gregariousness and that human co-operation therefore reflects a unique sociability.

Behaviorist psychology, Kohler's studies of apes, Pavlov's experiments, as well as the recent resurgence of primitive savagery in Europe have cast doubt on the traditional psychology of human nature, especially on any claim to superior distinctiveness; indeed, it is

recognized that no mere beast is capable of the inordinate cruelty of *homo sapiens*. These challenges
require drastic modification of optimistic psychologies
just as they compel us to read the traditional Natural
Law postulates as emphases on certain differentials
rather than as assertions that men are wholly rational
and social.

But they do not invalidate the traditional insights.
We have only to point to the theoretical structure of
science, to philosophy, to advanced legal systems, and
to the progress in political ideals as evidence of human
rationality. It is significant that this is the position of
a distinguished biologist, Julian Huxley, who writes,
"The first and most obviously unique characteristic of
man is his capacity for conceptual thought . . .;" "a
cumulative tradition . . . capable of indefinite improvement in quality and increase in quantity" is
another distinctively human attribute. He notes that
". . . man is the only organism normally and inevitably
subject to psychological conflict." He stresses man's
"conscious reason," his "conscious purpose and his set
of values." "There may be other beings in this vast
universe," concludes Mr. Huxley, "endowed with reason, purpose and aspiration; but we know nothing
of them. So far as our knowledge goes, human mind
and personality are unique and constitute the highest
product yet achieved by the cosmos." "Biology thus
reinstates man in a position analogous to that conferred on him as Lord of Creation by theology."[2a]

❋   ❋   ❋

The law of democratic societies is distinguishable
from that of other polities in that it represents the
maximization of values. It facilitates more and higher
value-experience than does that of any other form of
polity because, in the first place, the conditions for
sound valuation are present in greater degree—democratic process, especially the activities which actualize
the Bill of Rights, means, in this connection, sound
methods for discovering the right answers to social
problems. Morality implies voluntary conduct, wherein obligations are recognized. Thus, secondly, regardless of how wise and good a dominating élite might

be, the rules they laid down could not begin to approximate the values experienced by a population legislating for itself, itself discovering the right answers and voluntarily laying down the rules to govern inter-personal relations, which are recognized as morally binding. Creativity in the realm of moral experience, no less than in the exact sciences, is stimulated by the quality of democratic law, which is the decisive relevant institution though not, of course, the only important influence in this regard.

That law is valuation also implies that law is an on-going process, that the process is meaningful in relation to the solution of social problems, and that legislation and adjudication are ways of discovering and using the ethically valid answers, which it is feasible to implement by force.

We must therefore question the common assertion that any legal order embodies only a minimum of morality. Sometimes, to be sure, it does even less than that. For example, even a minimum of morality would oblige an expert swimmer to save a drowning child if he could do so without endangering himself. But, though he need only reach out his arm to rescue the child, our law requires no such action by him. So, too, a minimum of morality would require individuals not to indulge in the vicious libel of minorities. But that and many other grossly immoral acts and omissions are legally privileged.

On the other hand, our law sometimes imposes a great deal more than a minimum of morality. For example, a railroad has been held to owe a duty of care to the heroic rescuer of a stranger. A right to privacy is becoming increasingly recognized. And, as regards trustees and guardians, our law has long imposed a standard of morality that is rigorous enough to satisfy the most sensitive conscience. Thus, it is not so much a minimum that is significant in legal valuation as are certain other criteria, namely, the feasibility of enforcement by coercive measures; the clash with other, superior values, e.g., whether it is possible to bar certain anti-social acts such as the libel of minorities, without at the same time repressing freedom of speech; and there is also the doctrine *de minimis,* which postulates the opposite of the traditional notion, namely, that the pettiest wrongs are too insignificant to receive legal recognition.

But if the theory that law enforces a minimum of morality is oversimple, it also contains an important truth. Its valid implication is the distinction which the Puritans drew between law and grace, *i.e.,* beyond the moral duty of the law, though not uninfluenced by that, is the boundless area of individual sacrifice and devotion.

The values incorporated in democratic law represent the more stable policy decisions which it is wise and feasible to implement by compulsion. But such value experience understood *vis à vis* problem-solving usually involves varying degrees of uncertainty not only up to the point where the goals are definable with sufficient precision to render group action possible but even after "the" correct answers have been discovered. The problematic aspect of law-as-valuation, especially the tensions between any given implemented valuation and competing values is a permanent phase of the democratic process.

This is perhaps most evident in the clash between the values of freedom and those of equality. The following dilemma is presented: The expansion of law limits freedom but may increase equality; on the other hand, if people are left free, inequality increases. It is possible to indicate what goes on incessantly in the democratic process by noting that the resolution of this dilemma involves evaluation in *specific* factual situations and with reference to relatively narrow issues; that any given determinations are held tentatively and subject to improvement; and that specific interpretations of the meaning of "liberty" and "equality" are derived, which are often formulated in precise laws.

It is in this context of specific problem-solving that one must interpret the ideal of legal equality implied in the uniformity of law. The generality (impersonality) of the substantive law as well as the objectivity of legal method are the corresponding, implementing constructs. But the generality and uniformity of law only guarantee that, if it is discriminatory, it discriminates against an entire class. "Equality before the law" therefore stipulates that the generalized rules must be ethically valid. But this criterion, related to actual social problems, also implies that certain kinds of inequality, *e.g.*, those indicative of superior merit, are desirable. Moreover, the grant of equal opportunities not only carries no assurance that inequalities will not arise; it can be confidently predicted that inequalities will arise. The social objective is to confine them to rational ones.

That equality does not mean that all persons must be treated alike in all situations and relationships may be seen in the legal cognizance taken of social and economic facts, differences in sex, age, income, and so on. Laws limiting the employment of children, the working hours of women, the labor contract, insurance, the operation of factories, railroads and banks, etc., single out certain classes of persons upon whom special limitations are imposed. This means differential legal treatment. But it is not discriminatory in an objectionable sense. There is often a conflict between the ideal and a specific obligation to care for certain persons. If one has only enough food to sustain his family, and a neighbor is hungry, the law of family relations imposes unequal distribution. Equal incomes would provide more wealth for more persons but it would also doom the efficient operation of the economy. So, too, income tax laws impose differential burdens. Finally, there are deeply rooted attitudes and loyalties which obstruct direct or early application of legal provisions for equality in some spheres of social life. Only a harsh egalitarianism would ignore these sensibilities. Only a smug complacency would ignore the problems.

Just as the ideal of political equality must not be confused with actual power to influence policy-determination, so, too, the ideal of legal equality must not be confused with the actual functioning of the legal system. The conditions of men vary in power, wealth, intelligence, and resourcefulness; these undoubtedly affect the operation of the law. There is certainly point in the criticism that it takes money to retain counsel, to appeal an adverse decision, and to employ lobbyists. The legal ideal falls short of complete realization because the facts often render that impossible; moreover, opposing values inhibit efforts to solve the problems by changing the facts. Solution takes the path of amelioration in specific areas, *e.g.*, legal aid societies, volunteer committees of Bar associations, public defenders, laws waiving court costs, and the organization of labor unions and other associations whose resources are sufficient to place their members on a parity with any litigant.

Thus, "freedom" and "equality" are not only essential democratic, though vague, ideals; they also raise many difficult problems. Democratic society holds fast to the central insight of the equal claims of personality, as such; hence, it seeks to determine what is arbitrary and to oppose unfair claims to special privilege. It provides the conditions wherein sound decisions can be reached regarding competing values. Its legal order represents a relatively refined instrument, stipulating and determining what values to advance, how far, and at what cost of other values. It represents a series of the more definite value judgments applied in limited areas, where not only equality but also many desirable inequalities are sanctioned. Actual capacity, need, merit, predictions regarding the consequences of certain policies, and many other factors are reflected in the legal system. The net result is a series of considered judgments representing differential specific applications of the principles of freedom and equality.

The problematic character of law in a democratic society is further revealed when we consider that, whereas morality presupposes freedom, law involves coercion. Yet, in law, morality is forcibly sanctioned, presenting a union of antimonies. We rationalize the situation by asserting that the law exists for bad people and that its purpose is to achieve a uniformity of conduct by compelling them to do what most persons do of their own volition. In addition, by restraining evil men, law enables good men to carry on worthy activities.

In a deeper sense, the legal order helps all of us to discover the correct solution of moral problems and to do the right thing. It aids solution of difficult moral problems by making readily and precisely available much of the accumulated ethical knowledge of the past. It stimulates us to do the right thing not so much because we are deterred by fear of sanctions as by rendering it easier for us, more or less unconciously, to repress our anti-social instincts and to remain emotionally satisfied despite our inhibitions.[3] That law checks the rush of destructive instinct is obvious. That, in doing so, it frees energy for devotion to worth-while endeavor is only slightly less apparent. In thus conditioning conduct, law functions as a major determinant of human nature. In this process men receive much of their moral education.

We may state the principal conclusions reached thus far: positive law consists of propositions stated in the form of hypothetical-imperative judgments; the formal source and the enforcer of these bilateral rules is the maximum power center in the society; the rules of law stand highest in the hierarchy of norms in the sense that, in case of conflict with other norms, law prevails; the sanction of legal rules is enforced, ultimately, by physical power which operates unconditionally; the rules of law, by and large, implement interests inclusive of the entire society; the rules of law are coalescences of the ideas, signified by the rules, with value; and this attribute is divisible into (a) conformity to ethical principles and (b) self-rule—the distinctive quality of the law of democratic society.

Edmond N. Cahn, Sense of Injustice (1949) pp. 11-27; reprinted by permission of the author and the New York University Press.

II. *The Sense of Injustice*

A Path to Justice. The stubborn survival of some sort of faith in *natural* justice should point to a nucleus of truth. Errors, whether sincere or interested, were committed by the natural-law philosophers; the pretensions of their systems became far too extravagant. Natural law sought to decide controversies in which it had no role and to offer absolute answers where only the tentative or relative would serve. It was guilty of the Duchess' fallacy in *Alice in Wonderland*: it insisted that everything must have a moral in a universe full of the irrelevant, the inane, the neutral, the fatuous, and the frolicsome. To make matters worse, its principles proved hopelessly discrete. The evolutionary connectedness of human life and of man's relations is the root fact of law; a collection, however ideal, of static, discontinuous maxims simply could not perform the task. Justice, as many attempted definitions have rather clearly demonstrated, is unwilling to be captured in a formula. Nevertheless, it somehow remains a word of magic evocations.

One clear occasion of these difficulties was the resort to rigorous deductive reasoning in the derivation of rules from ambitious axioms. Here it is proposed to pursue a different route. Perhaps the human mind does contain self-evident truths concerning justice, from which legal norms less obvious in their nature may be deduced; we shall, all the same, feel safer in trusting to experience and observation. What is given in experience appears, of course, less orderly and consecutive than any categorical maxim, but it at least offers a point of return in the cycle of ratiocination. As general propositions concerning law must ultimately succeed or fail in terms of their verifiable consequences, one would suppose that they can best be obtained in the very market place where they are to be realized upon. Justice is, of course, an ideal value of highest rank, but its positive embodiments are so thoroughly alloyed with other values and interests that it can never be completely refined out. Generalizing from particular rules and judgments will not assist us, for how are we to know that the instances selected are themselves wholly "just"? The lofty abstract concept lurks somewhere beyond our discernment; it offers no incarnation which may be trusted as quite unmixed and pure.

Thus we might be left entirely without empirical guidance, were it not for what we are about to call *the sense of injustice*. This sense is clearly and frequently manifested; it is a familiar and observable phenomenon. Its incidences show how justice arises and what biologic purpose it serves in human affairs.

Why do we speak of the "sense of injustice" rather than the "sense of justice?" Because "justice" has been so beclouded by natural-law writings that it almost inevitably brings to mind some ideal relation or static condition or set of preceptual standards, while we are concerned, on the contrary, with what is active, vital, and experiential in the reactions of human beings. Where justice is thought of in the customary manner as an ideal mode or condition, the human response will be merely contemplative, and contemplation bakes no loaves. But the response to a real or imagined instance of injustice is something quite different; it is alive with movement and warmth in the human organism. For this reason, the name "sense of injustice" seems much to be preferred. What then would be meant by "justice" in the context of the approach adopted in this book? The answer would appear to be: not a state, but a process; not a condition, but an action. "Justice," as we shall use the term, means the *active process* of remedying or preventing what would arouse the sense of injustice.

And now for some instances:

Instance A. Five men who had met to dine together are brought before a judge, on the complaint of the same police officer that each of them parked his automobile one hour overtime in the same block. All plead "not guilty" but offer no evidence or explanation. The testimony of the policeman is uniform, regarding each alleged offense. The judge acquits three, imposes a five-dollar fine on one, and sends the fifth defendant to jail for ninety days. This evokes the sense of injustice.

Obviously, in a given ethos all five might have been acquitted; alternately, all might have been convicted and punished in some appropriate manner. Regardless of the individual dispositions, the inequalities arbitrarily created arouse the sense of injustice, because equal treatment of those similarly situated with respect to the issue before the court is a deep implicit expectation of the legal order.

Now equality is in general the creature of positive law.[4] Courts and legislatures establish classes of humanity, categorizing for one or another purpose the duties and rights they desire to effect, to destroy, or to qualify. Thus, before a court, those only are equal whom the law has elected to equalize. The point is that the inequalities resulting from the law must make sense. If decisions differ, some discernible distinction must be found bearing an intelligible relation to the difference in result. The sense of injustice revolts against whatever is unequal by caprice. The arbitrary, though indispensable to many of law's daily operations, is always suspect; it becomes unjust when it discriminates between indistinguishables.

As human integers, men are indistinguishables. This natural fact imposes a limit on the classificatory discretion of positive law. The sense of injustice does not tolerate juridic classes by which the integral status of man is violated. Legal slavery, for example, was doomed to disappear everywhere, for no other reason than that a slave is a man. Here we recognize one of the fixed stars of an anthropocentric jurisprudence: nature has made man a prime which positive law cannot justly differentiate.

Why does the sense of injustice call actively for equality? One explanation is that equal treatment of all within a recognized class is a necessary attribute of any legal order; the very concept of law requires this minimal regularity. In terms of pure intellection, such an analysis appears quite persuasive, but it can hardly account for the sense of injustice. One does not become outraged and furious merely because some decision has violated a dialectic pattern. The true reason must go considerably deeper, below the threshold of feeling. It must make clear why the humble and illiterate, the drawers of water and hewers of wood can hate injustice with a burning hatred. The roots of this demand for equality will be exposed when we come later to describe the sense of injustice as a general phenomenon.

Instance B. Two shoe-factory employees, carrying a large amount of money, are waylaid, robbed, and fatally injured. The incident occurs during a period of intense public feeling against radicals of every kind. Subsequently, a shoemaker and a fish peddler are charged with the crime and though entirely innocent, are convicted on flimsy circumstantial evidence. The fact that the fish peddler is an avowed anarchist influences the decisions of the trial judge, the jury, the appellate court, and an advisory commission appointed by the governor. After languishing in jail for seven years, the accused are executed. This is felt to be unjust.

Here the sense of injustice attaches itself to the notion of desert. The law is regarded as an implement for giving men what they deserve, balancing awards and punishments in the scale of merit. As *general* merit is so difficult of admeasurement, legal action is usually expected to relate to particular merit; that is, to the right, duty, or guilt acquired in a specific circumstance. Sometimes, because of its own clumsiness, the law cannot fulfill this function. Then it may convict a murderer for a murder he has not committed, or a gangster for failure to report his income. In such case, the legal subterfuge does not evoke a keen sense of injustice, for desert has been somehow accorded. Thus, not merely the truth or falsity of a verdict but its relation to desert is a criterion of approval.

Nothing can so heartily satisfy this sense as an incident of "poetic" justice. That he who lives by the sword shall die by the sword, who digs a pit for his neighbor shall fall therein, who builds a high gallows for the innocent shall hang thereon—all these denouements seem peculiarly fitting. But the law cannot so variously adapt the punishment to the crime; it has a limited stock of beneficences and sanctions, limited by the need of legislative control over the inventive imagination of judges. Poetic justice, rare enough as it is, is also imperfect, for the wholesale malefactor can die only once. The sense of injustice does not call for highly dramatic or individualized awards. It adjusts to familiar imperfections. What it cannot stomach is the use of law to raise up the guilty or to punish the innocent.

Instance C. The defendant is convicted of treasonable utterances by which he successfully sought to impair the morale and obedience of combat soldiers in time of war. The sentence of the court is that he be compelled to submit to a surgical operation on his vocal chords, so that thereafter he may only bark like a dog. This affronts the sense of injustice.

Here the main concern is with human dignity. From early times, cruel and unusual punishments have been relegated to the discretion of deity or destiny; law has pulled away from vengeance and humiliation. Vicious and debasing punishments are felt to dishonor the court and the humanity whose authority it wields. Forty stripes were the ancient limit, not so much in the interest of the criminal as of the general respect for man.[5] On the same theory, an alien visitor was considered to be entitled to legal safeguards. In Athens, it was an execrable crime *erranti viam non monstrare,*[6] because the stranger who had lost his way had a residual status as a man.

Human dignity is one of the tacit assumptions of the law.[7] It expresses itself generally in the deep distinctions among accidental, innocent intentional, and guilty intentional conduct. Motives count because man is assumed to be primarily rational, free of will, and capable of choice. When he acts accidentally, he is regarded as the mere instrument of external forces; when he acts intentionally but in good faith, guilt may attach within circumscribed areas: only evil purpose will invoke mortal guilt. No one judges Oedipus as he does Nero, though each intentionally killed a person who was his parent.[8]

Positive law, building upon this dignity, may make it expensive. Thus the ancient Pharisees held that it precluded vicarious responsibility in law, *e.g.*, liability for the wrongful acts of one's slave.[9] And, in our own times, dignity has been held incompatible with requiring collective action in employee relations or prohibiting child labor. The sense of injustice is not so easily taken in: it can penetrate the masquerade.

Instance D. An important patent litigation is pending before an appellate court of three judges. One of them, having received a bribe from the appellant's attorney, succeeds in persuading his honorable colleagues to join with him in deciding for the appellant.

Here we have an example of injustice involved in the operation of the judicial process. The nature of that process requires certain familiar attributes and procedures, such as impartiality, notice, fair hearing, and judgment of defined issues predicated upon identifiable evidence. Of course, the judicial process, even when ideally applied, does not lead to ascertainment of all the truth, for there are subliminal values in most disputes which not even the most thorough hearing will disclose. Nor does it lead to judgments of perfect wisdom: the law cannot so individualize its operations as to meet the idiosyncrasy, the irreducible uniqueness of each case. Patterns are developed in the light of the repetitive aspects of litigation, and much that protrudes beyond the pattern must be ignored. But, whatever its pragmatic limitations, the judicial process is required to exhibit a fair effort at finding truth and exercising wisdom. Without that effort—involving notice, hearing, and deliberation—it loses its rank as process; it becomes gross will. Informed by this view, the sense of injustice protests all the more angrily against abuse of legal procedures to serve oppressive or vindictive ends.

Instance E. Some workmen engaged in excavation dig up certain ancient Pythagorean manuscripts and turn them over to the owner of the land. Their contents, hitherto unknown, excite much discussion, which reaches the ears of the city magistrate. He borrows the manuscripts, reads only the table of contents, and determines that the text will have a tendency to undermine established religion. Thereupon the legislature is consulted and, after hearing the magistrate take oath that the books ought not to be read or preserved, decrees that they be publicly burned.[10] This is felt to be unjust.

The concern in this instance is with the authorized functions of government, its right of censorship and relation to freedom of inquiry. There is hardly a conceivable function that government has not arrogated to itself at one time or another, under pretext of divine authority, public welfare, or bald caprice; and judgments of propriety on this score are almost completely relative.[11] Yet censorship of thought somehow remains the most obnoxious of all such interferences, perhaps because it eventually prevents all intelligent amelioration of government itself, perhaps because it insults and degrades the rational claims of the citizen.

What powers men delegate to their governments depend upon what they think of themselves and of their needs. Recognized needs may call for severe abnegation, especially in times of great public emergency. But if the citizenry thinks well of its own intelligence and wisdom, it will bridle at censorship; it will struggle for access to facts and to ideas. Men who do not respect human capacity will raise no such objections. They will feel no loss in being closed out from what they cannot use. Thus, here again the view of law parallels closely the view of human capacities.

Instance F. Relying on a series of formal charters, colonists set out from their homeland and, despite fearful perils and hardships, succeed in building the beginnings of a new pioneer society. They organize local governments and militia, open courts and schools, construct highways, harbors, and trading centers. Fighting back the savage aborigines, they hew down forests, plough and plant the land, and establish their councils of self-rule. Just at the dawn of their success, the home legislature, thousands of miles away from their new problems and free mores, passes a decree that it has the right to bind the colonies in all cases whatsoever. The sense of injustice is outraged.

In this instance, normal expectations have been disappointed—a species of injustice that embraces many varied actions of legislatures and courts. Any retroactive change in substantive law would, of course, furnish a conspicuous example of such disappointment, for the law itself creates expectation of the consistency and continuity of its own operations. But expectations may arise from other sources, such as the moral views and practices of the community and its economic fabric. The positive law may be unjust in breaking not only its promise of regularity but likewise its promise of adequacy and utility. What is the law good for, if it is deaf to patent needs?

One of these is the need for evolutionary change in the law itself. There is a legitimate expectation that courts and legislatures will discern what is useful and good in new occasions. The sense of injustice may find as much offense in a regularity that is slavish as in an inconsiderate change. In the former case, the provocation generally seems lighter, for the expectation has not been weighted with reliance and the direction of legal progress remains debatable. A prestige of legitimacy attaches to the known law, rebuttable only by showing that it is substantially wrong. At times, there arise revolutionary needs that demand a clean sweep of the established order and will not permit vested rights to stand in the way; but in the usual situation the law can fulfill its function best by seeing that contracts are performed, existing social standards are enforced, and relations which it invited men to create are sustained. Thus it is that judges in moving the law forward, case by case, are always impeded; attitudes and reliances intervene between the precedent and the attempt to improve it. Positive law as it progresses must weigh the utility of the new rule against that of confidence and certainty. The sense of injustice warns against either standing still or leaping forward, it calls for movement in an intelligible design.

What the Instances Show. These instances prick the

contours of our topic. The sense of injustice may now be described as a general phenomenon operative in the law. Among its facets are the demands for equality, desert, human dignity, conscientious adjudication, confinement of government to its proper functions, and fulfillment of common expectations. These are facets, not categories. They tend to overlap one another and do not together exhaust the sense of injustice. They should be thought of as facets, each partially shaping the outlines of the others in an almost fluid continuity. They do not resemble a neat row of discrete ice cubes or even the rigid mold that shapes the cubes, for they are only aspects, not parts, of the sense of injustice.

Are these aspects ethical in their nature? They are, for they posit certain explicit values in the realm of human conduct. But they are not merely ethical: as they enter into the shaping of positive law, they acquire a special direction and form qualified by the past history and present felt needs of the juridic system, and modified again by the factor of sanction. An ethical impulse to which legal sanctions have been attached is not quite the same as it was; its content and intensity must shrink to the size of its new responsibility.

Are these aspects of justice universal? Hardly. The claim might be made that they are limits which the variables of positive law tend to approach, and as we presently consider the sources of the sense of injustice that claim may gain some support. It must be remembered, however, that most of these aspects pertain to the operation of law rather than to its substance, and that positive rules contribute a great deal to the body and meaning of equality, legitimacy of expectations, and so forth. The universal element would thus appear exceedingly narrow, and may be restricted to inescapable natural dimensions such as the integral status of individual man.

Concepts may be real without being universal. In any sound pragmatic sense, principles are real so far as they have meaningful consequences. Of course, their rank may be made to vary with their universality, but loftiness of rank is all too often achieved by means of dilution and excessive thinning. Our interest here is rather in the real qua efficacious. Utterly universal operation of one cause would crowd out all others; it would destroy the dynamism of nature and level human life to monotony. Insistence on perfect universality would lead only to an ultimate colorless abstraction "sans everything." In the finite world of which we speak, the genuinely efficient causes are finite and plural; finite effects suggest and indicate finite causes. The justice that we can learn to know is neither completely universal nor categorically right; by that token, it is real in human affairs. It makes a practical difference.

Nor need we view the sense of injustice as dangling beneath some hypostatic framework of natural law, itself suspended from divine law in a chain of infinite regress. The law of nature may exist, may not exist, or may linger in the limbo of doubt for purposes of this inquiry, whose movement is forward to consequences, not backward to origins. We are concerned with studying the sense of injustice, not as a product or effect, but as an operative cause in the law. Thus it is that Ockham's razor excises natural law from our present interest; it does not excise the sense of injustice unless all the phenomena of positive law could be explained without it.

Finally, the sense of injustice is no mere generic label for the concepts already reviewed. It denotes that sympathetic reaction of outrage, horror, shock, resentment, and anger, those affections of the viscera and abnormal secretions of the adrenals that prepare the human animal to resist attack. Nature has thus equipped all men to regard injustice to another as personal aggression. Through a mysterious and magical *empathy* or imaginative interchange, each projects himself into the shoes of the other, not in pity or compassion merely, but in the vigor of self-defense. Injustice is transmuted into assault; the sense of injustice is the implement by which assault is discerned and defense is prepared.

Justice thus acquires its public meaning, as those

in a given ethos perceive the same threat and experience the same organic reactions. It is possible to speak of justice without utter relativism or solipsism, just because of this astonishing interchangeability within man's imagination. If a man did not have the capacity to recognize oppression of another as a species of attack upon himself, he would be unready—in the glandular sense—to face the requirements of juridic survival. In fine, the human animal is predisposed to fight injustice.

This predisposition like other natural capacities is designed to end in action. The individual man stands at the center of all thngs, bound by the perspective predicament to his own brief time and narrow place. The sense of injustice gives him a lengthening tether so that he may wander away from self and its setting. But tethered he remains. His survival does not require that the sense of injustice encompass infinitude; at a certain distance from the center in sympathy and circumstance, his reaction will shade off into contemplation, cool appraisal, and ultimate indifference. There are wrongs that retain only literary concernment. Iphigenia and her sorrows are such an instance.

Our awareness, however, is not necessarily lulled by mere disparity of culture, law, or ethical tradition, for Socrates' fate haunts the thoughts of every generation. The criterion is whether the circumstances permit imaginative interchange. If the specific threat be such as to project itself out of history and into the radius of possible experience, it becomes real, it calls for action. For example, corrupt judges and mob passion are ominous in every age.

The experience of the sense of injustice is of a social nature, enlarging the calculus of individual chances. What may or may not affect the particular human being in his own small ambit will inevitably, in the course of sufficient time, touch someone somewhere. That is why the jural status of each is felt to depend upon a just order of increasingly wide extension.

The sense of injustice now appears as an indissociable blend of reason and empathy. It is evolutionary in its manifestations. Without reason, it could not serve the ends of social utility, which only observation, analysis, and science can discern. Without empathy, it would lose its warm sensibility and its cogent natural drive. It is compounded, indissolubly, of both and can subsist on neither alone. For sheer rationality without an empathic fundament would usually degenerate to extreme skepticism and doubt; while empathy, uninformed by reason, would serve up only the illiterate gropings of animal faith. Together reason and empathy support our juridic world. Through them men may learn to identify their own interests with those of an unlimited community, no longer doubting in philosophy what they do not doubt in their hearts.[12]

Is the sense of injustice right? Certainly not, if rightness means conformity to some absolute and inflexible standard. There is nothing so easy or mechanical about it. Blended as it is of empathy and reason, its correctness in particular cases will vary greatly, for how can we know that the intellect has understood and that projection has comprehended every last relevant factor? Who will measure the limits of inquiry or affix the seal of completeness?

Fortunately we appear able to dispense with such a seal, accepting in its stead the assurances that come from inner conviction and from juridic experience. The sense of injustice is right in so far as its claims are recognized in action. Its logical justification must be found in its efficacy, for it succeeds in fact precisely to the extent that relevant circumstances have been understood, felt, and appreciated. Like other biological equipment it endures because it serves, and serves better through progressive adaptation. So, despite all blunders and insensibilities, the sense of injustice is on the right side, the side of fallible men. Offering a common language for communication and mutual defense, it reduces the perils of isolation. It affords some warrant of a progressively better legal order, and thus makes law a vehicle of persuasion. Plato has said that the creation of the world is the victory of persuasion over force;[13] the instrument of that victory is justice.

❋   ❋   ❋   ❋   ❋

Lon L. Fuller, Law in Quest of Itself (1940) pp.
5-6; 99-104; 135-137; reprinted by permission of the
author and the Foundation Press.

By legal positivism I mean that direction of legal
thought which insists on drawing a sharp distinction
between the law *that is* and the law *that ought to be*.
Where this distinction is taken it is, of course, for the
sake of the law *that is*, and is intended to purify it by
purging it of what Kelsen calls "wish-law." Generally
—though not invariably—the positivistic attitude is
associated with a degree of ethical skepticism. Its
unavowed basis will usually be found to rest in a conviction that while one may significantly describe the
law *that is*, nothing that transcends personal predilec-
tion can be said about the law *that ought to be*.

Natural law, on the other hand, is the view which
denies the possibility of a rigid separation of the *is*
and the *ought*, and which tolerates a confusion of
them in legal discussion. There are, of course, many
"systems" of natural law. Men have drawn their
criteria of justice and of right law from many sources:
from the nature of things, from the nature of man,
from the nature of God. But what unites the various
schools of natural law, and justifies bringing them
under a common rubric, is the fact that in all of them
a certain coalescence of the *is* and the *ought* will be
found. Though the natural law philosopher may
admit the authority of the state even to the extent of
conceding the validity of enacted law which is obviously "bad" according to his principles, it will be
found in the end that he draws no hard and fast line
between law and ethics, and that he considers that the
"goodness" of his natural law confers on it a kind of
reality which may be temporarily eclipsed, but can
never be wholly nullified, by the more immediately
effective reality of enacted law. So far as the question
of ultimate motives is concerned, it is fairly obvious
that if the positivist insists on separating the *is* and
the *ought* for the sake of the *is*, the natural-law
philosopher is attempting to serve the *ought* when he

refuses to draw a sharp distinction between it and the *is*.

* * *

So far we have been almost exclusively concerned with the difficulties encountered in the search for some criterion which will separate the law that is from the law that ought to be. Our attention has been concentrated on the obstacles which beset the law's quest of itself. I have attempted to reveal the essentially sterile nature of any form of legal positivism which purports to divorce itself from a definite ethical or practical goal; I have tried to demonstrate the bankruptcy of those formalized varieties of positivism which purport to deal analytically and descriptively with an assumed "pure fact of law." Does this rejection of the claims of "scientific" positivism imply a recommendation that we should go the whole way in the opposite direction of legal thought? Am I to be understood as asserting, in effect, that almost any system of natural law is to be preferred to legal positivism? If not, then what attitude is here implied toward the various theories of natural law that have come down to us from the speculations of the past?

In answering these questions, I should like to have it understood at the outset that any compliments which may here be cast in the direction of natural law are not addressed to the doctrine of natural and inalienable rights. This warning would probably be unnecessary if it were not for the fact that we have got into the habit of identifying these two notions and of assuming that some conception of the natural rights of man must lie at the heart of every system of natural law. As a matter of fact, if we take into account the whole course of legal philosophy from its beginnings with the Greeks, the notion of natural rights appears not as an integral part of the theory of natural law but as a passing episode in the history of ethical and legal speculation. Even in its heyday the view was neither received unanimously, nor entertained by its philosophic adherents in the unqualified form it assumed in political documents. But there is no need here either to beat dead horses or to review their pedigrees. I am not advocating the doctrine of natural rights, and I may add that in my opinion the notion of "imputed rights," or rights in the positivistic sense, is open to many of the objections which have been advanced against natural rights.

Not only am I not proposing to re-fight the philosophic battles of the American and French Revolutions, but I am not attempting to set myself up as sponsor for any of the various systems of natural law which have been advocated in the past. In particular, I should dislike being called upon to undertake a defense of all the things which have been said in the name of that excellent philosopher, Saint Thomas Aquinas. On the other hand, I believe that there is much of great value for the present day in the writings of those thinkers who are classified, and generally dismissed, as belonging to the school of natural law, and I regard it as one of the most unfortunate effects of the positivistic trend still current that it has contributed to bring about the neglect of this important and fruitful body of literature. Ironically enough, one of the things which has rendered this literature unacceptable to the modern legal mind is a quality which ought really to have had precisely the opposite effect. It is one of the tenets of modern legal science that law is an integral part of the whole civilization of a society, and that fruitful work in the law presupposes a familiarity with the other social sciences such as psychology, economics and sociology. Yet this is only the rediscovery of a point of view which has always been taken for granted in natural law speculation. Unfortunately for the natural law philosopher, however, this interest in subjects outside his immediate field has as its price the possibility that his work may soon become dated. By relating his legal philosophy to the other social sciences, he runs the risk that the progress of those sciences may leave his work behind. So today, when we read in Ahrens' *Cour de Droit Naturel* that the theory of evolution is disproved by the fact that monkeys cannot be taught to talk,[14] we put the book back on the shelf in disgust and we forget, or fail to learn, that it contains an excellent discussion of the function of contract law, a discussion which is perhaps even more valuable today than when it was written. We fail also to realize that it was after all more significant that Ahrens' conception of law should have been broad enough to make the truths of biology legally relevant, than that he should have rejected a particular biological theory which was still a great novelty in his day. Of course the work of the positivists is essentially timeless; by abstracting law entirely from its environment and defining it not in terms of its content, but of its form and sanction, they run no risk either of being outdated or of ever contributing anything to the development of the law except restraints and inhibitions. Austin's theory, which suffered no contamination from the backward state of the social sciences of his day, remains today just as true, and just as lacking in significance for human affairs, as in 1832.

The chief value of the older books on natural law for us of the present day does not lie so much in the systems they expound, as in the kind of legal thinking they exemplify. The broader and freer legal method of these books is in a double sense "natural law." In the first place, it is the method men naturally follow when they are not consciously or unconsciously inhibited by a positivistic philosophy. When there is no warning stop sign, reason naturally pushes as far ahead as it can. In the second place, when reason is unhampered by positivistic restraints, it tends inevitably to find anchorage in the natural laws which are assumed to underlie the relations of men and to determine the growth and decay of civilizations.

* * *

It has been the service of a vigorous Swedish school of legal thought to bring home to us a realization of the extent to which the law, particularly judge-made law, shapes common morality.[15] They have shown us how false is the common picture according to which there exists outside the law, and wholly independent of it, a body of moral precepts which exerts a kind of one-way gravitational pull on the law, against which the law opposes a constant inertia, so that it lags always behind morality and only meets those minimum ethical demands which relate to the most pressing social needs. This whole "extra-legal" body of moral precepts is to a large extent a creature compounded of paper and ink and philosophic imagination. Actually, if we look to those rules of morality which have enough teeth in them to act as serious deterrents to men's pursuit of their selfish interests, we will find that far from being "extra-legal" they are intimately and organically connected with the functionings of the legal order. I may think that I drive carefully because it is my moral duty to do so as a good citizen, and I may suppose that the law merely takes over my standard of driving—which is, of course, that of the prudent man—as a test to apply to drivers less virtuous than myself. I forget to what extent my conceptions of my duty as a driver have been shaped by the daily activities of the traffic police. I forget that behind my standard of driving there may lie a vague fear of the ignominy involved in having to appear in traffic court, and that this fear may have had a great deal to do with shaping my conceptions of traffic morality.

It should be noted that the view I am expounding here does not assert that men are, in the ordinary affairs of life, consciously deterred by legal penalties. It concedes that the effective deterrents which shape the average man's conduct derive from morality, from a sense of right and wrong. What it asserts is that these conceptions of right and wrong are themselves significantly shaped by the daily functionings of the legal order, and that they would be profoundly altered if this legal order were to disappear. As business men we may perform our contracts not because we are afraid of a law suit, but because we feel that it is our duty to do so. But would this same conception of duty exist if the law enforced no contracts at all? In the moral environment out of which this conception of duty arises, is not the law itself one of the most important elements?

C. Natural Law

"It is not an accident that something very like a resurrection of natural law is going on the world over," Roscoe Pound, 25 Harvard Law Review (1911) p. 162, quoted in Haines, Revival of Natural Law Concepts (1930) p. 309.

The question whether law is founded on "convention" or exists by "nature" is one that was old when it was formulated by the Greek Sophists and Socrates. It is still with us. While *analytical jurisprudence* rests almost exclusively on the positive law, natural law theorists speak of a higher law behind or above all explicit legal prescriptions. Whether this "higher law" is deemed to originate in the universal elements of human reason, or in postulates of rational activity, or in the law of God, it has this characteristic in common: it is more authoritative than any specific human enactment and it serves as a critique of all existing law.

IN COURT: STATE v. TUNE[*]

The charge is murder in the first degree, allegedly committed on August 22, 1952. In the early morning hours from 12:20 A.M. to 5 A.M. of August 24, in custody and without counsel and surrounded only by police officers, the accused had "conversations" with Detective Lieutenant Neidorf during which not the accused but the lieutenant wrote down 14 pages of "narrative" which when completed the accused read aloud, had it read back to him by one of the officers, and signed.

It was not until over two months later that defendant, being without means to employ counsel, was assigned counsel in his defense. Assigned counsel have been members of the bar of this State for 37 years and 20 years respectively, and are practitioners of acknowledged standing, ability and integrity. The accused told them that he had signed a statement but that "he could tell us nothing about the contents of any statement that he may have signed." Counsel sought out the prosecutor, who acknowledged that he had such a "signed confession" but refused to permit counsel to examine either it or the statements of other

---

[*] Dissenting opinion of Justice Brennan in the Supreme Court of New Jersey, 13 N. J. 203 (1953) at pp. 230-235.

persons also in his possession. He also refused to disclose the names of such other persons.

Such investigation as counsel were able to make satisfied them, however, that there were "material discrepancies between the facts as we have been able to ascertain them and the theory of the homicide indicated by the State, and to ascertain the real truth of the matter and to prevent an injustice from being done," they sought from Judge Speakman and were granted the order directing that they be allowed "to inspect and make a copy of" the alleged confession, but their application for inspection of the statements of other persons, or, in the alternative, that they be supplied with the names of such other persons, was denied. * * *

It shocks my sense of justice that in these circumstances counsel for an accused facing a possible death sentence should be denied inspection of his confession which, were this a civil case, could not be denied.

* * * * *

In the ordinary affairs of life we would be startled at the suggestion that we should not be entitled as a matter of course to a copy of something we signed. Granted that there is a public interest present in the case of the confession of one accused of crime which makes generally inapplicable this rule of everyday affairs, how possibly can we say that counsel for the accused should be denied a copy in face of the affirmative findings by Judge Speakman, certainly supported by what was before him, that neither the public interest nor the prosecution of the State's case will suffer? Surely we have come a long way since the day when Mr. Justice Cardozo was able to discern only "The beginnings or at least the glimmerings" of a "power in courts of criminal jurisdiction to compel the discovery of documents in furtherance of justice." *People v. Supreme Court,* 245 N. Y. 24, 156 N. E. 84, 86 (*Ct. App.* 1927).

* * * * *

The implication in the majority's argument is that the accused is guilty so that not only is he not to be heard to complain of the use of the confession by the police as evidence to prove that fact and as a source of leads to make the case against him as ironclad as possible, but also that he has no complaint that his counsel are denied its use to aid them better to develop the whole truth. In other words, the State may eat its cake and have it too. To that degree the majority view sets aside the presumption of innocence and is blind to the superlatively important public interest in the acquittal of the innocent. To shackle counsel so that they cannot effectively seek out the truth and afford the accused the representation which is not his privilege but his absolute right seriously imperils our bedrock presumption of innocence. And the assertion that counsel will be allowed "ample time" at the trial to examine the confession is disingenuous to a fault. "Ample time" is no more than time to read the writing, perhaps a half-hour or an hour or two at best, hardly enough even for counsel to organize a proper cross-examination, let alone initiate and complete an investigation to satisfy themselves upon the vital question which is the essence of the inquiry, namely, the credibility of what appears in the confession.

The holding of this case gives the majority's protestation that "In this State our courts are always mindful of the rights of the accused" a hollow ring. The assurance seems doubly hollow in light of the emphasis upon formalism in this case while it has been our boast in all other causes that we have subordinated the procedural niceties to decisions on the merits.

Charles G. Haines, The Revival of Natural Law Concepts (1930) pp. 309-310; 316-319; 323; reprinted by permission of the Harvard University Press.

OBJECTIVES IN THE MODERN REVIVAL OF NATURAL LAW THINKING

Though no effort has been made to review any but a few of the many indications of the revival of natural law theories or of other types of higher law notions, sufficient evidence has been given to show that the return to these concepts, as criteria to measure the justice or validity of civil enactments, is more than a casual phase of current legal thought. Many factors are combining to bring to the fore again some of the ideas involved in the ancient doctrines of natural law. With widely differing purposes in view and with varying approaches to the fundamental and permanent principles of the law, legal philosophers, jurists, and judges, in applying concrete formulae of written charters, codes, or statutes, are wont to turn to modernized versions of the law of nature or of its counterpart, the law of reason. It is obvious of course that there are many thinkers in all countries who deny that there is such a thing as natural law with anything more than moral import, and who doubt the possibility of any such thing as a true philosophy of law. This point of view is so well known and is so general in legal thought that it seems unnecessary to elaborate on it in a treatise the object of which is primarily to indicate the significance of opposite opinions.

Among some of the prevailing tendencies in legal thinking which are giving an impetus to the revival of higher law theories are: first, the efforts to introduce in a more direct way ethical concepts into the law; second, the attempts to formulate ideal or philosophical standards to measure positive laws; third, the establishment of criteria for judges and administrators when they act as legislators; fourth, a justification for limits on the sovereignty of states. Each of these modern applications of natural law concepts deserves brief consideration.

1. *Natural Law as a Device to introduce Ethical Concepts into the Law.* It is apparent that natural law thinking has served many purposes in the process of the evolution of legal systems. None of these purposes has been more constant and influential than the effort to infuse ethical concepts into the practical application of the law by means of natural law principles. Every stage in legal evolution bears witness to the

close relation between law and morals and not infrequently the law of nature served as a convenient connecting link. A reference to the stages of legal history previously outlined will indicate some of the obvious relations between these concepts.

❋   ❋   ❋   ❋   ❋

2. *Natural Law as an Ideal or Philosophical Standard.* Beginning at least with the Greeks and the Romans natural law was thought of as an ideal or philosophical standard toward which temporary enactments or ordinary civil laws were to approximate. Similar use was made of the concept during the Middle Ages. And it is an ideal standard to which appeal may be made when other sources failed to give justice that judges and jurists frequently referred to natural law, natural justice, and natural rights. There are times, as in the seventeenth and eighteenth centuries, when natural law as an ideal was subordinated to certain fixed and immutable conceptions of law and right, but these were only temporary deviations from the main purpose of natural law ideas. For centuries law was liberalized chiefly "by a juristic doctrine that all legal institutions and all legal rules were to be measured by reason and that nothing could stand in law that could not maintain itself in reason."[1] The use of natural law as a standard to guide law in its progressive development is again receiving serious consideration. Law must take its bearings from the ethical standards of justice. This gives rise to certain requirements, as, for example, equality before the law, which involves the idea of fair play. Speaking of the attempts to put in opposition to positive law, the law of nature in the seventeenth and eighteenth centuries, Sir Paul Vinogradoff suggests that "unless I am much mistaken we witness another wave of this kind in our own time."[2] During ancient and mediaeval times, he observes, two purposes of natural law were gradually evolved, one in which it served a theoretic foundation for axiomatic truths from which a rational system of positive law could be derived. According to this purpose existing legal rules were accepted as manifestations of permanent legal principles. On the

other hand, the concept was used as a critical standard to distinguish between reasonable and unreasonable rules. It was used by Rousseau and Kant to serve as a philosophical basis for revolutionary ideas. Modern exponents of the law of nature, such as Charmont, Saleilles, and Stammler recur to natural law as a critical standard. The new natural law is regarded as a pervasive method by the help of which rules of law are to be criticized and estimated. Thus the evolution of natural law has been influenced by the tendency toward the scientific treatment of social life in distinction from the rationalistic individualism of the eighteenth century. The problem today is regarded as one of ascertaining certain standards of social value, and in this process the new natural law takes a prominent place, not as a fixed and immutable standard as of the eighteenth century, but as a standard which changes to suit the conditions of various races and divergent times and conditions.

There is a better appreciation today of the fact that in certain divisions of the law there are few rules and that judicial decisions are based chiefly on standards and degrees.[3] The application of such phrases as those of "fair conduct" in the case of a fiduciary, "due care" in the law of negligence, "good faith" and "fair competition" in business transactions, "reasonable facilities" in furnishing public utility services, "fair return" on property invested in a business, and, "due process of law" in depriving an individual of life, liberty, and property are well-known illustrations of the method of determining rights on the basis of standards rather than rules. In cases involving such concepts the judge must form his own standard and measure the degree of agreement or variation of conduct with the standard. "He must balance all his ingredients, his philosophy, his logic, his analogies, his history, his customs, his sense of right, and all the rest, and, adding a little here and taking out a little there, must determine, as wisely as he can, which weight shall tip the scales."[4] Some of these standards found their way into the law through the frank recognition of natural law theories.[5] And there are abundant indications that natural law methods of thinking are conditioning their application in various branches of modern law.

Instead of seeking a law of absolute significance, modern jurists find in natural law an ideal with changing content which furnishes a standard to test what is theoretically and practically just under certain given conditions.[6] This natural law is regarded as "an idealized ethical custom and an ideal picture of the end of law, painted, it may be, with reference to the institutions and ethical customs of the time and place, which may serve as an instrument of shaping and developing legal materials and of drawing in and fashioning materials from outside of law."[7]

We are witnessing, then, the rehabilitation of natural law theories, not as a formal part of positive law, but as conceptions wielding influence on the opinions of judges and legislators.[8]

❀   ❀   ❀   ❀   ❀

3. *Higher Laws to guide Judges as Legislators.* Modern exponents of natural law theories reject the mechanical notion of the place and function of the judge whereby he is expected merely to seek and apply predetermined rules and is not permitted to mold the law in the course of his application of these rules. They believe that whether legal traditions admit it openly or conceal the practice judges necessarily take a prominent part in the lawmaking process as they adapt legal rules to the unusual conditions of concrete cases. They maintain that "the judge who would think and act rightly in his function of rendering judgment must be able, as far as inelastic provisions of the statute do not prevent him, to discover in the law and make effective that which he himself, if placed in the situation of the parties, would feel right and just."[9]

Roscoe Pound, An Introduction to the Philosophy of Law (1922) pp. 49-53; reprinted by permission of the author and the Yale University Press.

In the United States, since the natural law of the eighteenth-century publicists had become classical, we relied largely upon an American variant of natural law. It was not that natural law expressed the nature of man. Rather it expressed the nature of government. One form of this variant was due to our doctrine that the common law of England was in force only so far as applicable to our conditions and our institutions. The attempt to put this doctrine philosophically regards an ideal form of the received common law as natural law and takes natural law to be a body of deductions from or implications of American institutions or the nature of our polity. But yesterday the Supreme Court of one of our states laid down dogmatically that primogeniture in estates tail (which by the way is still possible in one of the oldest of the original states) could not co-exist with "the axioms of the constitution" which guarantees to each state a republican form of government. More generally, however, the American variant of natural law grew out of an attempt at philosophical statement of the power of our courts with respect to unconstitutional legislation. The constitution was declaratory of principles of natural constitutional law which were to be deduced from the nature of free government. Hence constitutional questions were always only in terms questions of constitutional interpretation. They were questions of the meaning of the document, as such, only in form. In substance they were questions of a general constitutional law which transcended the text; of whether the enactment before the court conformed to principles of natural law "running back of all constitutions" and inherent in the vary idea of a government of limited powers set up by a free people. Now that courts with few exceptions have given over this mode of thinking and the highest court in the land has come to apply the limitations of the fifth and fourteenth amendments as legal standards, there are some who say that we no longer have a constitutional law. For how can there be law unless as a body of rules declaring a natural law which is above all human enactment? The interpretation of a written instrument, no matter by whom enacted, may be governed by law, indeed, but can yield no law. Such ideas die hard. In the language of the eighteenth century, our courts sought to make our positive law, and in particular our legislation, express the nature of American political institutions, they sought so to shape it and restrain it as to make it give effect to an ideal of our policy.

Later in the nineteenth century natural law as a deduction from American institutions or from "free government" gave way to a metaphysical-historical theory worked out in Continental Europe. Natural rights were deductions from a fundamental metaphysically demonstrable datum of individual free will, and natural law was an ideal critique of positive law whereby to secure these rights in their integrity. History showed us the idea of individual liberty realizing itself in legal institutions and rules and doctrines; jurisprudence developed this idea into its logical consequences and gave us a critique of law whereby we might be delivered from futile attempts to set up legal precepts beyond the necessary minimum for insuring the harmonious co-existence of the individual and his fellows. This mode of thought was well suited to a conception of law as standing between the abstract individual and society and protecting the natural rights of the former against the latter, which American law had derived from the seventeenth-century contests in England between courts and crown. It was easy to generalize this as a contest between the individual and society, and it became more easy to do so when the common-law rights of Englishmen secured by common-law courts against the crown had become the natural rights of man secured to individual men as against the state by the bills of rights.

Brendan F. Brown, The Natural Law, the Marriage Bond, and Divorce, 24 Fordham Law Review pp. 83-84 (1955) (footnotes omitted); reprinted by permission of the Fordham Law Review.

CATHOLIC TRADITION

Natural law is that objective, eternal and immutable hierarchy of moral values, which are sources of obligation with regard to man because they have been so ordained by the Creator of nature. This law conforms to the essence of human nature which He has created. It is that aspect of the eternal law which directs the actions of men. Although this law is divine in the sense that it does not depend on human will, nevertheless, it is distinguishable from divine positive law, which has been communicated directly from God to men through revelation, for natural law is discoverable by reason alone. Natural law has been promulgated in the intellect. At least as regards its more fundamental principles it is knowable proximately through the conscience.

The most basic ideal of this law, namely, that every man must live in accordance with his rational nature, so that he will do good and avoid evil, is self-evident to all. No reasoning is required to reach a knowledge of this ideal. But other parts of the natural law are not perceivable with an equal degree of facility. Varying gradations and types of reasoning are necessary to ascertain the sub-norms of that law. Some of these are discoverable by an immediately derived deduction, which is almost obvious, such as the requirement of *some* form of marriage or contractual agreement before a man and a woman can lawfully have sexual relations. But other sub-norms are ascertainable only after observation, study, and experience, both individual and sociological. Examples are the secondary goal of marriage, and the precise means for the just and adequate effectuation of the primary and secondary purposes of marriage.

Anton-Hermann C. Chroust, Natural Law and Legal Positivism, 13 Ohio State Law Journal pp. 178-186 (1952); reprinted by permission of the author and the Ohio State Law Journal.

A frequently heard complaint among present day lawyers and jurists is that they can no longer look to real legal authority. We have just been told by Julius Stone that even the slender traditional authority of the common law, the "jurisprudence of stare decisis," is at best a wishful thought.[10] Our learned judges, speaking from the highest tribunal, are bluntly informing us that their decisions are valid for one day and that day only. How, then, can we resort to authority, if we are surrounded by what might be called an anti-authoritarian experimental jurisprudence, already degenerating into a purely experimental "method of social engineering."

The advocates of this social experimentation admit that if there is at all such a strange thing as law or justice, it is at best a crudely pragmatic hit and miss affair. We might even use reason as an instrument to find out something about the law. But, again, we have been told by philosophers now in fashion that reason is an instrument to be used sparingly and then only as a means of clarifying what comes to us by experience. And experience—the positive law—itself has become a tenuous term which today is more elusive than ever.

It is suggested here that we should define natural law above all as a "knowledge situation" or "truth situation" which renders the term law in a broader sense than the legal positivist or realist would probably concede.

In other words, law is interpreted here to include a type of understanding which to some extent is outside the narrow limits drawn by the legal positivist, without thereby becoming "illegal" or "irrational." We shall attempt to indicate that natural law is a form of eminently valid legal knowledge; that like all other forms of valid knowledge it consists of critical judgments organized in a coherent body of supersensorial data; and that these judgments are based on reason and fact as well as the rational awareness and acceptance of the existence of objective values, standards, or norms of proper conduct. At the same time natural law constitutes a form of legal knowledge which cannot be restricted by legal empiricism to judgments confirmed by what courts, legislators, or administrative agencies actually do or have done in a given situation. This knowledge which stands for natural law is tantamount to the apprehension of certain decent propositions as well as their rationally cogent implications. Hence we shall conclude that natural law is above all not so much the establishment of a particular and limited legal datum or the description of such an isolated datum, but rather the fuller realization of all relevant legal data and their ultimate overall significance. Being able to point out the profounder meaning of the many and at times confusingly complex legal facts by showing us their inner structure, natural law can also tell us what the presuppositions are which enable us to deal with all these facts in an intelligent manner.

Properly understood, natural law will not ignore or discriminate against the present status of social, sociological, or legal theories concerning the derivation and validation of certain ethico-practical judgments or facts. Neither does it depreciate an empirical explanation of the multifarious experiences that comprise legal controversy, legal adjudication and law-making.

Natural law, by conforming to the dispassionate process of intelligent argument, claims truth for the judicious assertion that the world as a whole no less than our total legal experience furnished actual support for the significance of values and objective standards. In this, natural law contributes decisively to the translation of mere hopes or dreams into the actual realization of what is good, true, and just. It is also declaratory of an eminently decent and intelligent attitude which continuously asserts that the standards of right and wrong, good and evil are real and as such are truly effective in the lives of men. It implies, finally, that any legal knowledge situation which fails to take account of these standards and their practical effectiveness, is incomplete and as such no true legal knowledge situation at all.

Although natural law at times lacks the detailedness and particularization of the positive law, like every form of rational knowledge, it presupposes participation in fundamental relationships which are reasonable. In this is signfies also a well grounded understanding of a basic situation expressed in rational judgments. In addition, natural law stands for what we may call a basic loyalty to something eminently intelligent in the domain of human conduct and human relations. Hence it is also a body of convictions as well as rational conclusions declaratory of the appropriateness of certain intelligent and voluntarist commitments. It might even be called a devotion to perfection.

Such commitments, to be sure, cannot always be verified empirically, particularly not by the positivist or realist who insists on limiting the meaning of law to whatever is done officially by the courts, the legislators, or the administrative agencies. But even the most adamant realist would not really deny that natural law, which he probably would call a "belief," leads to a kind of assurance which cannot be considered more arbitrary than the positivist or realist position itself.

The positive law, which is a purely experimental knowledge situation, also claims to be true—a claim which must still be submitted to the approved tests of truth. Obviously, the positive law cannot test itself as regards this particular claim. For what sincere legal positivist or realist could really tell us which of two decisions is "the correct one," and which is "the false one." And still he is somehow aware that one of these two decisions is the "correct one" or at least the one he "likes better," unless he would concede, in a spirit of cynical resignation, that "correct" is whatever the last and hence technically unimpeachable court of appeals has said in its latest decision. But such a dispirited surrender to mere "legal do-ism" cannot satisfy and never has satisfied the more ambitious mind.

Some opponents of the natural law might point out here that it has not as its primary object theoretical truth, at least not according to their pragmatic or realist conception of truth; that it has not the detached impartiality which is considered by the scientific realist, positivist, or semanticist an indispensable part of the truth seeker's attitude. But what does he actually mean by truth? Truth to him is perhaps contained in the following formula: Any assertion which is not an assertion of fact is not a true assertion; any assertion of fact which is not based on sense experience is not a true assertion of fact; any sense experience which cannot be verified by scientific experiment is not a true sense experience; and any scientific experiment which does not lend itself to quantitative measurement is not a true scientific experiment. But what bearing has all this on the problem of law? How can this formula be transposed into the domain of legal science? Let me suggest the following answer: in the light of such a naturalistic view, and in keeping with the now so prominent faith in "scientific realism," psychologism, or plain statistical method, the truth meaning of law would have to be reduced to a quantitative analysis of glandular secretions, appetitive droolings, and reflex, random, or artificial responses to stimuli. Obviously, the truth situation connected with natural law does not meet these particular truth requirements.

But if we are willing to concede that the methods with which we seek truth are so complex and often so different from one another that different forms of approach to truth at times become necessary, then we may discuss natural law as a truth situation. Hence the argument in favor of natural law will rest on the assumption that the approach to natural law requires a different and less restricted method than a purely realistic treatment of the law, often referred to as "legal scientism." If, in other words, we should admit that there exists a type of truth which we affirm even through its complete verification by sense data, sense observation, and quantitative experimentation alone is beyond our reach, then a more fruitful approach to the larger legal truth situation may be established. Perhaps the most eloquent defense of this broader view on the legal truth situation is stated by William James in a letter addressed to Professor Leuba: "I find it preposterous," James claims, "that if there be a feeling of unseen reality shared by large numbers of men in their best moments, responded to by other men in their deepest moments, good to live by, strength-giving—I find it preposterous, I say, to suppose that the goodness of that feeling for living purpose should be held to carry no objective significance, and especially preposterous if it combines harmoniously with our otherwise grounded philosophy of objective truth." [11]

In a general way the legal positivist or realist starts out with the ambitious but never realized claim that he would establish once and for all the foundation of legal truth. Putting the emphasis on certainty and clarity at the expense of its range and profundity, he has gradually and progressively restricted the area to which the term "law" can be applied. No one, to be sure, will quarrel with a procedure which, if applied to a limited field of human understanding and human inquiry, assists us in distinguishing what from the standpoint of purely experimental knowledge is clearly known, and what is less clearly known. But this method certainly goes too far when, as a by-product of this procedure, the domain of the less clearly known —less clearly known according to the truth criteria of the positivist or realist—suddenly becomes the unknowable or not-known or, as in the case of natural law, the "non-sensical." Issues and problems which are at best but dimly perceived by the positivist or realist, and which do not lend themselves to quantitative analysis or statistical experimentation, are thus banished in a rather arbitrary manner from the area of the total truth situation and simply declared the equivalent of matters which are not known at all.

Many jurists have looked to legal positivism or realism for a scientific solution to the many complex questions posed by the law. They hoped that this positivism would offer some intelligent answer to the many vexing problems connected with the law. But they were sorely disappointed. For the only real answer which legal positivism or realism can offer to the problem of law is in fact the denial of the significance of the problem itself. What the legal positivist can actually supply is nothing other than a factual description or recitation of decisions, statutes, procedural rules, or perhaps congressional debates in terms of naive observations or manipulations. But what might be fully adequate for the descriptive sciences, could be and probably is, somewhat inadequate for the solution or understanding of the many problems arising from the practically significant conduct of man. Hence we might ask here the question whether this kind of scientific simplicity in the province of experimental knowledge is not won at the dire expense of adequacy in our treatment of the problem of legal knowledge in general, in that we lose at the outset every chance of expanding the domain of truth and the area of the knowable. Because in doing this we refuse at the very outset to admit the possibility of such an extension beyond mere sensate experience and experiment.

At this point we should also inquire whether the positivist or realist position itself is not confronted with serious difficulties of its own: the positivist must assume without proof the accessibility of the past through memory; the communication or communicability of ideas, concepts, or symbols through identical meaning; the consonance of other experiences with his own; the acceptability of his hypothetical purpose; the dependability of induction; and the validity of his insight into logical relations as well as into the connection between initial hypothesis and final verification. All these "postulates," on which he bases his whole method, his procedures, and, hence, his whole claim to truth, are nothing but "gratuitous dogmas." The exclusive reliance on actual pronouncements of the courts, the dicta of legislators, or the acts of administrative agencies, in itself always implies and presupposes the assumption of, and reliance on, something more than these pronouncements. And finally, we should also point out that by his reliance on actual pronouncements, he is forced to assume the existence of other minds—an assumption which he himself cannot verify satisfactorily by his own scientific method. But he must nevertheless make this unscientific and, as a mater of fact, totally unwarranted assumption— unwarranted from his own point of view—in order to justify his own use of intersubjective language and symbols.

In sum, the legal positivist or realist always assumes or presupposes certain "unscientific" beliefs which, in the final analysis, turn out well for him. These beliefs actually do not belong in the province of verifiable sense-experience, but are outside the particular truth situation which he so jealously tries to establish and defend. The legal positivist or realist openly scoffs at such "bed-time stories" as the "moral dignity of man" or the "natural rights of man." But from experience we know that in practice there is hardly a more eloquent claimant of these rights than the legal positivist or realist who spends most of his time disproving "scientifically" the very existence or truth of these rights. Since natural law frequently fulfills the latent purposes even of those who rebel against it, it seems to provide also for those who are totally blind to its existence. Hence the question arises whether we are actually improving the total legal knowledge situation by following the positivist position in refusing to permit the term knowledge or truth to be applied to insights which are the result of analysis of a body of given facts. The intelligent person, it appears, is always suspicious of those efforts to establish truth which limit themselves to mere sense perception and sense data. He consistently denies the existence of a purely experimental knowledge or truth situation. At the same time, in one way or another, he emphatically disclaims that all super-sensual assertions are meaningless. He insists that, if certain assertions made by positivist philosophers are provisionally accepted as true, then we should also investigate the assertions made by non-positivist philosophers.

Whenever we are dealing incompetently with a type of knowledge such as natural law, we are apt to tread on perilous ground. It appears that the perils of natural law arise from several sources. One peril stems from a shocking misunderstanding or misconception of natural law. Another proceeds from the unwillingness of some men to face its demands whenever these demands are opposed to their prejudices, traditions, interests, or aspirations. These men, at least outwardly, "accept" natural law by professing to be its supporters. But actually, in the application of its principles to social problems they succeed in undermining it in the eyes of its adherents and the sceptic. A third peril arises from the failure to re-apply the principles of natural law to changing conditions and changing needs. This peril becomes particularly serious in times of crisis or rapid socio-economic change. We may, for instance, falsely identify natural law with an established economic, political, or social system, or, on the other hand, we may be so convinced of the desirability of a new economic or political order that we are inclined to abandon the principles of natural law altogether in order to bring about this new economic, social, or political system. We may even be so misguided about the meaning of natural law that we claim thereby to be setting up a new and allegedly superior kind of natural law.

Hence there seem to be five major difficulties with natural law which we have often experienced from the manner in which it is being treated by certain questionable experts on the natural law. The first difficulty is caused by a misunderstanding which proceeds from the methods applied by some of the defenders of natural law. This particular defense overlooks four important factors: First, it is made in behalf of all manner of conflicting notions as to what constitutes natural law; secondly, the rather crude but frequently encountered efforts to identify natural law exclusively with property rights at the expense of human rights at times have actually turned it into the handmaid of unrestrained greed and economic domination; thirdly, there is always a glaring incongruity between the notion of a natural law which gives special favors to one, while at the same time denying the other the prerequisites of a minimum of decent human existence —and the idea of the universal validity of the natural law advanced by the defenders or authors of such a "preferential natural law"; fourthly, the manner in which this type of preferential natural law is woven into the general fabric of legal ideas and the concept of universal justice approved by ordinary standards arising from common and healthy experiences, has never been satisfactorily explained.

The second difficulty about natural law arises from the frequently reiterated claim that some men possess what I would call a mystical experience of natural law—an immediate and personal conviction which supposedly reveals to some select people the "mystery of natural law." In essence, this particular attitude towards natural law is merely another form of "special revelation" frequently claimed by such clairvoyants as Hitler or Stalin.

The third difficulty about natural law seems to be related to the question as to how its principles could be applied to an existing, that is to say, historically developed socio-economic situation. This acute and perhaps even crucial problem is often disposed of in a most perfunctory, not to say callous and irresponsible manner. The historical complexities of the many economic, social, political, and moral issues to total human existence thus remain wholly unrelated to the natural law principles professed. Such an attitude towards natural law is clearly one of shallow generalization bordering on meaningless or platitudinous equivocations.

The fourth difficulty about the natural law comes from an uncritical definition of natural law, coined and employed by people who have tried to manipulate natural law and its meaning in order to advance selfish interests or to defend, on an allegedly supernatural basis, what nature and natural reason have unmasked as being indefensible. In their hands it has become a more or less systematic effort to justify strange practices of somewhat objectionable men trying to use and abuse some of the loftiest aspirations of mankind for their own crude purposes. By its very motives and results this type of natural law stands condemned in the eyes of all intelligent and decent men.

The fifth and perhaps most serious difficulty about natural law must be recognized in the fact that natural law has been invoked, though falsely, by certain questionable experts on the natural law in order to justify, and even glory in, their anti-intellectual, anti-progressive, and anti-humanitarian bias. This irresponsible and immoral policy, parading under the name of natural law, has done almost irreparable damage to the cause of natural law. It has, in many instances, alienated from the natural law many people who, under more favorable circumstances, would have become its most persuasive adherents and spokesmen.

Some people seem to be ready to take natural law for granted—to regard it as somthing self-explanatory. There are indeed those who sing its praises, as there are those who denounce it. But there are only a very few who genuinely study and properly interpret it. Whenever we think that natural law, being something allegedly self-explanatory, needs no explanation or special understanding, we are particularly apt to misunderstand it completely. It is most deplorable that this thing called natural law frequently is not deemed to need or deserve the patient and faithful exercise of the intelligence we apply to so many things which matter to us much less. Here as elsewhere we fail to see the importance of things we simply take for granted. But this alleged familiarity with natural law may in fact breed misunderstanding and even contempt. Many advocates of the natural law, aside from clinging to antique expressions, outmoded conceptions, or outworn phrases of the past, also make the serious if not fatal mistake of limiting both its meaning and content to thunderous and often ill-advised tirades against legal positivism, legal pragmatism, and legal realism. Such a purely negative attitude, aside from being totally devoid of any constructive or positive elements, is not apt to clarify what natural law actually means and for what it stands.

Natural law, by its very definition, reflects the true dignity of individual man as a person and as a social being. By giving expression to elementary human interests and aspirations, it endows man with the power to assert himself within proper limits and to work out his own happiness. But these powers or rights of every human individual do not presume his independence of other individuals. They do not separate his affairs or interests from the affairs or interests of other men. They do not permit him to conduct his affairs without concern for the effects which his actions may have upon other men. Natural law, by succeeding in making man aware of fundamental rights or powers to act, assures him a moral equality in the exercise of these rights. Under natural law one man's rights are another man's obligations. No man can claim rights the exercise of which is demonstrably injurious to another man. And no man has a right to exploitation. For natural law, properly understood, will never condone man's inhumanity to man. It does not merely establish the liberties and rights of individual man, but also the liberties, rights, and obligations of social man. It sustains man's claim as a person; it affirms his quality as an individual human being. At the same time it confronts man with serious social obligations. Hence natural law is not merely a body of rights, often loosely referred to as "the liberties of the individual." Such a generalization is both thoughtless and dangerous in that it connotes "rights in detachment," that is, rights-apart from the human community and rights unrelated or even antagonistic to the common good and the common welfare. It is dangerous in that it conceives of the individual as existing in a social vacuum; and in that it completely ignores the question, so basic to natural law, how far can one's liberty or one's rights co-exist or conflict with the liberties and rights of others, and how far certain liberties and rights of some individuals can be adverse to certain liberties or rights cherished by others, or even to the elementary needs of life itself. Natural law by its very nature is the great and eternal restraint imposed on all men by virtue of their humanity. Because of the failure to perceive this, a gross and vulgar individualism or naturalism has frequently paraded itself as natural law or natural rights.

There exists also an alarming confusion concerning the relation of natural law and human equality. Natural law, by assuring all men of certain fundamental rights, also assures them of a moral equality in the exercise of these rights. Now it is claimed that men cannot exercise their natural rights effectively unless they are equal in all other aspects as well. This claim is justified to a degree, and then only if the problem of limitation is clearly understood. For beyond certain limits equality and liberty may become opposed to one another in that the passion for equality can destroy liberty. Any attempt to achieve absolute equality would most surely result in regimentation or totalitarianism in one form or another. The kind of equality which is most clearly in harmony with natural law is the equality of opportunity in order that all men may develop their natural gifts and talents to their own advantage and the service of the common good. This equality of opportunity, proclaimed by the natural law, is based on the realization that man has his irreplaceable worth and irrepressible dignity. By conferring as well as declaring the equal dignity of all men, natural law actually combines opportunity with dignity—the opportunity to realize one's own moral nature and thus live in accord with one's own dignity.

D. Pragmatism

This word is hardly a designation for a philosophical system. It is rather an attempt to give a philosophical name to the American way of doing philosophy. Its founders were American: the scientist Charles Peirce, the psychologist William James, the lawyer Nathaniel Green, and the educator John Dewey.

Pragmatism is a philosophy of action and of consequences, of observation rather than reflection, of the practical rather than the ideal in human behavior. It is well suited to the

American legal temperament. Its emphasis is on the positive law and on its ideals as working influences. In jurisprudence it substitutes a theory of law as a system of conflicting interests for the older notion of law as a system of rights and obligations. It is the major philosophical basis for Sociological Jurisprudence which is to be studied in Part III of this book.

Thomas A. Cowan's article on Legal Pragmatism and Beyond, in Interpretations of Modern Legal Philosophies: Essays in Honor of Roscoe Pound (1947) pp. 137-138; reprinted by permission of The Oxford University Press, Inc.

❈   ❈   ❈   ❈   ❈

PRAGMATISM

Pragmatism combines insistence on uncertainty of generalization or rational intuition with uncertainty of sense data or the facts of experience. Each rational intuition has meaning only as it is worked out in experience. Each fact of experience has meaning only in a whole context of knowledge. Fact becomes generalization and generalization becomes fact in an unending vortex of change. The last word can never be spoken. The ultimate truth is the possession of no one. The game of knowledge is a process; its reward is to be found in the striving. There is no certainty except this: there is no certainty.

In jurisprudence, the effect of this philosophical relativism was to broaden the borders of law immeasurably. All species of legal autonomy disappears. The law becomes merely a part of a larger context: society, which itself is but a small part of the sum total of human experience, the world. Basic legal conceptions are thought to rest on psychological concepts of "interest" or on sociological notions of "drives." Law as an autonomous discipline disappears, but with it disappears also the possibility of law as a science, whether autonomous or co-ordinate. For it is the inescapable fate of philosophical relativism to pass into skepticism. It possesses no method that can bring its relativism to a halt. Its root principle that nothing is certain is self-destructive as the ancient Skeptics showed. Neo-realistic skepticism is the outcome of philosophical relativism, and the present century has witnessed this late flowering of the fruit of philosophical relativism in the movement which denies reality to anything but the unique instance, the single case. Why the adherents of neo-realism stop at the unique case is hard to understand. Ancient skepticism showed that to stop at this point is idiosyncratic: How does one know that a case is unique? How does one know what the alleged case is a "case of"? Hegel showed that the unique case is unique only in the absence of thought. Reflection turns it immediately into a universal. In fact, uniqueness is the "most universal" of all qualities. Everything possesses it.

Thus seen, the history of philosophy has run into a dead end. The product of three centuries of thought is self-devouring skepticism. Every pragmatist, legal or otherwise, falls prey to his own attempt to widen the boundaries of knowledge. Soon the law knows no bounds, and the pragmatist disappears into the receding horizon, pursued by the hounds of skepticism.

How fares our foremost legal pragmatist, Roscoe Pound, on this score? Beset on every side by the legal nihilists whose every insistence is that the bounds of the law be completely set aside, Pound has sturdily resisted the temptation to do so. His refuge has been to erect borders beyond which he will not go in pursuit of the legal "uncertainty." The instinct is the healthy one. When pressed too hard Pound returns to the wellsprings of legal scholarship. And yet it would be too much to say that skeptical attacks have not resulted in his setting the bounds arbitrarily in some instances. Nor can the onslaughts of the legal skeptics be met successfully in any way other than by a principled answer to their objections. For we must remember that the skeptic fulfills a necessary though often thankless role in the history of philosophy. In effect, the skeptic points out that one's own account of one's philosophy leads to contradiction. Thus Hume showed that empiricism's own account of the learning process made knowledge impossible. And thus modern legal skeptics show that pragmatism's insistence on generalizing uncertainty leads inescapably to the uncertainty of all generalizing. The skeptics, the legal gadflies, force a re-examination of pragmatism. Evidently uncertainty alone cannot do. We seemed prepared to stake our whole future on the gains which pragmatism sums up: the last word in science can never be spoken. What plagues us is the skeptic's reply: the first word can't be spoken either. We must return to the history of philosophy to see how to escape the dilemma.

E. Logical Positivism

There are several transition points between Philosophical Jurisprudence as studied in Part I and Analytical Jurisprudence which is to be the subject of Part II. One of them might well have been the philosophical movement known as Analysis. Another is logical positivism with its theory that the knowing process rests on two ultimate methods of human reasoning: the logical and the positivistic. The following brief selection serves to show the relation between logical positivism and analytical jurisprudence.

> William Ebenstein, The Pure Theory of Law (1945) p. 70; reprinted by permission of the University of Wisconsin Press.

NATURAL LAW AND LEGAL POSITIVISM

In the previous chapter the delimitation of law from nature served only to establish the *genus proximum*, the character of law as a category of the Ought. It did not establish the *differentia specifica*, for law is only one of the concepts which fall under the ruling concept of the Ought.

The relation of law to morals and ethics has preoccupied jurists since law began. Sufficient to say, without embarking on a doctrinal history of the subject, that the recognition of law as an independent department of human behavior is of comparatively recent date. Even Maitland, who did attempt to distinguish ethics from jurisprudence, maintained that "the jurist, if indeed such an animal exists, plays, and of right ought to play, a subordinate, if not subservient, part."[1] It is Austin's contribution to have emphasized the character of jurisprudence as a science of positive law. The introductory words of the first of his *Lectures on Jurisprudence* sound like the proclamation of a program: "The matter of jurisprudence is positive law." Two generations have passed, the face of the world has changed, but the conflict of ideas proceeds undiminished and often over the same set of problems. Now it is Kelsen whose *Pure Theory of Law* opens programmatically as did Austin's theory: "The Pure Theory of Law is a theory of the positive law."[2]

FOOTNOTES TO SECTION I-A

1. 59 Yale L. J. 273 (1950).
2. For a comprehensive survey of American philosophic opinion, see Philosophic Thought in the United States and France (Farber ed. 1950).
3. See, *e.g.*, Contemporary Idealism in America (Barrett ed. 1932); Naturalism and the Human Spirit (Krikorian ed. 1944); Philosophy for the Future (Sellars, McGill and Farber ed. 1949); Value—A Cooperative Inquiry (Lepley ed. 1949).
4. Contemporary American Philosophy (Adams and Montague ed. 1930).
5. See, *e.g.*, Lovejoy, *The Thirteen Pragmatisms*, 5 J. Phil. Nos. 1, 2 (1908).
6. Outside these major movements, several specialized activities, of which language analysis and philosophy of science are two, occupy the attention of many American philosophers.
7. See, generally, Bodenheimer, Jurisprudence (1940); Pound, Outlines of Lectures on Jurisprudence (5th ed. 1943); My Philosophy of Law (1941); Annual Survey of American Law (1942-49); Cohen, *A Critical Sketch of Legal Philosophy in America* in 2 Law: A Century of Progress 266 (1937); Yntema, *Jurisprudence on Parade,* 39 Mich. L. Rev. 1154 (1941).
8. For his recent contributions to sociological jurisprudence, see Patterson in My Philosophy of Law 231-43 (1941); Patterson, *Pound's Theory of Social Interests* in Interpretations of Modern Legal Philosophy 558-73 (1947); Patterson, *Bentham on the Nature and Method of Law,* 33 Calif. L. Rev. 612 (1945); Patterson, *Logic in the Law,* 90 U. of Pa. L. Rev. 875 (1942); Patterson, Book Review of Radin, Law as Logic and Experience, 41 Columbia L. Rev. 562 (1941); Patterson, Book Review of Hexner, Studies in Legal Terminology, 54 Harv. L.

Rev. 1419 (1941); Patterson, Book Review of Fuller, The Law in Quest of Itself, 26 Iowa L. Rev. 166 (1940).

9. For a bibliography of Max Radin's voluminous writings, see 36 Calif. L. Rev. 163, 165 (1948). His most recent writing on jurisprudence is *Natural Law and Natural Rights,* 59 Yale L. J. 214 (1950).

10. Stone, The Province and Function of Law (1946).

11. Stone and Simpson, Law and Society (1948).

12. See, *e.g.,* Pound, The Task of Law (1944); Pound, Social Control Through Law (1942); Pound, Contemporary Juristic Theory (1940); Pound, *Fifty Years Growth of American Law,* 18 Notre Dame Law, 173 (1943); Pound, *Fifty Years of Jurisprudence,* 50 Harv. L. Rev. 557 (1937), 51 Harv. L. Rev. 444, 777 (1938). Some of these latest productions are in a pessimistic vein and are extremely critical of the realistic position, although the opposition is not fundamental since the basic philosophic orientation is the same.

13. See, *e.g.,* Cairns, Legal Philosophy from Plato to Hegel (1949); Cairns, The Theory of Legal Science (1941); Cairns, Law and the Social Sciences (1935); Cairns, *Philosophy as Jurisprudence* in Interpretations of Modern Legal Philosophies, Essays in Honor of Roscoe Pound (1947).

14. For a more extended exposition of the present author's views on this point, see Cowan, *The Relation of Law to Experimental Social Science,* 96 U. of Pa. L. Rev. 484 (1948).

15. Cowan, *A Postulate Set for Experimental Jurisprudence,* to be published in 18 J. Phil. Science No. 1 (1951).

16. Levi, Introduction to Legal Reasoning (1949); Levi, *Natural Law, Precedent and Thurman Arnold,* 24 Va. L. Rev. 587 (1938).

17. Murphy, *Free Speech and Atom Bombs,* 2 Ala. L. Rev. 24 (1949).

18. My Philosophy of Law (1941).

19. See Cowan, *Legal Pragmatism and Beyond* in Interpretations of Modern Legal Philosophies, Essays in Honor of Roscoe Pound (1947).

For a philosophical analysis of the position of the legal realists in this country see Garlan, Legal Realism and Justice (1941). This book also contains an extensive bibliography on legal realism.

20. Professor McDougal of Yale recently took cognizance of this change. McDougal, *The Law School of the Future: From Legal Realism to Policy Science in the World Community,* 56 Yale L. J. 1345 (1947).

21. Uniform Commercial Code (Proposed Final Draft, Spring 1950); Llewellyn, *Law and the Social Science—Especially Sociology,* 62 Harv. L. Rev. 1286 (1949).

22. See Frank, Law and the Modern Mind (1949); Frank, Fate and Freedom: A Philosophy for Free Americans (1945); Frank, If Men Were Angels (1942); Frank, *Epithetical Jurisprudence and the Work of the Securities and Exchange Com-*

mission in the Administration of Chapter X of the Bankruptcy Act, 18 N. Y. U. L. Q. Rev. 317 (1941); Frank, *A Sketch of an Influence* in Interpretations of Modern Legal Philosophies 189 (1947); Frank, *Modern and Ancient Legal Pragmatism, John Dewey & Co. vs. Aristotle*, 25 Notre Dame Law, 207 (1950); Frank, *Legal Thinking in Three Dimensions*, 1 Syracuse L. Rev. 9 (1949); Frank, *Say It With Music*, 61 Harv. L. Rev. 921 (1948).

23. Frank, *A Plea for Lawyer-Schools*, 56 Yale L. J. 1303 (1947).

24. See Fuller, Problems of Jurisprudence (1949); Fuller, The Law in Quest of Itself (1940); Fuller, *Place and Uses of Jurisprudence in the Law School Curriculum*, 1 J. Legal Educ. 495 (1949); Fuller, *Reason and Fiat in Case Law*, 59 Harv. L. Rev. 376 (1946).

25. See Hall, Living Law in Democratic Society (1949); Hall, General Principles of the Criminal Law (1947); Hall, *Integrative Jurisprudence* in Interpretations of Modern Legal Philosophies (1947); Hall, *Place and Uses of Jurisprudence*, 1 J. Legal Educ. 475 (1949).

26. See Cahn, The Sense of Injustice (1949); Cahn, *Jurisprudence* in Annual Survey of American Law (1944-49); Cahn, *Goethe's View of the Law*, 49 Columbia L. Rev. 904 (1949).

27. Fuller, *op. cit. supra* note 24.

28. Hall, *op. cit. supra* note 25.

29. Positivism, on the other hand, is a throwback beyond Hegel to seventeenth century empiricism. And it is melancholy, though perhaps inevitable, that eighteenth century intuitional idealism should be resurrected today to lay the still more ancient ghost of seventeenth century positivistic empiricism.

30. Cahn, *op. cit. supra* note 26.

31. The present author has attempted to adjust the pure theory of law to serve the purposes of experimental science. See Cowan, *Experimental Jurisprudence and the Pure Theory of Law*, 11 Philosophy and Phenomenological Research (1950) 164.

32. Kelsen, General Theory of Law and State (1945); Kelsen, Society and Nature: A Sociological Inquiry (1943); Kelsen, Law and Peace in International Relations (1942); Kelsen, *The Pure Theory of Law and Analytical Jurisprudence*, 55 Harv. L. Rev. 44 (1941); Kelsen, *The Law as a Specific Social Technique*, 9 U. of Chi. L. Rev. 75 (1941).

33. Ebenstein, Man and the State (1947); Ebenstein, Pure Theory of Law (1945).

34. But see M. R. Cohen, Preface to Logic (1945); Radin, Law as Logic and Experience (1940); F. S. Cohen, *Field Theory and Judicial Logic*, 59 Yale L. J. 238 (1950); Patterson, *Logic in the Law*, 90 U. of Pa. L. Rev. 875 (1942).

35. See Silving, *Analytical Limits of the Pure Theory of Law*, 28 Iowa L. Rev. 1 (1942).

36. Our Legal System and How It Operates (1951).

37. For a survey of neo-scholastic philosophy in this country see Rooney, Special Report of the Committee on Philosophy of Law in Government (1942); Relativism in American Law (American Catholic Philosophic Ass'n 1945); Brown, *A Scholastic Curriculum and Teaching Method for the Catholic Law School in War Time,* 10 Catholic U. Bul. No. 4, p. 7 (1943); Chroust, *Aristotle's Conception of "Equity" (Epieikeia),* 18 Notre Dame Law. 119 (1942); Chroust, *Law and the Administrative Process: An Epistemological Approach to Jurisprudence,* 58 Harv. L. Rev. 573 (1945); Chroust and Collins, *The Basic Ideas in the Philosophy of Law of St. Thomas Aquinas as found in the "Summa Theologica,"* 26 Marq. L. Rev. 11 (1941); Chroust and Osborn, *Aristotle's Conception of Justice,* 17 Notre Dame Law. 129 (1942); Kennedy, *Storm over Law Schools,* 18 Ford. L. Rev. 41 (1943); *A New School of Juristic Thought,* 10 Int. L. Publ. and Jur. 507 (1943); *The Philosophy of Law from St. Augustine to St. Thomas Aquinas,* 20 New Scholasticism 26 (1946).

38. See Lucey, *Natural Law and American Legal Realism: Their Respective Contributions to a Theory of Law in a Democratic Society,* 30 Geo. L. J. 493 (1942).

39. See Northrop, The Logic of the Sciences and the Humanities (1947); Northrop, The Meeting of East and West, An Inquiry Concerning World Understanding (1946); Northrop, *Jurisprudence in the Law School Curriculum,* 1 J. Legal Educ. 482 (1949); Northrop, *The Criterion of the Good State,* 52 Ethics 309 (1942); Northrop, *The Philosophical Presuppositions of Democracy Necessary for the Solution of Social Problems,* 38 J. Phil. 687 (1941).

40. See pp. 1093-94 and note 15 *supra.*

41. Beutel, *Some Implications of Experimental Jurisprudence,* 48 Harv. L. Rev. 169 (1934).

42. Yntema, *Jurisprudence of Codification* in David Dudley Field; Centenary Essays 251 (1949). See also Morrow, *Louisiana Blueprint: Civilian Codification and Legal Method for State and Nation,* 17 Tulane L. Rev. 351 (1943).

43. See F. S. Cohen, *Field Theory and Judicial Logic,* 59 Yale L. J. 238 (1950).

44. See Lasswell and McDougal, *Legal Education and Public Policy: Professional Training in the Public Interest,* 52 Yale L. J. 203 (1943); McDougal, *The Role of Law in World Politics,* 20 Miss. L. J. 253 (1949); McDougal and Leighton, *The Rights of Man in the World Community,* 14 Law & Contemp. Prob. 490 (1949).

45. See Moore and Callahan, *Law and Learning Theory: A Study in Legal Control,* 53 Yale L. J. 1 (1943); Yntema, *"Law and Learning Theory" Through the Looking Glass of Legal Theory,* 53 Yale L. J. 338 (1944).

FOOTNOTES TO SECTION I-B

1. Fearne on Contingent Remainders, First American Edition, p. 170.

2. Cassirer, An Essay on Man, 223-224 (1944).

2a. Huxley, The Uniqueness of Man, 28 Yale Review 475, 491, 500 (1939).

3. West, Conscience and Society (1945).

4. The instance given is advisedly extreme, but so extensive is the operation of positive law on this issue of equality that we should have to add that all five men were duly licensed to drive and that none of them had a previous unfavorable record.

5. Deuteronomy 25:3. It was reduced by the rabbis to a maximum of thirty-nine. Tract Maccoth III, VI, in 9 (XVII). Rodkinson, Babylonian Talmud 48 (1918); II Corinthians 11:24.

6. Cicero, De officiis III, xiii (Loeb's trans. 1928), 323.

7. The development of Roman tort law may be attributed in substantial part to assimilation of Greek standards of human dignity. *See* Buckland, A Text-Book of Roman Law from Augustus to Justinian 589, *et seq.* (2d ed. 1932); Taubenschlag, The Law of Greco-Roman Egypt in the Light of the Papyri 329, *et seq.* (1944). *Cf.* our own recent discovery of the right of privacy, still inadequately safeguarded.

8. This reference was lifted baldly from David Hume's An Enquiry Concerning the Principles of Morals (1740), where I thought it originated until, as usual, I found the archetype in Aristotle (Nicomachean Ethics, 1135a).

9. Finkelstein, The Pharisees 283-85 (1938).

10. This instance was taken almost literally from Livy XL. 29 (Bohn's trans. 1915), 1885-86.

11. A negative instance would also have been appropriate; that is, one of the failure of government to fulfill functions that custom or circumstances rendered obligatory. Failure to provide opportunity for productive employment of those able to work might illustrate the case.

12. A paraphrase of two unrelated sentences of C. S. Peirce. The Philosophy of Peirce 163, 229 (Buchler ed. 1940).

13. Using Dr. Whitehead's summary of various sentiments in the Timaeus (particularly at 48A). Whitehead, Adventures of Ideas 105 (1937). *See also* Laws IV, 718B-723D (Loeb's trans. 1926), 300-18.

14. Vol. 1 (8th ed. 1892) p. 254. The discussion of contract law is found in Vol. 1, p. 143, and Vol. 2, p. 223.

15. See Olivecrona Law as Fact (1939); Lundstedt, Superstition or Rationality in Action for Peace? (1925); Lundstedt, Die Unwissenschaftlichkeit der Rechtswissenschaft (1932). The leader of this school is Axel Hägerström, whose principal works are unfortunately available only in Swedish.

In connection with the point made in the text, it is interesting to compare the observations of Timasheff in An Introduction to the Sociology of Law (1939) 132, n. 17, concerning the effect of Soviet legal reforms on Russian, conceptions of morality.

FOOTNOTES TO SECTION I-C

1. Pound, *The Spirit of the Common Law*, p. 81.
2. Sir Paul Vinogradoff, "Legal Standards and Ideals," *Michigan Law Review*, XXXIII (November, 1924), 1 ff. For reference by the same writer to the revival of a modified conception of the law of nature as one of the significant currents of thought in jurisprudence, see *Historical Jurisprudence*, I, 144, 145.
3. Benjamin N. Cardozo, *The Nature of the Judicial Process* (New Haven, 1922), pp. 161, 162.
4. Cardozo, *op. cit.*, p. 162.
5. See Pound, *Law and Morals*, p. 60.
6. Stammler, *Wirtschaft und Recht* (2d ed.), p. 181, and *Die Lehre von dem richtigen Rechte* (Berlin, 1902), pp. 116-121; Saleilles, "L'École historique et droit naturel," *Revue trimestrielle de droit civil*, I, 80, 98; R. Demogue, *Notions fondamentales du droit privé*, p. 22.

Vinogradoff characterized this phase of natural law thinking as follows: "The law of nature is an appeal from Caesar to a better informed Caesar. It is an appeal by society at large, or by the best spirits of a given society, not against single decisions or rules, but against entire systems of positive law. Legislators are called in to amend law by separate statutes; judges may do a great deal in amending the law by decisions in individual cases, but the wisdom of legislators and equity of judges are by themselves powerless against systems, because they start from the recognition of the authority of positive law in general. And yet law, being a human institution, ages not only in its single rules and doctrines, but in its national and historical setting, and the call for purification and reform may become more and more pressing with every generation. Public opinion, then, turns from reality to ideals. Speculation arises as to the essentials of law as conceived in the light of justice. Of course these conceptions of justice are themselves historical, but they are drawn not from the complicated compromises of positive law but from the simpler and more scientific teaching of philosophical doctrine. Thus the contents of the law of nature vary with the ages, but their aim is constant; it is justice; and though this species of law operates not in positive enactments, but in the minds of men, it is needless to urge that he who obtains command over minds will in the end master their institutions." *Common Sense in Law*, pp. 244, 245. See also, by the same author, "Reason and Conscience in Sixteenth Century Jurisprudence," *Law Quarterly Review*, XXIV (October, 1908), 379.

7. Pound, *Law and Morals,* p. 113.

8. Vinogradoff, *Common Sense in Law,* pp. 235 ff., and *Central Law Journal,* LXXX (May, 1915), 346.

9. Gmelin, *The Science of Legal Method* (Boston, 1917), p. 89; for a thorough discussion of the function of the judge as a lawmaker, see other selections in this volume. *Cf.* also my article on "General Observations on the Effects of Personal, Political, and Economic Influences in the Decisions of Judges," *Illinois Law Review,* XVII (June, 1922), 96.

10. *Cf.* Julius Stone, Fallacies of the Logical Form in English Law, in Interpretations of Modern Legal Philosophies (1947) pp. 696-735.

11. Quoted in Perry, The Thought and Character of William James, vol. 2, p. 350.

FOOTNOTES TO SECTION I-E

1. Frederick W. Maitland, *Collected Papers* (Cambridge, 1911), 3:304.

2. Kelsen, *Reine Rechtslehre,* 1. Among the many positivists who follow Austin is Holland, who writes: "Jurisprudence . . . is the science of actual or positive law." *Jurisprudence,* 12.

Part II

ANALYTICAL JURISPRUDENCE

Analytical jurisprudence is the study of the *structure* of the law. In its simplest manifestation it is the shredding apart of a single judicial decision, statutory enactment, or executive regulation to see what are its component parts. The study may then go on to compare one case with another, or one bunch of cases with others, or one branch of the law with another. It may compare decisional law with legislative enactment and with executive regulation. In any event it confines itself fairly well to authoritative legal materials. It studies, in brief, the law as it now is, not the law as it ought to be in the future nor as it was in the past.

Analytical jurists are much concerned with examining the nature of authoritative legal materials. They put great emphasis on the task of clearly separating law from other human activities and from other means of social control. They tend to deny the name law to any proposition which does have an authoritative sanction behind it. In the past, analytical jurists were wont to define law merely and simply as the will of the sovereign expressed in political institutions and in the organs of government, particularly the legislature and the courts. They were thus much impressed with the element of force which they see as the defining mark of law.

The analytical jurists reverence two virtues: clarity and consistency. They desire to make legal terms and legal conceptions as clear as possible so that ambiguities lurking in them may be cleared up. This is obviously a practice calling for much experience in the law. Ambiguities usually generate contradictions. To remove such contradictions and to make law consistent with itself is the chief function of this school.

Analytical jurisprudence has thus been called legal logic since clarity and consistency are the cardinal marks of that discipline. It would not be impossible to trace the close relation between the development of analytical jurisprudence and the history of logic although this specialized study is beyond our intent here. Suffice it for us to know that at present analytical jurisprudence is coming into close relation with that branch of philosophy which is known as *analysis*. Indeed, one prominent English analytical jurist (Professor Hart of Oxford University) is also a student of analytical philosophy.

Analytical jurisprudence is of great consequence for political science. Since the analytical jurist tends to deny that anything can be law save what is enforced by some political institution of the state, he must perforce study the nature of government and the results are of interest to the political theorist. Also of consequence is the older analytical jurist's conclusion that "international law" is not law.

I have included a fragment from the work of the "founder" of English analytical jurisprudence, John Austin.

A. Analytical Jurisprudence in Court

Palsgraf v. *Long Island R. R.*, 248 N. Y. 339, 162 N. E. 99 (1928).

[This is one of the most celebrated American cases in the law of torts, that branch of the law which seeks in a general way to compensate those who are injured by the wrongful conduct of others. The issue in the case turns on the definition of the word *negligence*. The majority (four) of the highest court of the state of New York, represented by Judge Cardozo took one view; the minority (three), represented by Judge Andrews took another. Judge Cardozo believed that if a person is acting negligently toward a group of people likely to be hurt by his misconduct he should not be liable to another person who is outside of that group. Judge Andrews felt that if one is acting carelessly and is likely to injure another he should be liable to anyone who in fact is hurt.

It is interesting to watch each judge at work supporting his view. Each picks up, uses, and lays aside one judicial instrument after another: history, precedent, social policy, instinctive ideas of justice, practical expediency.

It is not necessary that the layman understand everything that is done to be fascinated by this piece of legal analysis. One need not be a student of anatomy to marvel at the work of a skilled dissectionist. The point to remember here is that the court is manufacturing the basic elements of analytical jurisprudence.]

HELEN PALSGRAF, *Respondent* v. THE LONG ISLAND RAILROAD COMPANY, *Appellant,* 248 N. Y. 339 (1928).

CARDOZO, Ch. J. Plaintiff was standing on a platform of defendant's railroad after buying a ticket to go to Rockaway Beach. A train stopped at the station, bound for another place. Two men ran forward to catch it. One of the men reached the platform of the car without mishap, though the train was already moving. The other man, carrying a package, jumped aboard the car, but seemed unsteady as if about to fall. A guard on the car, who had held the door open, reached forward to help him in, and another guard on the platform pushed him from behind. In this act, the package was dislodged, and fell upon the rails. It was a package of small size, about fifteen inches long, and was covered by a newspaper. In fact it contained fireworks, but there was nothing in its appearance to give notice of its contents. The fireworks when they fell exploded. The shock of the explosion threw down some scales at the other end of the platform, many feet away. The scales struck the plaintiff, causing injuries for which she sues.

The conduct of the defendant's guard, if a wrong in its relation to the holder of the package, was not a wrong in its relation to the plaintiff, standing far away. Relatively to her it was not negligence at all. Nothing in the situation gave notice that the falling package had in it the potency of peril to persons thus removed. Negligence is not actionable unless it involves the invasion of a legally protected interest, the violation of a right. "Proof of negligence in the air, so to speak, will not do" (Pollock, Torts [11th ed.], p. 455; *Martin* v. *Herzog*, 228 N. Y. 164, 170; cf. Salmond, Torts [6th ed.], p. 24). "Negligence is the absence of care, according to the circumstances" (Willes, J., in *Vaughan* v. *Taff Vale Ry. Co.*, 5 H. & N. 679, 688; 1 Beven, Negligence [4th ed.], 7; *Paul* v. *Consol. Fireworks Co.*, 212 N. Y. 117; *Adams* v. *Bullock*, 227 N. Y. 208, 211; *Parrott* v. *Wells-Fargo Co.*, 15 Wall. [U. S.] 524). The plaintiff as she stood upon the platform of the station might claim to be protected against intentional invasion of her bodily security. Such invasion is not charged. She might claim to be protected against unintentional invasion by conduct involving in the thought of reasonable men an unreasonable hazard that such invasion would ensue. These, from the point of view of the law, were the bounds of her immunity, with perhaps some rare exceptions, survivals for the most part of ancient forms of liability, where conduct is held to be at the peril of the actor (*Sullivan* v. *Dunham*, 161 N. Y. 290). If no hazard was apparent to the eye of ordinary vigilance, an act innocent and harmless, at least to outward seeming, with reference to her, did not take to itself the quality of a tort because it happened to be a wrong, though apparently not one involving the risk of bodily insecurity, with reference to some one else. "In every instance, before negligence can be predicated of a given act, back of the act must be sought and found a duty to the individual complaining, the observance of which would have averted or avoided the injury." . . .

The argument for the plaintiff is built upon the shifting meanings of such words as "wrong" and "wrongful," and shares their instability. What the plaintiff must show is "a wrong" to herself, *i.e.,* a violation of her own right, and not merely a wrong to some one else, nor conduct "wrongful" because unsocial, but not "a wrong" to any one. . . .

Negligence, like risk, is thus a term of relation. Negligence in the abstract, apart from things related, is surely not a tort, if indeed it is understandable at all (Bowen, L. J., in *Thomas* v. *Quartermaine,* 18 Q. B. D. 685, 694). Negligence is not a tort unless it results in the commission of a wrong, and the commission of a wrong imports the violation of a right, in this case, we are told, the right to be protected against interference with one's bodily security. But bodily security is protected, not against all forms of interference or aggression, but only against some. One who seeks redress at law does not make out a cause of action by showing without more that there has been damage to his person. If the harm was not willful, he must show that the act as to him had possibilities of danger so many and apparent as to entitle him to be protected against the doing of it though the harm was unintended. Affront to personality is still the keynote of the wrong. Confirmation of this view will be found in the history and development of the action on the case. Negligence as a basis of civil liability was unknown to mediaeval law (8 Holdsworth, History of English Law, p. 449; Street, Foundations of Legal Liability, vol. 1, pp. 189, 190). For damage to the person, the sole remedy was trespass, and trespass did not lie in the absence of aggression, and that direct and personal (Holdsworth, op. cit. p. 453; Street, op. cit. vol. 3, pp. 258, 260, vol. 1, pp. 71, 74). Liability for other damage, as where a servant without orders from the master does or omits something to the damage of another, is a plant of later growth (Holdsworth, op. cit. 450, 457; Wigmore, Responsibility for Tortious Acts, vol. 3, Essays in Anglo-American Legal History, 520, 523, 526, 533). When it emerged out of the legal soil, it was thought of as a variant of trespass, an off-shoot of the parent stock. This appears in the form of action, which was known as trespass on the case (Holdsworth, op. cit. p. 449; cf. *Scott* v. *Shepard,* 2 Wm. Black, 892; Green, Rationale of Proximate Cause, p. 19). The victim does not sue derivatively, or by right of subrogation, to vindicate an interest invaded in the person of another. Thus to view his cause of action is to ignore the fundamental difference between tort and crime (Holland, Jurisprudence [12th ed.], p. 328). He sues for breach of a duty owing to himself.

The law of causation, remote or proximate, is thus foreign to the case before us. The question of liability is always anterior to the question of the measure of the consequences that go with liability. If there is no tort to be redressed, there is no occasion to consider what damage might be recovered if there were a finding of a tort. We may assume, without deciding, that negligence, not at large or in the abstract, but in relation to the plaintiff, would entail liability for any and all consequences, however novel or extra-ordinary (*Bird* v. *St. Paul F. & M. Ins. Co.*, 224 N. Y. 47, 54; *Ehrgott* v. *Mayor, etc., of N. Y.*, 96 N. Y. 264; *Smith* v. *London & S. W. Ry. Co.*, L. R. 6 C. P. 14; 1 Beven, Negligence, 106; Street, op. cit. vol. 1, p. 90; Green, Rationale of Proximate Cause, pp. 88, 118; cf. *Matter of Polemis*, L. R. 1921, 3 K. B. 560; 44 Law Quarterly Review, 142). There is room for argument that a distinction is to be drawn according to the diversity of interests invaded by the act, as where conduct negligent in that it threatens an insignificant invasion of an interest in property results in an unfor-seeable invasion of an interest of another order, as, *e.g.*, one of bodily security. Perhaps other distinctions may be necessary. We do not go into the question now. The consequences to be followed must first be rooted in a wrong.

The judgment of the Appellate Division and that of the Trial Term should be reversed, and the complaint dismissed, with costs in all courts.

* * * * *

ANDREWS, J. (dissenting). Assisting a passenger to board a train, the defendant's servant negligently knocked a package from his arms. It fell between the platform and the cars. Of its contents the servant knew and could know nothing. A violent explosion followed. The concussion broke some scales standing a considerable distance away. In falling they injured the plaintiff, an intending passenger.

Upon these facts may she recover the damages she has suffered in an action brought against the master? The result we shall reach depends upon our theory as to the nature of negligence. Is it a relative concept— the breach of some duty owing to a particular person or to particular persons? Or where there is an act which unreasonably threatens the safety of others, is the doer liable for all its proximate consequences, even where they result in injury to one who would generally be thought to be outside the radius of danger? This is not a mere dispute as to words. We might not believe that to the average mind the dropping of the bundle would seem to involve the probability of harm to the plaintiff standing many feet away whatever might be the case as to the owner or to one so near as to be likely to be struck by its fall. If, however, we adopt the second hypoth-
however, we adopt the second hypothesis we have to inquire only as to the relation between cause and effect. We deal in terms of proximate cause, not of negligence. . . .

* * * * *

It may well be that there is no such thing as negligence in the abstract. "Proof of negligence in the air, so to speak, will not do." In an empty world negligence would not exist. It does involve a relationship between man and his fellows. But not merely a relationship between man and those whom he might reasonably expect his act would injure. Rather, a relationship between him and those whom he does in fact injure. If his act has a tendency to harm some one, it harms him a mile away as surely as it does those on the scene. We now permit children to recover for the negligent killing of the father. It was never prevented on the theory that no duty was owing to them. A husband may be compensated for the loss of his wife's services. To say that the wrongdoer was negligent as to the husband as well as to the wife is merely an attempt to fit facts to theory. An insurance company paying a fire loss recovers its payment of the negligent incendiary. We speak of subrogation—of suing in the right of the insured. Behind the cloud of words is the fact they hide, that the act, wrongful as to the insured, has also injured the company. Even if it be true that the fault of father, wife or insured will prevent recovery, it is because we consider the original negligence not the proximate cause of the injury. (Pollock, Torts [12th ed.], 463.) . . .

The proposition is this. Every one owes to the world at large the duty of refraining from those acts that may unreasonably threaten the safety of others. Such an act occurs. Not only is he wronged to whom harm might reasonably be expected to result, but he also who is in fact injured, even if he be outside what would generally be thought the danger zone. . . .

The judgment appealed from should be affirmed, with costs.

POUND, LEHMAN and KELLOGG, JJ., concur with CARDOZO, Ch. J.; ANDREWS, J., dissents in opinion in which CRANE and O'BRIEN, JJ., concur.

Judgment reversed, etc.

B. Analytical Jurisprudence Defined

John Austin, The Province of Jurisprudence
Determined (1832).

The Matter of the Science of Jurisprudence is Law
(strictly so called).

But this, as I stated in the preceding lecture, is
liable to be confounded with certain objects, to which
it is allied or related in the way of resemblance or
analogy: viz: Divine Laws and Religious Precepts;
Moral Rules or the Laws of Morality; and Laws
merely improper, or purely metaphorical.

To extricate the subject of Jurisprudence from these
foreign, though related, objects is the purpose which
I am trying to accomplish in this earlier portion of
my course: and in order to accomplish this purpose,
the following, I think, is the obvious and convenient
method:—

1st, To enumerate the essentials of a law or rule
(as taken in the largest signification which can be
given to the term with propriety).

2ndly, Having stated the essentials of a law (in
the largest signification of the term), to distinguish
divine and moral laws from laws, strictly so called.

3rdly, To advert, briefly, to the metaphorical applications of the term, and to cleanse it of the other
ambiguities by which its import is obscured.

Accordingly, I endeavoured, in my last lecture, to
explain the essentials of a law (as taken in the largest
signification which can be given to the term with
propriety) as embracing *every* object to which we
can apply the term without extending its import
analogically, and without deviating into sheer meta-
phor: as comprising religious precepts and certain
moral rules, together with the laws which are
strictly so styled.

Subject to the restrictions which I there stated,
and which it were extremely inconvenient to repeat
here, the result of the analysis which I applied to
the term law, is this:—

1st, That a law or rule is a command.

2ndly, That, as distinguished from the commands which may be named occasional or particular, a law is a command, which obliges to a *course* of conduct; or which obliges, *generally* and *indefinitely,* to acts or forbearances of a *class.*

But laws which are strictly so called (laws established by political superiors) are not the *only* objects which this definition embraces. It comprises every object to which the term law can be extended, unless it be used with a meaning which is purely metaphorical and improper. It applies, with perfect precision, to religious precepts; or to the laws which are established immediately by God himself: And it also applies (although with a little inaccuracy) to those laws of human, but not of political institution, which may be styled the moral law, or the rules or precepts of morality. In short, I have stated the essentials of a law (in the *large* signification of the term) and have still to distinguish the laws which are the matter of the science of jurisprudence, from the laws divine and human which are the matter of other sciences.

C.   Definition of Legal Conceptions

Wesley Newcomb Hohfeld, Fundamental Legal Conceptions (1923); Introduction by Walter Wheeler Cook pp. 3-9; 11-12 (footnotes omitted); reprinted by permission of the Yale University Press.

It is a commonplace that the vast majority of the members of the legal profession in English-speaking countries still regard "jurisprudence" in all its manifestations, and especially that branch of it commonly known as "analytical jurisprudence," as something academic and without practical value. It is believed that the chief reason of at least one of the reasons, for this view is not hard to discover. Almost without exception the writers who have dealt with the subject seem to have proceeded upon the theory that their task was finished when they had set forth in orderly and logical array their own analysis of the nature of law, of legal rights and duties, and similar things. That the making of this analysis—aside from the mere intellectual joy of it—is not an end in itself but merely a means to an end, these writers perceive only dimly or not at all; that the analysis presented has any utility for the lawyer and the judge in solving the problems which confront them, they do not as a rule attempt to demonstrate; much less do they show that utility by practical application of the analysis to the solution of concrete legal problems.

In the opinion of the present writer one of the greatest messages which the late Wesley Newcomb Hohfeld during his all too short life gave to the legal profession was this, that an adequate analytical jurisprudence is an absolutely indispensable tool in the equipment of the properly trained lawyer or judge — indispensable, that is, for the highest efficiency in the discharge of the daily duties of his profession. It was Hohfeld's great merit that he saw that, interesting as analytical jurisprudence is when pursued for its own sake, its chief value lies in the fact that by its aid the correct solution of legal problems becomes not only easier but more certain. In this respect it does not differ from any other branch of pure science. We must hasten to add, lest we do an injustice to Hohfeld's memory by thus emphasizing his work along the line of analytical jurisprudence, that no one saw more clearly than he that while the analytical matter is an indispensable tool, it is not an all-sufficient one for the lawyer. On the contrary, he emphasized over and over again — especially in his notable address before the Association of American Law Schools upon *A Vital School of Jurisprudence* — that analytical work merely paves the way for other branches of jurisprudence, and that without the aid of the latter satisfactory solutions of legal problems cannot be reached. Thus legal analysis to him was primarily a means to an end, a necessary aid both in discovering just what the problems are which confront courts and lawyers and in finding helpful analogies which might otherwise be hidden.

If attention is here directed chiefly to Hohfeld's work in the analytical field, it is by reason of the fact that the larger portion of his published writings is devoted to that subject, in which he excelled because of his great analytical powers and severely logical mind.

* * *

Before we examine the main outlines of the structure which Hohfeld had planned and started to build, let one thing be clearly said. No one realized more clearly than did he that none of us can claim to have been the originator of any very large portion of any science, be it legal or physical. It is all that can be expected if each one of us succeeds in adding a few stones, or even one, to the ever-growing edifice which science is rearing. It follows that anything which one writes must largely be made up of a restatement of what has already been said by others in another form. Each one of us may congratulate himself if he has added something of value, even if that consists only in so rearranging the data which others have accumulated as to throw new light upon the subject — a light which will serve to illuminate the pathway of those who come after us and so enable them to make still further progress.

In the first of the two essays upon *Fundamental Legal Conceptions* Hohfeld sets forth the eight fundamental conceptions in terms of which he believed all legal problems could be stated. He arranges them in the following scheme:

Jural Opposites	(right (no-right	privilege duty	power disability	immunity liability
Jural Correlatives	(right (duty	privilege no-right	power liability	immunity disability

One thing which at once impresses itself upon one who is familiar with law, and especially with the work of writers upon jurisprudence who preceded Hohfeld, is that the terms found in this scheme are with one exception not new, but have always been more or less frequently used. To be sure, they have not ordinarily been used with precision of meaning as in the table we are considering; on the contrary, they have been given one meaning by one person, another by another, or indeed, different meanings by the same person upon different occasions. It is also true that nearly all the concepts which these terms represent in Hohfeld's system have been recognized and discussed by more than one writer upon jurisprudence. A brief consideration serves to show, however, that the concepts and terms which are new are needed to logically complete the scheme and make of it a useful tool in the analysis of problems. When so completed, these legal concepts become the "lowest common denominators" in terms of which all legal problems can be stated, and stated so as to bring out with greater distinctness than would otherwise be possible the real questions involved. Moreover, as previously suggested, the writers who did recognize many of these concepts failed to make any real use of them in other portions of their work.

That the word *right* is often used broadly to cover legal relations in general has probably been at least vaguely realized by all thoughtful students of law. Thus, to take a concrete example, nearly all of us have probably noted at some time or other that the "right" (privilege) of self-defense is a different kind of "right" from the "right" not to be assaulted by another; but that legal thinking can never be truly accurate unless we constantly discriminate carefully between these different kinds of rights, few of us have sufficiently realized. We constantly speak of the right to make a will; the right of a legislative body to enact a given statute; of the right not to have one's property taken without due process of law, etc. In these and innumerable other instances it turns out upon examination that the one word "right" is being used to denote first one concept and then another, often with resulting confusion of thought.

With the clear recognition of the fact that the same term is being used to represent four distinct legal conceptions comes the conviction that if we are to be sure of our logic we must adopt and consistently use a terminology adequate to express the distinctions involved. The great merit of the four terms selected by Hohfeld for this purpose—right, privilege, power and immunity — is that they are already familiar to lawyers and judges and are indeed at times used with accuracy to express precisely the concepts for which he wished always to use them.

Right in the narrow sense — as the correlative of *duty* — is too well known to require extended discussion at this point. It signifies one's affirmative claim against another, as distinguished from "privilege," one's freedom from the right or claim of another. *Privilege* is a term of good repute in the law of defamation and in that relating to the duty of witnesses to testify. In defamation we say that under certain circumstances defamatory matter is "privileged," that is, that the person publishing the same has a *privilege* to do so. By this statement we are not asserting that the person having the privilege has an affirmative claim against another, i. e., that that other is under a duty to refrain from publishing the defamatory matter, as we are when we use "right" in the strict sense, but just the opposite. The assertion is merely that under the circumstances there is *an absence of duty* on the part of the one publishing the defamatory matter to refrain from doing so under the circumstances. So in reference to the duty of a witness to testify: upon some occasions we say the witness is privileged, i. e., that under the circumstances there is an absence of duty to testify, as in the case of the privilege against self-incrimination. "Privilege" therefore denotes absence of duty, and its correlative must denote absence of right. Unfortunately there is no term in general use which can be used to express this correlative of privilege, and the coining of a new term was necessary. The term devised by Hohfeld was "no-right," obviously fashioned upon an analogy to our common words *nobody* and *nothing.* The exact term to be used is, of course, of far less importance than the recognition of the concept for which a name is sought. The terms "privilege" and "no-right," therefore, denote respectively absence of duty on the part of the one having the privilege and absence of right on the part of the one having the "no-right."

All lawyers are familiar with the word "power" as used in reference to "powers of appointment." A person holding such a "power" has the legal ability by doing certain acts to alter legal relations, viz., to transfer the ownership of property from one person to another. Now the lawyer's world is full of such legal "powers," and in Hohfeld's terminology any human being who can by his acts produce changes in legal relations has a legal *power* or powers. Whenever a power exists, there is at least one other human being whose legal relations will be altered if the power is exercised. This situation Hohfeld described by saying that the one whose legal relations will be altered if the power is exercised is under a *"liability."* Care must be taken to guard against misapprehension. "Liability" as commonly used is a vague term and usually suggests something disadvantageous or burdensome. Not so in Hohfeld's system, for a "liability" may be a desirable thing. For example, one who owns a chattel may "abandon" it. By doing so he confers upon each person in the community a legal power to acquire ownership of the chattel by taking possession of it with the requisite state of mind. Before the chattel is abandoned, therefore, every person other than the owner is under a legal "liability" to have suddenly conferred upon him a new legal power which previously he did not have. So also any person can by offering to enter into a contract with another person confer upon the latter—without his consent, be it noted—a power by "accepting" the offer to bring into existence new legal relations. It follows that every person in the community who is legally capable of contracting is under a *liability* to have such a power conferred upon him at any moment.

Another use of the term "right," possibly less usual but by no means unknown, is to denote that one person is not subject to the power of another person to alter the legal relations of the person said to have the "right." For example, often when we speak of the "right" of a person not to be deprived of his liberty

or property without due process of law, the idea
sought to be conveyed is of the exemption of the person concerned from a legal power on the part of the
persons composing the government to alter his legal
relations in a certain way. In such cases the real concept is one of exemption from legal power, i. e.,
"immunity." At times, indeed, the word "immunity"
is used in exactly this sense in constitutional law. In
Hohfeld's system it is the generic term to describe
any legal situation in which a given legal relation
vested in one person can not be changed by the acts
of another person. Correlatively, the one who lacks
the power to alter the first person's legal relations is
said to be under a *"disability,"* that is, he lacks the
legal power to accomplish the change in question.
This concept of legal "immunity" is not unimportant,
as Salmond in his *Jurisprudence* seems to indicate
by placing it in a brief footnote. For example, the
thing which distinguishes a "spendthrift trust" from
ordinary trusts is not merely the lack of power on
the part of the *cestui que trust* to make a conveyance
of his interest, but also the *immunities* of the *cestui*
from having his equitable interest divested without his
consent in order to satisfy the claims of creditors.
Ordinary exemption laws, homestead laws, etc., also
furnish striking illustrations of immunities.

A power, therefore, "bears the same general contrast to an immunity that a right does to a privilege.
A right is one's affirmative claim against another, and
a privilege is one's freedom from the right or claim
of another. Similarly, a power is one's affirmative
'control' over a given legal relation as against another;
whereas an immunity is one's freedom from the legal
power or 'control' of another as regards some legal
relation." * * *

The credit for the logical completion of the scheme
of classification and the recognition of the importance
of each element in it may thus fairly be given to
Hohfeld. It is believed also that his presentation of it
in the form of a table of "jural correlatives" and "jural
opposites" has done much to clarify and explain it. A
still more important thing, as has been suggested

above, is that he demonstrated how these fundamental legal concepts were of the utmost utility and importance in bringing about a correct solution of concrete legal problems. Here also credit to some extent must in all fairness be given to Terry, as above indicated, but Hohfeld seems to the present writer to be the first one who appreciated to the full the real significance of the analysis. In the first of the articles upon *Fundamental Legal Conceptions* he demonstrated its utility by many examples from the law of contracts, torts, agency, property, etc., showing how the courts are constantly confronted by the necessity of distinguishing between the eight concepts and are all too often confused by the lack of clear concepts and precise terminology. On the other hand, so clear a thinker as Salmond has shown himself to be in his *Jurisprudence* fails to make any substantial use of the analysis in his book on *Torts*. Indeed, so far as the present writer has been able to discover, one might read his *Torts* through and never realize that any such analysis as that found in the *Jurisprudence* had ever been made. Yet the problems involved in such subjects as easements, privilege in defamation, and other portions of the law of torts too numerous to mention, require for their accurate solution careful discrimination between these different concepts.

Even in the work on *Jurisprudence* itself Salmond completely fails in certain chapters to show an appreciation of the meaning of these fundamental conceptions. Consider, for example, the following passage from the chapter on "Ownership":

"Ownership, in its most comprehensive signification, denotes the relation between a person and any right that is vested in him. That which a man *owns* is in all cases *a right*. When, as is often the case, we speak of the ownership of a material object, this is merely a convenient figure of speech. To *own* a piece of land means in truth to *own a particular kind of right* in the land, namely *the fee simple of it*."

From the point of view of one who understands the meaning of the eight fundamental legal concepts, it would be difficult to pen a more erroneous passage. To say that A owns a piece of land is really to assert that he is vested by the law with a complex—exceedingly complex, be it noted—aggregate of legal rights, privileges, powers and immunities—all relating of course to the land in question. He does not *own* the rights, etc., he *has* them; because he has them, he "owns" in very truth the material object concerned; there is no "convenient figure of speech" about it. To say that A has the "fee simple" of a piece of land is, therefore, to say not that he "owns *a* particular kind of *right* in the land" but simply that he has a very complex aggregate of rights, privileges, powers and immunities, availing against a large and indefinite number of people, all of which rights, etc., naturally have to do with the land in question.

The full significance and great practical utility of this conception of "ownership" would require a volume for its demonstration. When one has fully grasped it he begins to realize how superficial has been the conventional treatment of many legal problems and to see how little many commonly accepted arguments prove. He discovers, for example, that "*a right* of way" is a complex aggregate of rights, privileges, powers and immunities; is able to point out precisely which one of these is involved in the case before him, and so to demonstrate that decisions supposed to be in point really dealt with one of the other kinds of "rights" (in the generic sense) and so are not applicable to the case under discussion. He soon comes to look upon this newer analysis as an extraordinary aid to clearness of thought, as a tool as valuable to a lawyer as up-to-date instruments are to a surgeon.

Roscoe Pound, Fifty Years of Jurisprudence, 50 Harvard Law Review pp. 571-576 (1937); reprinted by permission of the author and the Harvard Law Review.

One of the notable achievements of jurisprudence in the last fifty years is the analysis of a "right" and resolving what had gone by that name into a number of components. The historical development of this differentiation is substantially this. Austin at least suggested the setting off of "liberties" from "rights." [1] He points out that a "liberty" (Hohfeld would say "privilege") is the absence of legal restraint, a condition or situation of legal nonrestraint of one's natural freedom of action, whereas a "right" is, as he puts it, a "faculty" residing in a determinate person by virtue of a given rule of law which avails against and answers to a duty lying on some other person.[2] He does not develop the distinction, but he evidently saw the difference between the so-called right of free contract or right to pursue a lawful calling and the right to free choice of location or right of corporal integrity. The German Pandectists analyzed what they called the "content of a right." That is, they set off various conceptions or "jural relations" involved in "a right" in the broader sense—in the legally recognized and delimited interest plus the complex of "faculties" or "capacities of influence" (*i. e.*, rights in the narrower sense, powers, liberties, and privileges) by which it is secured. Thus Windscheid in 1862 differentiated (under *subjektives Recht*) a right from a power.[3] Thon in 1878 differentiated *Anspruch* (claim), *Genuss* (enjoyment, largely Austin's liberty), and *Befugung* (power).[4] Bierling in 1883 made it *Anspruch* (claim), *Dürfen* (liberty), and *Können* (power).[5] But these distinctions did not affect English analytical jurisprudence for some time. The terms "power" and "liberty" are not in the index to the third edition of Holland's *Jurisprudence* (1886) and he uses "privilege" in the French sense to mean a pledge right taking precedence irrespective of its date.[6] In his discussion of "ambiguous uses" of the term "right" he speaks of the languages of Continental Europe in which what is right, law, and a right are denoted by one word, and the English confusion of what is right with a right. But he conceives that "the simple meaning of the term 'a right' is for the purposes of the jurist entirely adequate."[7] At length in 1902 Salmond (following Jhering in setting off the secured interest, but calling interest and securing apparatus a right) adopted Bierling's distinctions but with an attempt at a system of correlatives which gave an unusual and forced meaning to "disability" (no power) and "liability" (risk of exercise of a power). He distinguished legal advantages (rights in the wider sense), including rights in the stricter sense, liberties, powers and immunities, from legal burdens including duties, disabilities, and liabilities.[8] Hohfeld in 1913,[9] a pupil of Howison, one of the chief American expounders of Hegel, building on Salmond and thus indirectly on Bierling, constructed an elaborate scheme of opposites and correlatives based on the Hegelian logic. The defects of Hegel's logic, now well understood, are brought out in this ingenious and in many ways useful scheme. Croce has pointed out that Hegel's opposites are often not opposites but only contrasts.[10] This is true also of the "opposites" in Hohfeld's scheme, *e. g.*, power and disability, right and no right. All we have here is a contrast of a right in the narrower sense with the absence of such a right and of a power with the absence of a power.[11]

Moreover Hohfeld's scheme presupposes that there can only be one opposite and one correlative and that there must be an opposite and a correlative. But there may be many contrasts and there are sometimes two correlatives. For example, correlative to one's right as owner of Blackacre is his neighbor's duty not to trespass and his liability for trespass by his servant, trespass by his cow, and (in England) for breaking loose of his ponded water and invasion of the land. If it is said that the liability in case of the servant is correlative to a power in the servant, it will hardly be maintained that we may go on and say that there was a power in the reservoir, and if it is sought to fit such situations into the scheme by speaking of a duty in each case, the result is that the neighbor would be said to be under a duty to prevent servant and cow and water from trespassing and a liability (in Hohfeld's sense) that the servant make him answerable in damages by exercising his power. But the legal situation is exactly the same whether it is servant or cow or water that gets out of hand.

Again Hohfeld's scheme requires the finding of "opposites" (*i. e.*, usually contrasts) and correlatives, whether they have significance or not. For example, "no right" is put as if there were such a legal conception or institution as "a no-right." But there is no such thing as "a no-right" parallel to a disability (in the usual sense, *e. g.*, coverture at common law) or on the same plane as a right in the strict sense or a power.[12] Simply there are situations in which one has no legal right in the narrower sense although he may have one in the wider sense. His having no right (narrower sense) may be because the law does not recognize the interest asserted (*e. g.*, in jurisdictions which do not recognize the "right to privacy") or because the law secures a recognized interest in some other way, *e. g.*, by a liberty or a privilege or a power. Take a pact in Roman law, which could be used defensively but not as the basis of an action. Here there is no duty in the promisor. But the promisee has a power of using the claim upon the promise defensively and his recognized interest is secured to that extent and in that way. At common law the wife cannot sue the husband to enforce her right to support. But she can pledge his credit for necessaries at the grocer's. Her recognized interest is secured by a power. Also at common law the parent cannot sue the child for disobedience. But he has a privilege of moderate correction to enforce obedience. If one who has a right in the wider sense has also "a no-right" in Professor Goble's sense, it is because the right is better or sufficiently secured by a power or a privilege and so a right in the narrower sense is not conferred.[13]

As to Hohfeld's "disability" (taken over from Salmond) the use of the term was unhappy because disability had a long settled meaning referring to such things as the disabilities of a married woman at common law, the disabilities of infants, and the like. It is obviously unwise to lump these significant positive conceptions with the absence of powers in a person *sui juris* because none have been conferred on him. Accordingly "inability" has been suggested instead.[14] But "inability" as the "opposite" of power is like no-right. It means merely no power, which is no more a legal conception or institution than no right.

Not only does Hohfeld's scheme include pseudo conceptions which are the absence of things put as things, but it excludes or ignores things which are of real significance. It ignores right in the broader sense, for which over and again we need a term. Often, for example, in the conflict of laws the recognized and delimited interest and the whole bundle of legal institutions securing it, as a totality, are significant. Also it ignores the legally recognized and delimited interest, which is often the most significant thing in the whole complex. Take for instance the natural obligation in Roman law. Here there is a recognized interest which has significance in itself. Compare also the recognized claim of the husband as against the wife to her society, which has legal significance even if the action for restitution of conjugal rights is obsolete.

Finally the exigencies of Hegelian triads require one category of "privileges" for the two kinds of condition of legal nonrestraint of natural powers. The one is the natural freedom of the individual—the *de facto* freedom of each of us to do as he likes—so far as it remains unrestricted by legal rules. It is a general condition of legal nonrestraint of natural powers. An owner's *jus utendi, jus fruendi,* and *jus abutendi* are of this sort. His natural powers are not restrained, and that is one way of securing his interest. The so-called "right of association" is of this type. The Austinian term "liberty" does very well here. The other category is one of definite special conditions of nonrestraint of natural powers on special occasions or in special situations. These are privileges in the stricter sense; situations in which on a weighing of the interests one is exempted from liability under the precepts which ordinarily apply to what he does.

Some improvements in Hohfeld's terminology have been suggested. One, to substitute "inability" for "disability", has been noted above. Another is to get rid of the awkward phrases "right in the wider sense" and "right in the narrower (or stricter) sense" by using "right" for the whole complex and "claim" (*i. e.*, the German *Anspruch*) for the legal right with correlative duty.[15] Hohfeld's scheme of triads had no place for the whole complex and he sought to limit the term "right" to the narrower sense. It might also be suggested that "risk" would be better for the Hohfeldian "liability", which takes a well known legal term with long settled meanings and puts it to a new use.

Finally Kocourek, who in a number of papers had subjected Hohfeld's scheme to acute and discriminating criticism, proceeding on the basis of Salmond's distinction between advantages and burdens, worked out a scheme of advantages (claim, immunity, privilege, power) and disadvantages (duty, disability, inability, liability) which brings out effectively the significant legal conceptions (claim, duty, power, liberty, and privilege) without the incumbrance of opposites and correlatives.[16] He makes it clear that the contrasted ideas, useful to bring out these conceptions and define them clearly, are not for that reason themselves legal conceptions or to be treated as such. But one cannot but feel that he carries out schematic exposition and terminology far beyond what is practically worth while. Thus the matter stands at present. One may feel that Occam's razor may well be applied to the hypertrophy of categories which analysis of "a right" produced for a time, and, in fact, current usage has pretty well settled down to caution in use of the conventional terms and realization that the four or five significant conceptions must be clearly understood, whatever they are called.

Hohfeld did a great service to the law in bringing this home to teachers, practitioners, and judges. It was a misfortune that his untimely death prevented the further working over of the subject which would have taken place had he lived to put his work—which he had hardly more than begun—in final form.

D. Hierarchy of Legal Norms

Hans Kelsen, General Theory of Law and the State (1945) pp. 123-126; 128-129; 132-133; 134-136; reprinted by permission of the Harvard University Press.

A. The Superior and the Inferior Norm

The analysis of law, which reveals the dynamic character of this normative system and the function of the basic norm, also exposes a further peculiarity of law: Law regulates its own creation inasmuch as one legal norm determines the way in which another norm is created, and also, to some extent, the contents of that norm. Since a legal norm is valid because it is created in a way determined by another legal norm, the latter is the reason of validity of the former. The relation between the norm regulating the creation of another norm and this other norm may be presented as a relationship of super- and sub-ordination, which is a spatial figure of speech. The norm determining the creation of another norm is the superior, the norm created according to this regulation, the inferior norm. The legal order, especially the legal order the personification of which is the State, is therefore not a system of norms co-ordinated to each other, standing, so to speak, side by side on the same level, but a hierarchy of different levels of norms. The unity of these norms is constituted by the fact that the creation of one norm—the lower one—is determined by another—the higher—the creation of which is determined by a still higher norm, and that this *regressus* is terminated by a highest, the basic norm which, being the supreme reason of validity of the whole legal order, constitutes its unity.

B. The Different Stages of the Legal Order

a. *The Constitution*

1. Constitution in a Material and a Formal Sense; Determination of the Creation of General Norms

The hierarchical structure of the legal order of a State is roughly as follows: Presupposing the basic norm, the constitution is the highest level within national law. The constitution is here understood, not in a formal, but in a material sense. The constitution in the formal sense is a certain solemn document, a set of legal norms that may be changed only under the observation of special prescriptions, the purpose of which it is to render the change of these norms more difficult. The constitution in the material sense consists of those rules which regulate the creation of the general legal norms, in particular the creation of statutes. The formal constitution, the solemn document called "constitution," usually contains also other norms, norms which are no part of the material constitution. But it is in order to safeguard the norms determining the organs and the procedure of legislation that a special solemn document is drafted and that the changing of its rules is made especially difficult. It is because of the material constitution that there is a special form for constitutional laws or a constitutional form. If there is a constitutional form, then constitutional laws must be distinguished from ordinary laws. The difference consists in that the creation, and that means enactment, amendment, annulment, of constitutional laws is more difficult than that of ordinary laws. There exists a special procedure, a special form for the creation of constitutional laws, different from the procedure for the creation of ordinary laws. Such a special form for constitutional laws, a constitutional form, or constitution in the formal sense of the term, is not indispensable, whereas the material constitution, that is to say norms regulating the creation of general norms and—in modern law—norms determining the organs and procedure of legislation, is an essential element of every legal order.

A constitution in the formal sense, especially provisions by which change of the constitution is made more difficult than the change of ordinary laws, is possible only if there is a written constitution, if the constitution has the character of statutory law. There are States, Great Britain for instance, which have no "written" and hence no formal constitution, no solemn document called "The Constitution." Here the (material) constitution has the character of customary law and therefore there exists no difference between constitutional and ordinary laws. The constitution in the material sense of the term may be a written or an unwritten law, may have the character of statutory or customary law. If, however, a specific form for constitutional law exists, any contents whatever may appear under this form. As a matter of fact, subject-matters which for some reason or other are considered especially important are often regulated by constitutional instead of by ordinary laws. An example is the Eighteenth Amendment to the Constitution of the United States, the prohibition amendment, now repealed.

2. Determination of the Content of General Norms by the Constitution

The material constitution may determine not only the organs and procedure of legislation, but also, to some degree, the contents of future laws. The constitution can negatively determine that the laws must not have a certain content, e.g., that the parliament may not pass any statute which restricts religious freedom. In this negative way, not only the contents of statutes but of all the other norms of the legal order, judicial and administrative decisions likewise, may be determined by the constitution. The constitution, however, can also positively prescribe a certain content of future statutes; it can, as does, for instance the Constitution of the United States of America, stipulate "that in all criminal prosecutions the accused shall enjoy the right to a speedy and public trial, by an impartial jury of the State and district wherein the crime shall have been committed, which district shall have been previously ascertained by law, etc. . . ." This provision of the constitution determines the contents of future laws concerning criminal procedure. The importance of such stipulations from the point of view of legal technique will be discussed in another context.

     ✿   ✿   ✿   ✿   ✿

b. General Norms Enacted on the Basis of the Constitution; Statutes, Customary Law

The general norms established by way of legislation or custom form a level which comes next to the constitution in the hierarchy of law. These general norms are to be applied by the organs competent thereto, especially by the courts but also by the administrative authorities. The law-applying organs must be instituted according to the legal order, which likewise has to determine the procedure which those organs shall follow when applying law. Thus, the general norms of statutory or customary law have a two-fold function: (1) to determine the law-applying organs and the procedure to be observed by them and (2) to determine the judicial and administrative acts of these organs. The latter by their acts create individual norms, thereby applying the general norms to concrete cases.

c. Substantive and Adjective Law

To these two functions correspond the two kinds of law, which are commonly distinguished: material or substantive and formal or adjective law. Beside the substantive criminal law there is an adjective criminal law of criminal procedure, and the same is true also of civil law and administrative law. Part of procedural law, of course, are also those norms which constitute the law-applying organs. Thus two kinds of general norms are always involved in the application of law by an organ: (1) the formal norms which determine the creation of this organ and the procedure it has to follow, and (2) the material norms which determine the contents of its judicial or administrative act. When speaking of the "application" of law by courts and administrative organs, one usually thinks only of the second kind of norms; it is only the substantive civil, criminal, and administrative law applied by the organs one has in mind. But no application of norms of the second kind is possible without the application of norms of the first kind. The substantive civil, criminal, or administrative law cannot be applied in a concrete case without the adjective law regulating the civil, criminal, or administrative procedure being applied at the same time. The two kinds of norm are really inseparable. Only in their organic union do they form the law. Every complete or primary rule of law, as we have called it, contains both the formal and the material element. The (very much simplified) form of a rule of criminal law is: If a subject has committed a certain delict, then a certain organ (the court), appointed in a certain way, shall, through a certain procedure, especially on the motion of another organ (the public prosecutor), direct against the delinquent a certain sanction. As we shall show later, a more explicit statement of such a norm is: If the competent organ, that is the organ appointed in the way prescribed by the law, has established through a certain procedure prescribed by the law, that a subject has committed a delict, determined by the law, then a sanction prescribed by the law shall be directed against the delinquent. This formulation clearly exhibits the systematic relation between substantive and adjective law, between the determination of the delict and the sanction, on the one hand, and the determination of the organs and their procedure, on the other.

❋   ❋   ❋   ❋   ❋

d. Creation of Law and Application of Law

1. Merely Relative Difference between Law-creating and Law-applying Function

The legal order is a system of general and individual norms connected with each other according to the principle that law regulates its own creation. Each norm of this order is created according to the provisions of another norm, and ultimately according to the provisions of the basic norm constituting the unity of this system of norms, the legal order. A norm belongs to this legal order only because it has been created in conformity with the stipulations of another norm of the order. This *regressus* finally leads to the first constitution, the creation of which is determined by the presupposed basic norm. One may also say that a norm belongs to a certain legal order if it has been created by an organ of the community constituted by the order. The individual who creates the legal norm is an organ of the legal community because and insofar as his function is determined by a legal norm of the order constituting the legal community. The imputation of this function to the community is based on the norm determining the function. This explanation, however, does not add anything to the previous one. The statement "A norm belongs to a certain legal order because it is created by an organ of the legal community constituted by this order" and the statement "A norm belongs to a legal order because it is created according to the basic norm of this legal order" assert one and the same thing.

A norm regulating the creation of another norm is "applied" in the creation of the other norm. Creation of law is always application of law. These two concepts are by no means, as the traditional theory presumes, absolute opposites. It is not quite correct to classify legal acts as law-creating and law-applying acts; for, setting aside two borderline cases of which we shall speak later, every act is, normally, at the same time a law-creating and a law-applying act. The creation of a legal norm is—normally—an application of the higher norm, regulating its creation, and the application of a higher norm is — normally — the creation of a lower norm determined by the higher norm. A judicial decision, e.g., is an act by which a general norm, a statute, is applied but at the same time an individual norm is created obligating one or both parties to the conflict. Legislation is creation of law, but taking into account the constitution, we find that it is also application of law. In any act of legislation, where the provisions of the constitution are observed, the constitution is applied. The making of the first constitution can likewise be considered as an application of the basic norm.

* * * * *

e. *Individual Norms Created on the Basis of General Norms*

1. The Judicial Act as Creation of an Individual Norm

As an application of law, traditional doctrine considers above all the judicial decision, the function of courts. When settling a dispute between two parties or when sentencing an accused person to a punishment, a court applies, it is true, a general norm of statutory or customary law. But simultaneously the court creates an individual norm providing that a definite sanction shall be executed against a definite individual. This individual norm is related to the general norms as a statute is related to the constitution. The judicial function is thus, like legislation, both creation and application of law. The judicial function is ordinarily determined by the general norms both as to procedure and as to the contents of the norm to be created, whereas legislation is usually determined by the constitution only in the former respect. But that is a difference in degree only.

2. The Judicial Act as a Stage of the Law-creating Process

From a dynamic standpoint, the individual norm created by the judicial decision is a stage in a process beginning with the establishment of the first constitution, continued by legislation and custom, and leading to the judicial decisions. The process is completed by the execution of the individual sanction. Statutes and customary laws are, so to speak, only semi-manufactured products which are finished only through the judicial decision and its execution. The process through which law constantly creates itself anew goes from the general and abstract to the individual and concrete. It is a process of steadily increasing individualization and concretization.

The general norm which, to certain abstractly determined conditions, attaches certain abstractly determined consequences, has to be individualized and concretized in order to come in contact with social life, to be applied to reality. To this purpose, in a given case it has to be ascertained whether the conditions, determined *in abstracto* in the general norm, are present *in concreto*, in order that the sanction, determined *in abstracto* in the general norm, may be ordered and executed *in concreto*. These are the two essential elements of the judicial function. This function has, by no means, as is sometimes assumed, a purely declaratory character. Contrary to what is sometimes asserted, the court does not merely formulate already existing law. It does not only "seek" and "find" the law existing previous to its decision, it does not merely pronounce the law which exists ready and finished prior to its pronouncement. Both in establishing the presence of the conditions and in stipulating the sanction, the judicial decision has a constitutive character. The decision applies, it is true, a preexisting general norm in which a certain consequence is attached to certain conditions. But the existence of the concrete conditions in connection with the concrete consequence is, in the concrete case, first established by the court's decision. Conditions and consequences are connected by judicial decisions in the realm of the concrete, as they are connected by statutes and rules of customary law in the realm of the abstract. The individual norm of the judicial decision is the necessary individualization and concretization of the general and abstract norm. Only the prejudice, characteristic of the jurisprudence of continental Europe, that law is, by definition, only general norms, only the erroneous identification of law with the general rules of statutory and customary law, could obscure the fact that the judicial decision continues the law-creating process from the sphere of the general and abstract into that of the individual and concrete.

3. The Ascertainment of the Conditioning Facts

The judicial decision is clearly constitutive as far as it orders a concrete sanction to be executed against an individual delinquent. But it has a constitutive character also, as far as it ascertains the facts conditioning the sanction. In the world of law, there is no fact "in itself," no "absolute" fact, there are only facts ascertained by a competent organ in a procedure prescribed by law. When attaching to certain facts certain consequences, the legal order must also designate an organ that has to ascertain the facts in the concrete case and prescribe the procedure which the organ, in so doing, has to observe. The legal order may authorize this organ to regulate its procedure at its own discretion; but organ and procedure by which the conditioning facts are to be ascertained must be— directly or indirectly—determined by the legal order, to make the latter applicable to social life. It is a typical layman's opinion that there are absolute, immediately evident facts. Only by being first ascertained through a legal procedure are facts brought into the sphere of law or do they, so to speak, come into existence within this sphere. Formulating this in a somewhat paradoxically pointed way, we could say that the competent organ ascertaining the conditioning facts legally "creates" these facts. Therefore, the function of ascertaining facts through a legal procedure has always a specifically constitutive character. If, according to a legal norm, a sanction has to be executed against a murderer, this does not mean that the fact of murder is "in itself" the condition of the sanction. There is no fact "in itself" that A has killed B, there is only my or somebody else's belief or knowledge that A has killed B. A himself may either acquiesce or deny. From the point of view of law, however, all these are no more than private opinions without relevance. Only the establishment by the competent organ has legal relevance. If the judicial decision has already obtained the force of law, if it has become impossible to replace this decision by another because there exists the status of *res judicata*—which means that the case has been definitely decided by a court of last resort—then the opinion that the condemned was innocent is without any legal significance. As already pointed out, the correct formulation of the rule of law is not "If a subject has committed a delict, an organ shall direct a sanction against the delinquent," but "If the competent organ has established in due order that a subject has committed a delict, then an organ shall direct a sanction against this subject."

FOOTNOTES TO SECTION II-C

1. 1 Lectures on Jurisprudence (5th ed. 1885) 274-75.
2. *Id.* at 285n.
3. 1 Lehrbuch des Pandektenrechts, §37.
4. Rechtsnorm und subjektives Recht, c. 5.
5. 2 Zur Kritik der juristischen Grundbegriffe (1877-83) 49-73.
6. Elements of Jurisprudence (3d ed. 1886) 192.
7. *Id.* at 69-70.
8. Jurisprudence, §§70-74.
9. What is Living and What is Dead in the Philosophy of Hegel, transl. by Ainslie, c. 4.
10. Some Fundamental Legal Conceptions as Applied in Judicial Reasoning, 36, reprint of article in (1913) 23 Yale L. J. 16, 30.
11. Professor Radin has called attention to this and also to a logical difficulty in Hohfeld's use of "correlative". *L'analisi dei rapporti giuridici secondo il metodo di Hohfeld* (1927) 7 Rivista Internazionale di Filosofia del Diritto 117, 124.
12. Professor Goble, *Affirmative and Negative Legal Relations* (1922) 4 Ill. L. Q. 94, speaks repeatedly of one having a no-right. *E.g.*, at 100, 105. Also Professor Cook speaks of "the one having 'the no-right'". *Hohfeld's Contributions to the Science of Law* (1919) 28 Yale L. J. 721, 725.

13. Professor Goble's contention that wherever a court decides that a plaintiff has not proved his case on the facts it decides he has a no-right (see the paper referred to *supra* note 12, at 98) is an example of what the schematism of Hegelian logic may lead to.

14. Randall, *Hohfeld on Jurisprudence* (1925) 41 L. Q. Rev. 86, 90.

15. Kocourek, Jural Relations (1927) 7, 14.

16. Jural Relations (1927) c. 13.

Part III
SOCIOLOGICAL JURISPRUDENCE

In widest terms, sociological jurisprudence is the study of the interaction of law and the rest of society. The phrase itself was introduced into American law by Roscoe Pound at the beginning of the century. At that time it was widely condemned as synonymous with "socialism." The intervening years however have shown that the movement was mainly interested in law as a *social* rather than a personal phenomenon, in the demands society makes on law, and in the conflicting interests of individuals and groups.

The dominance of sociological jurisprudence in this country is waning. It is being challenged on many sides, particularly by natural law. But almost all American scholars accept its major contributions. Their criticism is generally directed at remedying its defects. The outstanding exponent of sociological jurisprudence in this country is of course Roscoe Pound.

Twenty-five years ago a group of legal educators who became known as the Neo-Realists started a vigorous campaign to study the way in which legal rules actually worked out in the living law. This movement was touched off by the work of an Austrian sociologist, Eugen Ehrlich, who called attention to the sharp differences between the law in books and the law in action. While taking issue with the adherents of all other schools of jurisprudence including the sociological, the Neo-Realists found their movement generally regarded as a continuation of sociological jurisprudence.

A. In Court

The Brandeis Brief

The famous Brandeis Brief introduced American courts dramatically to the use of social science materials in legal proceedings. The lawyer whose exploit is here referred to is of course he who later became the celebrated Justice Louis D. Brandeis of the Supreme Court of the United States.

Mr. Brandeis, in arguing for the constitutionality of an Oregon statute which provided that no female should work in certain establishments more than ten hours a day, presented the court with materials gathered from many sources. He did not follow the practice then prevalent of restricting himself to authoritative legal sources as the sole guides to decision.

What interests us here is the way the court used these materials in sustaining the constitutionality of the statute. *Muller* v. *Oregon*, 208 U. S. 412 at 419-421 (1908).

MR. JUSTICE BREWER delivered the opinion of the court.

In patent cases counsel are apt to open the argument with a discussion of the state of the art. It may not be amiss, in the present case, before examining the constitutional question, to notice the course of legislation as well as expressions of opinion from other than judicial sources. In the brief filed by Mr. Louis D. Brandeis, for the defendant in error, is a very copious collection of all these matters, an epitome of which is found in the margin* (citations omitted).

    ✿   ✿   ✿   ✿   ✿

The legislation and opinions referred to in the margin may not be, technically speaking, authorities, and in them is little or no discussion of the constitutional question presented to us for determination, yet they are significant of a widespread belief that woman's physical structure, and the functions she performs in consequence thereof, justify special legislation restricting or qualifying the conditions under which she should be permitted to toil. Constitutional questions, it is true, are not settled by even a consensus of present public opinion, for it is the peculiar value of a written constitution that it places in unchanging form limitations upon legislative action, and thus gives a permanence and stability to popular government which otherwise would be lacking. At the

---

* Then follow extracts from over ninety reports of committees, bureaus of statistics, commissioners of hygiene, inspectors of factories, both in this country and in Europe, to the effect that long hours of labor are dangerous for women, primarily because of their special physical organization. The matter is discussed in these reports in different aspects, but all agree as to the danger. It would of course take too much space to give these reports in detail. Following them are extracts from similar reports discussing the general benefits of short hours from an economic aspect of the question. In many of these reports individual instances are given tending to support the general conclusion. Perhaps the general scope and character of all these reports may be summed up in what an inspector for Hanover says: "The reasons for the reduction of the working day to ten hours—(a) the physical organization of women, (b) her maternal functions, (c) the rearing and education of the children, (d) the maintenance of the home— are all so important and so far reaching that the need for such reduction need hardly be discussed."

same time, when a question of fact is debated and debatable, and the extent to which a special constitutional limitation goes is affected by the truth in respect to that fact, a widespread and long continued belief concerning it is worthy of consideration. We take judicial cognizance of all matters of general knowledge.

* * * * *

B. General Theory of Sociological Jurisprudence

Roscoe Pound, The Scope and Purpose of Sociological Jurisprudence, 25 Harvard Law Review pp. 489-490 (1912); reprinted by permission of the author and the Harvard Law Review.

Sociological Jurisprudence is still formative. In diversity of view the sociological jurists but reflect the differences that exist among sociologists. This is no more a ground for denying that there is a sociological school or denying that there is a sociological method in jurisprudence, than the differences among philosophical jurists are ground for denying that there is a philosophical method.

In common with sociology, sociological jurisprudence has its origin in the positivist philosophers in the sense that each subject has a continuous development from Comte's positive philosophy. But both have long got beyond this and are now wholly independent of it. Nevertheless, there are those who appear to insist that sociological jurisprudence must be identified with a philosophical jurisprudence of the positivist type.[1] Others, also, because sociological thought went through an anthropological-ethnological stage, both in the social sciences generally and in jurisprudence, assume that sociological jurisprudence can mean only a science of law based on anthropology and ethnology.[2] In other words, some insist it must stand for a mechanical interpretation that regards law as the product of an inexorable mechanism of social forces. Others insist that it must stand for an ethnological interpretation; for a science of law developed from comparative study of primitive institutions or for a generalization from the jural materials gathered by a purely descriptive social science. Today, such views are held chiefly by the critics of sociological jurisprudence. But they have a certain warrant in an unhappy tendency in the earlier stages of the development of the new school to insist exclusively upon some one phase of social science or some one mode of investigation or some one interpretation. It is to be remembered, however, that all the methods of jurisprudence have suffered from a like tendency; that extreme assertions of an imperative theory at one time brought analytical jurisprudence into disfavor, that historical jurisprudence is now under a cloud because it was so long identified with Savigny's views as to law-making, and that philosophical jurisprudence has still to recover in some countries the ground it lost when it became identified with the metaphysical method of the last century. Sociological jurisprudence did not find itself at once, and some assert it has not yet done so.

Benjamin N. Cardozo, Nature of Judicial Process (1921) in Selected Writings of Benjamin Nathan Cardozo pp. 135-140; reprinted by permission of the Yale University Press and the Fallon Book Company.

It is true, I think, today in every department of the law that the social value of a rule has become a test of growing power and importance. This truth is powerfully driven home to the lawyers of this country in the writings of Dean Pound. "Perhaps the most significant advance in the modern science of law is the change from the analytical to the functional attitude." [3] "The emphasis has changed from the content of the precept and the existence of the remedy to the effect of the precept in action and the availability and efficiency of the remedy to attain the ends for which the precept was devised." [4] Foreign jurists have the same thought: "The whole of the judicial function," says Gmelin,[5] "has . . . been shifted. The will of the State, expressed in decision and judgment is to bring about a just determination by means of the subjective sense of justice inherent in the judge, guided by an effective weighing of the interests of the parties in the light of the opinions generally prevailing among the community regarding transactions like those in question. The determination should under all circumstances be in harmony with the requirements of good faith in business intercourse and the needs of practical life, unless a positive statute prevents it; and in weighing conflicting interests, the interest that is better founded in reason and more worthy of protection should be helped to achieve victory." [6] "On the one hand," says Gény,[7] "we are to interrogate reason and conscience, to discover in our inmost nature, the very basis of justice; on the other, we are to address ourselves to social phenomena, to ascertain the laws of their harmony and the principles of order which they exact." And again:[8] "Justice and general utility, such will be the two objectives that will direct our course."

All departments of the law have been touched and elevated by this spirit. In some, however, the method of sociology works in harmony with the method of philosophy or of evolution or of tradition. Those, therefore, are the fields where logic and coherence and consistency must still be sought as ends. In others, it seems to displace the methods that compete with it. Those are the fields where the virtues of consistency must yield within those interstitial limits where judicial power moves. In a sense it is true that we are applying the method of sociology when we pursue logic and coherence and consistency as the greater social values. I am concerned for the moment with the fields in which the method is in antagonism to others rather than with those in which their action is in unison. Accurate division is, of course, impossible. A few broad areas may, however, be roughly marked as those in which the method of sociology has fruitful application. Let me seek some illustrations of its workings. I will look for them first of all in the field of constitutional law, where the primacy of this method is, I think, undoubted, then in certain branches of private law where public policy, having created rules, must have like capacity to alter them, and finally in other fields where the method, though less insistent and pervasive, stands ever in the background, and emerges to the front when technicality or logic or tradition may seem to press their claims unduly.

I speak first of the Constitution, and in particular of the great immunities with which it surrounds the individual. No one shall be deprived of liberty without due process of law. Here is a concept of the greatest generality. Yet it is put before the courts *en bloc*. Liberty is not defined. Its limits are not mapped and charted. How shall they be known? Does liberty mean the same thing for successive generations? May restraints that were arbitrary yesterday be useful and rational and therefore lawful today? May restraints that are arbitrary today become useful and rational and therefore lawful tomorrow? I have no doubt that the answer to these questions must be yes. There were times in our judicial history when the answer might have been no. Liberty was conceived of at first as something static and absolute. The Declaration of Independence had enshrined it. The blood of Revolution had sanctified it. The political philosophy of Rousseau and of Locke and later of Herbert Spencer and of the Manchester school of economists had dignified and rationalized it. *Laissez faire* was not only a counsel of caution which statesmen would do well to heed. It was a categorical imperative which statesmen, as well as judges, must obey. The "nineteenth century theory" was "one of eternal legal conceptions involved in the very idea of justice and containing potentially an exact rule for every case to be reached by an absolute process of logical deduction."[9] The century had not closed, however, before a new political philosophy became reflected in the work of statesmen and ultimately in the decrees of courts. The transition is interestingly described by Dicey in his "Law and Opinion in England."[10] The movement from "individualistic liberalism to unsystematic collectivism" had brought changes in the social order which carried with them the need of a new formulation of fundamental rights and duties. In our country, the need did not assert itself so soon. Courts still spoke in the phrases of a philosophy that had served its day.[11] Gradually, however, though not without frequent protest and intermittent movements backward, a new conception of the significance of constitutional limitations in the domain of individual liberty, emerged to recognition and to dominance. Judge Hough, in an interesting address, finds the dawn of the new epoch in 1883, when Hurtado v. California, 110 U. S. 516, was argued.[12] If the new epoch had then dawned, it was still obscured by fog and cloud. Scattered rays of light may have heralded the coming day. They were not enough to blaze the path. Even as late as 1905, the decision in Lochner v. N. Y., 198 U. S. 45, still spoke in terms untouched by the light of the new spirit. It is the dissenting opinion of Justice Holmes, which men will turn to in the future as the beginning of an era.[13] In the instance, it was the voice of a minority. In principle, it has become the voice of a new dispensation, which has written itself into law. "The Fourteenth Amendment does not enact Mr. Herbert Spencer's Social Statics."[14] "A constitution is not intended to embody a particular economic theory, whether of paternalism and the organic relation of the citizen to the state, or of *laissez faire.*"[15] "The word liberty in the Fourteenth Amendment is perverted when it is held to prevent the natural outcome of a dominant opinion, unless it can be said that a rational and fair man necessarily would admit that the statute proposed would infringe fundamental principles as they have been understood by the traditions of our people and our law."[16] That is the conception of liberty which is dominant today.[17] It has its critics even yet,[18] but its dominance is, I think, assured. No doubt, there will at times be difference of opinion when a conception so delicate is applied to varying conditions.[19] At times, indeed, the conditions themselves are imperfectly disclosed and inadequately known. Many and insidious are the agencies by which opinion is poisoned at its sources. Courts have often been led into error in passing upon the validity of a statute, not from misunderstanding of the law, but from misunderstanding of the facts. This happened in New York. A statute forbidding night work for women was declared arbitrary and void in 1907.[20] In 1915, with fuller knowledge of the investigations of social workers, a like statute was held to be reasonable and valid.[21] Courts know today that statutes are to be viewed, not in isolation or *in vacuo,* as pronouncements of abstract principles for the guidance of an ideal community, but in the setting and the framework of present-day conditions, as revealed by the labors of economists and students of the social sciences in our own country and abroad.[22] The same fluid and dynamic conception which underlies the modern notion of liberty, as secured to the individual by the constitutional immunity, must also underlie the cognate notion of equality. No state shall deny to any person within its jurisdiction "the equal protection of the laws." [23] Restrictions, viewed narrowly, may seem to foster inequality. The same restrictions, when viewed broadly, may be seen "to be necessary in the long run in order to establish the equality of position between the parties in which liberty of contract begins." [24] Charmont in "La Renaissance du Droit Naturel," [25] gives neat expression to the same thought: "On tend à considerer qu'il n'y a pas de contrat respectable si les parties n'ont pas été placées dans les conditions non seulement de liberté, mais d'égalité. Si l'un des contractants est sans abri, sans ressources, condamné à subir les exigences de l'autre, la liberté de fait est supprimée." [26]

From all this, it results that the content of constitutional immunities is not constant, but varies from age to age. "The needs of successive generations may make restrictions imperative today, which were vain and capricious to the vision of times past." [27] "We must never forget," in Marshall's mighty phrase, "that it is a *constitution* we are expounding." [28] Statutes are designed to meet the fugitive exigencies of the hour. Amendment is easy as the exigencies change. In such cases, the meaning, once construed, tends legitimately to stereotype itself in the form first cast. A *constitution* states or ought to state not rules for the passing hour, but principles for an expanding future. In so far as it deviates from that standard, and descends into details and particulars, it loses its flexibility, the scope of interpretation contracts, the meaning hardens. While it is true to its function, it maintains its power of adaptation, its suppleness, its play. I think it is interesting to note that even in the interpretation of ordinary statutes, there are jurists, at any rate abroad, who maintain that the meaning of today is not always the meaning of tomorrow. "The President of the highest French Court, M. Ballot-Beaupré, explained, a few years ago, that the provisions of the Napoleonic legislation had been adapted to modern conditions by a judicial interpretation in *'le sens évolutif.'* 'We do not inquire,' he said, 'what the legislator willed a century ago, but what he would have willed if he had known what our present conditions would be.'" [29] So Kohler: "It follows from all this that the interpretation of a statute must by no means of necessity remain the same forever. To speak of an exclusively correct interpretation, one which would be the true meaning of the statute from the beginning to the end of its day, is altogether erroneous." [30] I think the instances must be rare, if any can be found at all, in which this method of interpretation has been applied in English or American law to ordinary legislation. I have no doubt that it has been applied in the past and with increasing frequency will be applied in the future, to fix the scope and meaning of the broad precepts and immunities in state and national constitutions. I see no reason why it may not be applied to statutes framed upon lines similarly general, if any such there are. We are to read them, whether the result be contraction or expansion, in *"le sens évolutif."* [31]

Roscoe Pound, Outlines of Lectures on Jurisprudence (1943) pp. 32-34 (omitting fine print); reprinted by permission of the author and the Harvard University Press.

THE PROGRAMME OF THE
SOCIOLOGICAL SCHOOL

Sociological jurists insist upon eight points:

(a) Study of the actual social effects of legal institutions, legal precepts, and legal doctrines.

* * * * *

(b) Sociological study in preparation for law-making.

* * * * *

(c) Study of the means of making legal precepts effective in action.

* * * * *

(d) Study of juridical method: psychological study of the judicial, legislative, and juristic processes as well as philosophical study of the ideals.

* * * * *

(e) A sociological legal history; study of the past social background and past social effects of legal institutions, legal precepts, and legal doctrines, and of how these effects were brought about.

* * * * *

(f) Recognition of the importance of individualized application of legal precepts—of reasonable and just solutions of individual cases.

* * * * *

(g) In English-speaking countries, a ministry of justice.

* * * * *

(h) That the end of juristic study, toward which the foregoing are but some of the means, is to make effort more effective in achieving the purposes of law.

* * * * *

Huntington Cairns, The Theory of Legal Science (1941) pp. 7-10; 22-25; reprinted by permission of the author and the University of North Carolina Press.

JURISPRUDENCE AS A SOCIAL SCIENCE

It requires little reflection, however, to realize that the characteristics exhibited by modern legal study are not characteristics of the principal social sciences. Contemporary legal study is a technology; but the social sciences are not technologies. Their ideal, like the ideal of those departments of knowledge commonly denominated the "natural sciences," is the discovery of general laws which unite a number of particular facts. We may pass over the circumstance that the successes of the social sciences in formulating laws have been relatively few in number. The ideal remains warranted in the absence of a demonstration—which is still to be offered—that its realization is impossible. Moreover, the fact that the social sciences have put forward some "general laws" which appear to be "true" with respect to the subject matter for which they were framed, is a positive indication that the ideal is permissible. The ideals of the technologies are, however, entirely different and vary from one technology to another. In the case of modern legal study, it is, as we have seen, law reform. It seems scarcely necessary to point out that this difference in ideals is a crucial one. Each ideal determines in large part the subject matter to be selected for examination, the methods to be adopted, even the facts which will be chosen for study. The possibility of legal study as a technology, moreover, raises a special question, one not peculiar to the other studies we know as technologies. It is the characteristic of a technology that it is indebted to many sciences, although it has in many cases its own contribution to make of matter and method. Mechanical engineering, which is beholden to a score or more of sources, is such a subject. This, however, although characteristic, is not always the case; psychology, which until recently was principally concerned with the gathering of facts as a basis for the formulation of general principles or "laws," has now felt that enough of such principles have been formulated to permit it to become also an "applied" science or technology. In its case, psychology is the principal source upon which psychologists draw in making their application. The important point with respect to every technology is, however, that it involves to an exclusive or considerable degree the application of principles or laws formulated by a "pure" science. But this is not the situation in which modern legal study finds itself. It is attempting to be an applied science, although there has been as yet no pure science of law in the sense of a study of the principles governing the relations of law and society. In the absence of such a previous study, the applications of modern legal research must necessarily be of a crude order. They would seem to be confined largely to such problems as the discovery of the manner in which legal procedure should be altered so as to make possible a more expeditious, and at the same time equitable, trial of issues. By its emphasis upon law reform, modern legal study overlooks the fact that it is limiting itself to a circumscribed field of study, and that no matter how successful its accomplishments in this field, it is not a social science nor will it ever become one so long as it maintains its present ideal. More important than these considerations, however, is the fact that modern legal study, by reason of its technological ideal, is overlooking a field of investigation which must be tilled before we can ever have a really fruitful applied legal science. It is the domain which legal research would necessarily explore if it were properly a social science.

Thus, the theory of jurisprudence as a social science marks off a field of inquiry which differs radically from that explored by the major present-day American schools. It differs first in its ideal, which is the ideal of the other social sciences, namely, the formulation of statements asserting invariant, or almost invariant, relationships among the facts in its specific field and, in its special case, the organization of such principles into a coherent system in conjunction with a rational theory of ethics. Secondly, it is concerned with a different subject matter. Its point of departure is not law as such, but human behavior as influenced by, or in relation to, the social factor of disorder. If the attempt is successful to create a jurisprudence which is in actuality a social science, it requires little reflection to grasp the importance of that result. We are living today in a human world which is under reconstruction. The focal point of legal action is shifting; new claims, new demands, are calling for recognition. Our theory of law as we know it now is founded upon a view of a society which is in a rapid state of transformation. It is obvious that the law itself must be modified to meet the forces of the new society. What are the principles which should guide us in that task of modification? In the present state of legal knowledge, we have no better method than that of trial and error. If we were to adopt any of the programs for law reform now urged upon us, we literally do not know whether the effects of those reforms would be beneficial or injurious. In the unlimited extravagance of nature the method of trial and error has proved itself successful; but it is a method too expensive for the limited resources of human society. The earth is peopled with a multitude of living things, but a vaster ill-adapted multitude were doomed to extinction in the fortuitous processes of that experiment. That process, although it is today still the customary one in social action, puts too great a strain upon the delicate balances of society; it is a wasteful method which efficient thought has taught us is within man's power to eliminate. A social science jurisprudence aims at revealing to us the consequences of the various courses of action open to us. It aims to tell us in advance the perils which attend our various programs; to tell us which is the rational and which the irrational course.

❖   ❖   ❖   ❖   ❖

In the world of order, law appears as one of the instruments which stabilize and modify modes of activity. It is one of the means of social control. In sociological literature the term "social control" has been used with a variety of meanings, dependent upon whether the source or the purpose of control was stressed. In its widest and most useful sense, however, it includes every way through which human society exercises a modifying influence upon itself or any part of itself.[32] Law is that means of social control regulating human conduct which, for its enforcement, embodies in itself, or has behind it, a definite agency which exerts, or through which may be exerted, the pressure of politically organized society. We must beware, Thurnwald has warned us, of assuming a supercilious egocentric position. Law in the forms we know it in the Western World is, as he remarked of the modern state, no more than several of many abstract possibilities. We must be prepared, upon the basis of the principle of equivalents, to recognize as law many social forms to which, if they obtain in our own society, the term could not properly be applied. In other words, we must not assume, as Durkheim[33] did in his study of the Australian totem system, that a painstaking study of the law of one people will reveal the essential elements of law in its generality. We are entitled to assume universally only that which we have in fact or in sound theory good reason to believe may be put universally.

Sociologists studying law as an instrument of social control have thought of that aspect of the legal order which Mr. Justice Cardozo has aptly termed the judicial process. They think about the machinery of law, its instruments of compulsion, what officials do about disputes and about the rules of law. It is in this sense that Ross examined law in his now classic work *Social Control*. From this position the judicial process is the "law" which is the means of social control. The set of rules of conduct which the English analytical jurists assumed was "law" is, in this theory, merely a formulation or abstract scheme of the legal order which obtains or results from the functioning of the judicial process. It is not the "law" but a series of shorthand descriptions of the legal order which, when taken in their total, describe the legal order in its entirety. Malinowski's[33a] much discussed conception of law in the Trobriands as a body of binding obligations, thought of as rightful claim on one side and as duty on the other, "kept in force by a specific mechanism of reciprocity and publicity inherent in the structure of their society" is included within this theory. In the Trobriands the principle of reciprocity is the "law"; it is the instrument of compulsion, the equivalent of the judicial process in Western society. The so-called body of binding obligations is the anthropologists' description of the legal order which results from the operation of the principle of reciprocity. But this is plainly a one-sided view of the facts. Law as a means of social control includes much more than merely the judicial process. It includes all aspects of the legal order which do in fact influence social behavior. One of these aspects, obviously, is the set of legal rules. They are imperatives or norms, ordering or indicating what men shall do, and, as such, exercise a modifying effect on human behavior. They may be, and frequently are, obeyed entirely apart from any thought of the judicial process or compulsion. In this respect they are on a plane with rules of custom, which, as Cicero[33b] pointed out, are precepts in themselves. They are distinguished from customary rules only in the respect that behind them lies a specific agency of political society for their enforcement. It must be granted also that the idealistic elements in law, our notions of what is just or natural, which the philosophical jurists since at least the days of Plato have endlessly debated, are embraced within the concept of law as an instrument of order. From time to time they assume the form of legal precepts and also directly influence judicial decision. A familiar example in our own system is the ideals which have found expression in the decisions of the United States Supreme Court construing the phrase "due process of law," which, by its very wording and absence of content directs judicial inquiry to conceptions of justice and right.

It is perhaps unnecessary, though no doubt safer, to add that the primary purpose of the definition of law here put forward is to distinguish it, as an instrument of control, from the other instruments of control such as custom, propaganda and public opinion. Clear thinking demands that we know as precisely as possible what it is we are to discuss; it is one of the chief weaknesses of Ehrlich,[33c] who, like Aristotle, Aquinas and Kant, sees law in terms of order, that he nowhere makes clear what he means by law or how it is to be distinguished from other orderings. There is no thought, in the definition here suggested, that an essential element of the law is that its rules are obeyed because of its compulsive aspect. Legal precepts in fact, in our society at any rate, are, more often than not, obeyed without the idea of compulsion ever entering men's minds. Compulsion, moreover, in this sense raises an entirely different question than the one we are now considering. We are here attempting a classification; compulsion is one aspect of the entirely different problem, Why is law obeyed? One other point with respect to the definition should be emphasized. The use of the term "political" is not meant to imply that law is determined exclusively by political factors, a view entertained by some jurists. Many factors—political, economic, ethical, psychologic, etc.—influence the legal order and none of them is exclusive. The use of the term "political" is meant only to indicate to which aspect of society the enforcement agency is to be assigned. The allotment to the political assists in the distinction. It rules out, for example, religious precepts supported by the force of that part of society.

Edwin W. Patterson, Jurisprudence: Men and Ideas of the Law (1953) pp. 518-524; reprinted by permission of the author and The Foundation Press.

Pound's theory of social interests, his most important contribution to legal philosophy, is one of the significant ideas of the century, not only because it preserves that continuity with the past which is inevitable and valuable, but also because it stands for the method of reason and compromise which is essential to the development of a democratic and free society. His table of social interests seems to embrace all of the public policies of which legislatures and courts should take account in their respective spheres of law-making and interpretation; or at least it can serve, as Mendelejeff's table of chemical elements has done, in looking for the missing ones. It is not composed of value-propositions, such as the jural postulates (§4.60), but of values, as ends and as means, for the construction of legal norms. Yet choices will remain. To illustrate: If the social interest in public safety and health ("general security") calls for the elimination of advertising billboards obstructing the view at high-way intersections, the social interest in the security of acquisitions (property rights, also classified under "general security") must give way to some extent; but whether the owner's loss of advertising revenue shall be compensated depends in part upon factors not covered by Pound's table. Indeed, the survey or inventory of social interests is only a part of his general plan for determining the scope and subject matter of a legal system. The plan includes also four other steps or processes: To determine the interests which the law should seek to secure; to determine the principles upon which such chosen interests should be defined and limited; to determine the means by which the law can secure them; and to take account of the limitations on effective legal action[34] (§4.60).

Pound was working on his theory of interests as early as 1913,[35] and brought it to fruition in an inaccessible publication of 1921.[36] He revised it and republished it in 1943.[37] The earlier draft is interesting because it showed that Pound tried to find in sociology, in theories of social instincts, the basis for a theory having the down-to-earth quality which Holmes had urged him to seek.[38] The law had to reckon with the instincts of self-assertion, of acquisitiveness, of gregariousness. However, he concluded that the jurist could not safely use social instincts as a basis of classification because sociologists were not agreed about them. Indeed, Dewey's work on social psychology showed that instincts were inadequate to explain human conduct and attitudes, without the mediation of custom and habit.[39] He then turned to a less pretentious method of finding a classification of social interests: By the study of legal phenomena as social phenomena. The lawyer can contribute to social science generally as well as to legal science, by surveying legal systems "to ascertain just what claims or wants or demands have pressed or are now pressing for recognition and satisfaction and how far they have been or are recognized or secured." [40] The data of the survey are chiefly judicial decisions and legislation; that is, for the most part they are propositions about valuations (to use Dewey's terms (§4.54)) as facts, from which the surveyor abstracts or generalizes values.

But this is getting ahead of our story. The term "interest" was used by Bentham as an indefinable or primitive term.[41] Pound combined Ihering's conception of the legal right as a legally protected interest (§4.44) with James' conception of a claim or demand as the source of ethical obligations (§4.52) to define individual interests as "claims or demands or desires involved immediately in the individual life and asserted in title of that life." [42] It is an alloy of social ethics and a social analysis of law. Alloys are often highly useful because they are stronger and more durable than the elements of which they are composed. Now two questions may be asked about Pound's conception of an individual interest. First, is it necessary that the claim or desire be actually and continuously asserted? Does the one-year-old infant who has just inherited a tract of land (which his deceased father owned) have an "interest" in the land? No, if interest means an asserted claim or desire. Yes, if interest means the kernel of a (primary) legal right. A radical operationalist, as Holmes was at times, might say that there is no legal right to the property until an action at law is brought in which that issue is adjudicated. A primary right is only a prophecy of what a court will do *if* certain things occur.[43] Yet this view recognizes a primary right as having a potential status even though no present claim or demand is being asserted. So the conception of individual interest includes the cases of *potential* claims or demands, such as those of the infant when he grows up, or of the idiot through his guardians or of the private corporation through its directors.[44] This extension is based not only upon law-buttressed customs and attitudes but also upon the need for maintaining an orderly society by channeling conduct in advance of controversy. Secondly, are individual interests "facts" or "values"? As Professor Dewey has protested against this contrast by asserting that values *are* facts,[45] the question may be rephrased, are individual interests the mere claims or demands of men, what Dewey calls their "prizings," regardless of an "appraisal" by someone else, *or* is the latter necessarily included? The answer is the first alternative. A pickpocket in the subway has (under certain circumstances) an "interest" in my watch (which is in my pocket), though not one that the law will legally protect.[46] Thus one function of law is to discriminate (a word having the same root as "crime") between the interests that will be and those that will not be protected. Pound has written valuable articles on the legal protection and means of protection of interests of personality and interests in the domestic relations.[47] A third class of individual interests he calls "interests of substance," property and contract rights.[48]

Pound's inventory includes two other classes of interests, public and social. In defining these he adheres to the basic notion of interest and changes the connections:

> "Public interests are claims or demands or desires involved in life in a politically organized society and asserted in title of that organization. They are commonly treated as the claims of a politically organized society thought of as a legal entity. Social interests are claims or demands or desires involved in social life in civilized society and asserted in title of that life. It is not uncommon to treat them as the claims of the whole social group as such." [49]

The state as a juristic person has "interests of substance," since it is a property owner. The interest of the United States in a post-office building is such an interest. It also has "interests of personality," in the sense that national dignity and honor are recognized in international law, and under recent statutes the state is suable in tort as well as in contract. The conception of public interest does not correspond to res publicae in Roman law[50] nor to "public policy" in Anglo-American law. The terminology is at first confusing. Yet Pound made a considerable advance over Ihering when he separated public from social interests. The state's property interests are not the same as the public policies which it enforces for the public good; the latter are the social interests.[51] They are the claims of the whole society, of which the political state is the guardian. Pound pointed out that the English common law had long recognized public policy as a ground for declaring contracts invalid, that English and American judges generally distrusted public policy because it had not been clearly worked out, and that the reasons for this distrust were upon analysis other public policies, such as the policy that private property rights must be protected against confiscation or impairment.[52] So the very same judges who in the nineteenth century and early twentieth century regarded "public policy" as an "unruly steed," had all along been riding another steed, called "freedom of contract" or "vested property rights" or "no liability without fault," which was only a different public policy, a horse of another color. Once it is recognized that policy-weighing goes on in the judicial process, the next step is to devise a method of balancing interests that will place them on the same plane. This is to be done, under Pound's plan, by subsuming the respective competing individual interests in a controversy under the social interests which support them and by weighing the consequences, in relation to social interests, of alternative modes of action. Thus the public policy against involuntary servitude was infringed *in fact* by a Georgia statute that imposed a penalty upon an employee who obtained money or property pursuant to a contract of employment and then failed to perform the contract; though the statute was apparently aimed at fraudulently obtaining money, in effect it could be used to hold employees in peonage.[53]

Pound's survey of social interests was intended to end the chaotic and episodic character of discussions of public policies by listing all of the main headings or classes of policies recognized in mature systems of law. He found six classes and several subclasses:[54]

I. *Social interest in general security.* This interest was protected in the period of strict law under the policy promoting certainty, later under the policy promoting individual liberty. The subdivisions are:

a. Safety from aggression, external and internal. (E.g., crimes of homicide, mayhem, assault and battery, and tort liability.)

b. Health, a concern of mature legal systems.

c. Peace and order. In mature systems, not only suppression of mobs but also of excessive noises.

d. Security of transactions, including the enforcement of contracts and giving effect to conveyances.

e. Security of acquisitions, the protection of property rights.

II. *Social interest in security of social institutions.*

a. Domestic, i.e., the domestic relations.

b. Religious, as indicated in penalties for blasphemy and other conduct injurious to religious feelings; but sometimes outweighed by the interest in free speech.

c. Political, i.e., the state and its subdivisions, and the political practices necessary to their maintenance, such as freedom of speech and freedom of the ballot; also protection against bribery of officials.

d. Economic, i.e., the convenience of commerce affecting commercial law (Mansfield). Overlaps "security of transactions," supra, I(d).

III. *Social interest in general morals,* that is, protection of the moral sentiments of the community. Includes policy of penalizing *dishonest* conduct in various ways; sexual immorality; obscene literature; other moral standards of the community.

IV. *Social interest in conservation of social resources.*

a. Physical resources. Conservation of forests, of gas and oil, of irrigation water, riparian rights, game laws.

b. Human resources. The protection and training of dependents and defectives, as represented in the English Chancellor's jurisdiction over infants, lunatics and idiots, and in juvenile court laws, reformation of delinquents; also in Social Security legislation, small loan legislation.

V. *Social interest in general progress.*

a. Economic: free trade, free competition, encouragement of invention and freedom of property from restrictions on alienation or use. (Note the similarity to II(d).)

b. Political: free criticism; free opinion. (Note similarity to II(c).)

c. Cultural: free science, free letters, encouragement of arts and letters and of higher education.

VI. *Social interest in the individual life.* Individual self-assertion, physical, mental, economic; individual opportunity, political, physical, cultural, social, economic; individual conditions of life (as expressed in Fair Labor Standards Act and state minimum wage laws, and earlier in bankruptcy acts and exemptions from execution).

This summary is inadequate to represent the richness and variety of his illustrations drawn from Roman, Continental, English and American law, both statutory and case law. A more thorough summary of the ends of a mature legal order, all directed to the common good or the greatest good of the greatest number, can scarcely be conceived.

C. The Realists

Beginning in the 1920's, a group of American jurists called for a more radical implementing of the program of sociological jurisprudence, particularly the doctrine which exposed the difference between "law in the books" and "law in action." What these thinkers were primarily interested in was factual study of the actual social effects of legal rules and doctrines. Their influence on taught law was and continues to be enormous. Although doctrinally diverse, and by nature not gladly yielding to classification, the realists have similar motives and the effect of their efforts is cumulative.

> Karl Llewellyn, Some Realism About Realism— Responding to Dean Pound,[1] 44 Harvard Law Review pp. 1222-1223; 1233-1238 (1931); reprinted by permission of the author and the Harvard Law Review.

Ferment is abroad in the law. The sphere of interest widens; men become interested again in the life that swirls around things legal. Before rules, were facts; in the beginning was not a Word, but a Doing. Behind decisions stand judges; judges are men; as men they have human backgrounds. Beyond rules, again, lie effects: beyond decisions stand people whom rules and decisions directly or indirectly touch. The field of Law reaches both forward and back from the Substantive Law of school and doctrine. The sphere of interest is widening; so, too, is the scope of doubt. *Beyond rules lie effects*—but do they? Are some rules mere paper? And if effects, what effects? Hearsay, unbuttressed guess, assumption or assertion unchecked by test—can such be trusted on this matter of what law is *doing*?

The ferment is proper to the time. The law of schools threatened at the close of the century to turn into words—placid, clear-seeming, lifeless, like some old canal. Practice rolled on, muddy, turbulent, vigorous. It is now spilling, flooding, into the canal of stagnant words. It brings ferment and trouble. So other fields of thought have spilled their waters in: the stress on behavior in the social sciences; their drive toward integration; the physicists' reexamination of final-seeming premises; the challenge of war and revolution. These stir. They stir the law. Interests of practice claim attention. Methods of work unfamiliar to lawyers make their way in, beside traditional techniques. Traditional techniques themselves are re-examined, checked against fact, stripped somewhat of confusion. And always there is this restless questing: what *difference* does statute, or rule, or court-decision, make?

Whether this ferment is one thing or twenty is a question; if one thing, it is twenty things in one. But it is with us. It spreads. It is no mere talk. It shows results, results enough through the past decade to demonstrate its value.

And those involved are folk of modest ideals. They want law to deal, they themselves want to deal, with things, with people, with tangibles, with *definite* tangibles, and *observable* relations between definite tangibles—not with words alone; when law deals with words, they want the words to represent tangibles which can be got at beneath the words, and observable relations between those tangibles. They want to check ideas, and rules, and formulas by facts, to keep them close to facts. They view rules, they view law, as means to ends; as only means to ends; as having meaning only insofar as they are means to ends. They suspect, with law moving slowly and the life around them moving fast, that some law may have gotten out of joint with life. This is a question in first instance of fact: what does law *do*, to people, or for people? In the second instance, it is a question of ends: what *ought* law to do to people, or for them? But there is no reaching a judgment as to whether any specific part of present law does what it ought, until you can first answer what it is doing now. To see this, and to be ignorant of the answer, is to start fermenting, is to start trying to find out.

All this is, we say, a simple-hearted point of view, and often philosophically naive—though it has in it elements enough of intellectual sophistication. It denies very little, except the completeness of the teachings handed down. It knows too little to care about denying much. It affirms ignorance, pitched within and without. It affirms the need to know. Its call is for intelligent effort to dispel the ignorance. Intelligent effort to cut beneath old rules, old words, to get sight of current things. It is not a new point of view; it is as old as man. But its rediscovery in any age, by any man, in any discipline, is joyous.

Speak, if you will, of a "realistic jurisprudence."

✿ ✿ ✿ ✿ ✿

REAL REALISTS[2]

What, then, *are* the characteristics of these new fermenters? One thing is clear. There is no school of realists. There is no likelihood that there will be such a school. There is no group with an official or accepted, or even with an emerging creed. There is no abnegation of independent striking out. We hope that there may never be. New recruits acquire tools and stimulus, not masters, nor over-mastering ideas. Old recruits diverge in interests from each other. They are related, says Frank, only in their negations, and in their skepticisms, and in their curiosity.[3]

There is, however, a *movement* in thought and work about law. The movement, the method of attack, is wider than the number of its adherents. It includes some or much work of many men who would scorn ascription to its banner. Individual men, then. Men more or less interstimulated—but no more than all of them have been stimulated by the orthodox tradition, or by that ferment at the opening of the century in which Dean Pound took a leading part. Individual men, working and thinking over law and its place in society. Their differences in point of view, in interest, in emphasis, in field of work, are huge. They differ among themselves well-nigh as much as any of them differs from, say, Langdell. Their number grows. Their work finds acceptance.

What one does find as he observes them is twofold. First (and to be expected) certain points of departure are common to them all. Second (and this, when one can find neither school nor striking likenesses among

individuals, is startling) a cross-relevance, a complementing, an interlocking of their varied results "as
if they were guided by an invisible hand." A third
thing may be mentioned in passing: a fighting faith
in their methods of attack on legal problems; but in
these last years the battle with the facts has proved
so much more exciting than any battle with tradi-
tionalism that the fighting faith had come (until the
spring offensive of 1931 against the realists) to manifest itself chiefly in enthusiastic labor to get on.

But as with a description of an economic order,
tone and color of description must vary with the
point of view of the reporter. No other one of the
men would set the picture up as I shall. Such a
report must thus be individual. Each man, of necessity, orients the whole to his own main interest of
the moment—as I shall orient the whole to mine: the
workings of case-law in appellate courts. Maps of the
United States prepared respectively by a political
geographer and a student of climate would show
some resemblance; each would show a coherent picture; but neither's map would give much satisfaction
to the other. So here. I speak for myself of that
movement which in its sum is realism; I do not speak
of "the realists"; still less do I speak *for* the participants or any of them. And I shall endeavor to keep
in mind as I go that the justification for grouping
these men together lies not in that they are *alike* in
belief or work, but in that from certain common
points of departure they have branched into lines of
work which seem to be building themselves into a
whole, a whole planned by none, foreseen by none,
and (it may well be) not yet adequately grasped by
any.

The common points of departure are several.[4]

(1) The conception of law in flux, of moving law,
and of judicial creation of law.

(2) The conception of law as a means to social
ends and not as an end in itself; so that any part
needs constantly to be examined for its purpose, and
for its effect, and to be judged in the light of both
and of their relation to each other.

(3) The conception of society in flux, and in flux typically faster than the law, so that the probability is always given that any portion of law needs reexamination to determine how far it fits the society it purports to serve.

(4) The *temporary* divorce of Is and Ought for purposes of study. By this I mean that whereas value judgments must always be appealed to in order to set objectives for inquiry, yet during the inquiry itself into what Is, the observation, the description, and the establishment of relations between the things described are to remain *as largely as possible* uncontaminated by the desires of the observer or by what he wishes might be or thinks ought (ethically) to be. More particularly, this involves during the study of what courts are doing the effort to disregard the question what they ought to do. Such divorce of Is and Ought is, of course, not conceived as permanent. To men who begin with a suspicion that change is needed, a permanent divorce would be impossible. The argument is simply that no judgment of what Ought to be done in the future with respect to any part of law can be intelligently made without knowing objectively, as far as possible, what that part of law is now doing. And realists believe that experience shows the intrusion of Ought-spectacles *during the investigation of the facts* to make it very difficult to see what is being done. On the Ought side this means an insistence on informed evaluations instead of armchair speculations. Its full implications on the side of Is-investigation can be appreciated only when one follows the contributions to objective description in business law and practice made by realists whose social philosophy rejects many of the accepted foundations of the existing economic order. (*E.g.,* Handler *re* trade-marks and advertising; Klaus *re* marketing and banking; Llewellyn *re* sales; Moore *re* banking; Patterson *re* risk-bearing.)

(5) Distrust of traditional legal rules and concepts insofar as they purport to *describe* what either courts or people are actually doing. Hence the constant emphasis on rules as "generalized predictions of what

courts will do." This is much more widespread as yet than its counterpart: the careful severance of rules *for* doing (precepts) from rules *of* doing (practices).

(6) Hand in hand with this distrust of traditional rules (on the descriptive side) goes a distrust of the theory that traditional prescriptive rule-formulations are *the* heavily operative factor in producing court decisions. This involves the tentative adoption of the theory of rationalization for the study of opinions. It will be noted that "distrust" in this and the preceding point is not at all equivalent to "negation in any given instance."

(7) The belief in the worthwhileness of grouping cases and legal situations into narrower categories than has been the practice in the past. This is connected with the distrust of verbally simple rules— which so often cover dissimilar and non-simple fact situations (dissimilarity being tested partly by the way cases come out, and partly by the observer's judgment as to how they ought to come out; but a realist tries to indicate explicitly which criterion he is applying).

(8) An insistence on evaluation of any part of law in terms of its effects, and an insistence on the worthwhileness of trying to find these effects.

(9) Insistence on *sustained and programmatic attack* on the problems of law along any of these lines. None of the ideas set forth in this list is new. Each can be matched from somewhere; each can be matched from recent orthodox work in law. New twists and combinations do appear here and there. What is as novel as it is vital is for a goodly number of men to pick up ideas which have been expressed and dropped, used for an hour and dropped, played with from time to time and dropped—to pick up such ideas and set about *consistently, persistently, insistently to carry them through.* Grant that the idea or point of view is familiar—the results of steady, sustained, systematic work with it are not familiar. Not hit-or-miss stuff, not the insight which flashes and is forgotten, but sustained effort to force an old insight

into its full bearing, to exploit it to the point where it laps over upon an apparently inconsistent insight, to explore their bearing on each other by the test of fact. This urge, in law, is quite new enough over the last decades to excuse a touch of frenzy among the locust-eaters.

Hessel E. Yntema, Legal Science and Reform, 34 Columbia Law Review pp. 209-211; 227-229 (1934); reprinted by permission of the author and the Columbia Law Review.

The idea that, for the purposes of scientific inquiry, law in action is more significant than law in books, has been challenged on grounds both theoretical and practical. The theoretical objections may first be briefly noticed.

Thus, for example, certain fixed notions as to scientific method have been made a ground of objection. Legal phenomena, it has been stated, cannot be measured with anything like the precision which has been attained in physical science. In the present state of knowledge, it has been suggested, law must be regarded as a complex of unpredictable, individual events, not susceptible of scientific "quantification." Accordingly, the denomination of any possible study of law as a science is branded a misleading euphemism.[5] It needs no quarrel with this argument to point out that this seems no more than a quibble about a name. Fortunately, the implied counsel of despair does not estop the effort to subject legal phenomena to scientific scrutiny, the more so as legal science is backward and its problems difficult. In any event, the argument fails on various counts. First, it is arbitrary to limit science to mathematics or, in other words, to define it by its quantitative tool. Second, legal phenomena are for some purposes measurable, and their significance is, therefore, in part revealed by statistical analysis. Third, legal phenomena are in some degree predictable. If it be not so, are not lawyers consummate charlatans!

Another theoretical criticism of the scientific study of law is based upon preconceptions which spring from the deep waters of philosophy. It is asserted that law is "normative" or, in other words, that it consists of ideas of what ought to be, not of facts that presently exist. This assumption is related to the more fundamental hypothesis that there are pure abstract ideas and there are pure concrete facts, and that these pertain to different realms of existence, divided by unbridgeable gulfs of separateness. The deduction is that no inferences can be drawn from a science of legal phenomena to the real law, *i.e.*, the ideal order.[6] For present purposes, this objection to obtaining more precise knowledge as to the operation of the legal system may be shortly dismissed as an incomplete hypothesis. Useful as the distinction between form and substance, idea and fact, may be for some purposes, it is not absolute. This is the point of Immanuel Kant's famous aphorism as to the emptiness of disembodied thought, the blindness of observation without concepts.[7] The refusal to recognize that the world we live in is relevant to the *juristischer Begriffshimmel,*—as Ihering termed the world of legal ideas—is a species of inverted nominalism, the persistence of which is due perhaps to desire to preserve the prerogative of abstract speculation in jurisprudence. It is briefly noticed in this connection only because it has been employed recently to support a direct attack on scientific legal studies,[8] and because it may seem otherwise to lend to the formal analysis of abstract rights a false inherent virtue.

     ❋   ❋   ❋   ❋   ❋

If, then, government be an essential element of society and law the chief force by which social ideals are translated into reality and the conditions of honor and happiness sought to be created, it is important to keep the wheels of justice in order. The more is this so as the problems of government by law become more difficult and complex with the increase of government under modern conditions. Recognition of the circumstances which at present limit both legal science and law reform, suggests the need of intensified and more intelligent effort to deal with them. The gist of the proposal which is here made, is that, if this be the case, it is expedient to make some provision, which should be neither expensive nor elaborate, for critical, independent, scientific inquiry as to the administration of justice. At the cost of repetition, this proposal may perhaps be made more explicit by a summary and a concrete application.

In sum, the argument is as follows:

1. That the conditions of modern civilization, reflected in the course of political opinion, increase the significance and difficulty of government by law and, consequently also, the need of knowledge as to how justice can be intelligently and efficiently administered;

2. That, in the attainment of such knowledge, common sense is only the beginning of wisdom, since the problems of judicial administration have become so complex as to require detailed scientific study for their understanding and solution;

3. That such study of law in action is an essential, if not under present conditions the most essential, object of a legal science which is not to remain esoteric;

4. That, on the other hand, the history of law reform leaves little reason to anticipate that the judicial system itself will be able, in any fundamental way, to deal with the causes of its own inefficiency, and with sufficient promptitude and decision;

5. That, on account of the very practical limitations of human effort, the activities of the bar and of the professional law schools as at present constituted, essential as they are, do not promise to be adequate to the situation;

6. That, in general, it is not desirable to leave the reform, as conditions require, of so important a branch of public administration as the law, to emergencies receptive to untried and possibly dangerous theories;

7. That, therefore, some independent provision should be made to promote the scientific study of the law in action, within or without the universities;

8. That, for its own purposes and to facilitate such

study, the judicial system itself should provide a sufficient judicial census and judicial clinics with appropriate powers for controlled experimentation in the methods of administering justice, preferably under the supervision of a ministry of justice;

9. That such provision for the practical scientific study of law can be made at relatively inconsiderable expense, if it is directed to the essential element,—critical, independent, individual scholarship.

In a concrete realization of this argument, certain conditions deserve attention: first, that the problems of the administration of justice reach their most acute and variegated forms in the large urban centers; second, that it is desirable to locate initial efforts where satisfactory cooperation can be had with other agencies concerned with these problems; third, that, among other things, it would be advantageous to conduct experiments in an effective forum. From these points of view, to give a specific instance, it will be remarked that the City of New York would in some respects form an exceptional center for the study of the administration of justice. Nowhere is there a more distinguished tradition of reform or such a vast laboratory of judicial machinery; no city has bar associations more active or effective; no state has a more enlightened judicial establishment. If there were added to this background a ministry of justice, such as Mr. Justice Cardozo advocated a decade since, at the instance perhaps of the temporary commission which was appointed in 1930 by then Governor Roosevelt to investigate and report upon the present administration of justice in New York State,[8] and if at the same time appropriate provision could be made, either in one of the large universities in the City or otherwise, for the scientific study of the operation of the judicial process in the light of the *data* collected by the ministry of justice and with such facilities for experimental observation as might be afforded, a situation would be created which could scarcely fail to stimulate a profitable conjunction of effort, both scientific and practical. At the same time, so great a hope of a successful attack on the perplexed problems of judicial administration would seem to be thereby assured, as can in the nature of things be offered by institutional arrangements as such.[9]

Jerome Frank, Law and the Modern Mind (1930, 1949) pp. 3-12; reprinted by permission of the author and Coward-McCann, Inc.

THE BASIC MYTH

The lay attitude towards lawyers is a compound of contradictions, a mingling of respect and derision. Although lawyers occupy leading positions in government and industry, although the public looks to them for guidance in meeting its most vital problems, yet concurrently it sneers at them as tricksters and quibblers.

Respect for the bar is not difficult to explain. Justice, the protection of life, the sanctity of property, the direction of social control—these fundamentals are the business of the law and of its ministers, the lawyers. Inevitably the importance of such functions invests the legal profession with dignity.

But coupled with a deference towards their function there is cynical disdain of the lawyers themselves. "Good jurist, bad Christian," preached Martin Luther in the sixteenth century. Frederick the Great and Herbert Hoover, Rabelais and H. G. Wells have echoed that sentiment. In varying forms it is repeated daily. The layman, despite the fact that he constantly calls upon lawyers for advice on innumerous questions, public and domestic, regards lawyers as equivocators, artists in double-dealing, masters of chicane.

The stage comedian can always earn a laugh with the pun on lawyers and liars. Still popular are Gay's couplets,

"I know you lawyers can, with ease,
Twist words and meanings as you please;
That language, by your skill made pliant,
Will bend to favor every client."

Not all the criticism is as gentle: "Going tew law," said Josh Billings, "is like skinning a new milch cow

for the hide and giving the meat tew the lawyers."
Butler in "Hudibras" was of like mind:

> "He that with injury is grieved
> And goes to law to be relieved,
> Is sillier than a Scottish chouse
> Who, when a thief has robbed his house,
> Applies himself to cunning men
> To help him to his goods again."

Arnold Bennett denounces the "lawyers as the most
vicious opponents of social progress today." Ambas-
sador Page wrote, "I sometimes wish that there were
not a lawyer in the world."

Diatribes against lawyers contain such words and
phrases as "duplicity," "equivocation," "evasions," "a
vast system of deception," "juggling," "sleight of
hand," "craft and circumvention," "the art of puzzling
and confounding," "darken by elucidation," "the petti-
foging, hypocritical, brigandage rampant under forms
of law." Kipling expresses the feeling of many in his
fling at the "tribe who describe with a gibe the per-
versions of Justice."

What is the source of these doubts of the lawyer's
honesty and sincerity?

A false tradition "invented by twelfth-century priests
and monks," replies Dean Roscoe Pound.[10] "For the
most part clerical jealousy of the rising profession of
non-clerical lawyers was the determining element.…
Naturally, the clergy did not relinquish the practice
of law without a protest." What those priests began,
says Pound, Luther developed, and since Luther's
day the other learned professions have taken over.
"Unless one perceives that a struggle of professions
for leadership is involved," one cannot understand the
distrust of the legal profession. The lawyer is today,
as he was in the twelfth century, in a marked position
of advantage. This irks the other learned men. "Their
minds are fertile soil for the time-worn tradition."

An ingenious explanation, but patently superficial.[11]
Surely twentieth-century mistrust of lawyers is based
on something more than a twelfth-century monkish
invention embodied in a tradition kept alive princi-

pally because the physicians, the engineers, and the journalists have been jealous of the lawyers' prestige. Modern dispraise of the Bar is not to be explained as merely an outcropping of angry rivalry; obviously it is not confined to members of competing professions. That lawyers are scheming hair-splitters is a popular commonplace.

What lies back of this popular criticism? It appears to be founded on a belief that the lawyers complicate the law, and complicate it wantonly and unnecessarily, that, if the legal profession did not interpose its craftiness and guile, the law could be clear, exact and certain. The layman thinks that it would be possible so to revise the law books that they would become something like logarithm tables, that the lawyers could, if only they would, contrive some kind of legal sliderule for finding exact legal answers. Public opinion agrees with Napoleon who was sure that "it would be possible to reduce laws to simple geometrical demonstrations, so that whoever could read and tie two ideas together would be capable of pronouncing on them." [12]

But the law as we have it is uncertain, indefinite, subject to incalculable changes. This condition the public ascribes to the men of law; the average person considers either that lawyers are grossly negligent or that they are guilty of malpractice, venally obscuring simple legal truths in order to foment needless litigation, engaging in a guild conspiracy of distortion and obfuscation in the interest of larger fees.[13]

Now it must be conceded that, if the law can be made certain and invariable, the lawyers are grievously at fault. For the layman is justified in his opinion that the coefficient of legal uncertainty is unquestionably large, that to predict the decisions of the courts on many a point is impossible. Any competent lawyer, during any rainy Sunday afternoon, could prepare a list of hundreds of comparatively simple legal questions to which any other equally competent lawyer would scarcely venture to give unequivocal answers.

Yet the layman errs in his belief that this lack of

precision and finality is to be ascribed to the lawyers. The truth of the matter is that the popular notion of the possibilities of legal exactness is based upon a misconception. The law always has been, is now, and will ever continue to be, largely vague and variable. And how could this well be otherwise? The law deals with human relations in their most complicated aspects. The whole confused, shifting helter-skelter of life parades before it—more confused than ever, in our kaleidoscopic age.

Even in a relatively static society, men have never been able to construct a comprehensive, eternized set of rules anticipating all possible legal disputes and settling them in advance. Even in such a social order no one can foresee all the future permutations and combinations of events; situations are bound to occur which were never contemplated when the original rules were made. How much less is such a frozen legal system possible in modern times. New instruments of production, new modes of travel and of dwelling, new credit and ownership devices, new concentrations of capital, new social customs, habits, aims and ideals—all these factors of innovation make vain the hope that definitive legal rules can be drafted that will forever after solve all legal problems. When human relationships are transforming daily, legal relationships cannot be expressed in enduring form. The constant development of unprecedented problems requires a legal system capable of fluidity and pliancy.[14] Our society would be strait-jacketed were not the courts, with the able assistance of the lawyers, constantly overhauling the law and adapting it to the realities of ever-changing social, industrial and political conditions; although changes cannot be made lightly, yet law must be more or less impermanent, experimental and therefore not nicely calculable. *Much of the uncertainty of law is not an unfortunate accident: it is of immense social value.*[15]

In fields other than the law there is today a willingness to accept probabilities and to forego the hope of finding the absolutely certain.[16] Even in physics and chemistry, where a high degree of quantitative exactness is possible, modern leaders of thought are recognizing that finality and ultimate precision are not to be attained.[17] The physicists, indeed, have just announced the Principle of Uncertainty or Indeterminacy. If there can be nothing like complete definiteness in the natural sciences, it is surely absurd to expect to realize even approximate certainty and predictability in law, dealing as it does with the vagaries of complicated human adjustments.

Since legal tentativeness is inevitable and often socially desirable, it should not be considered an avoidable evil. But the public learns little or nothing of this desirability of legal tentativeness from the learned gentlemen of the law. Why this concealment? Have the lawyers a sinister purpose in concealing the inherent uncertainty of law? Why, it may fairly be asked, do they keep alive the popular belief that legal rules can be made predictable? If lawyers are not responsible for legal indefiniteness, are they not guilty, at any rate, of duping the public as to the essential character of law? Are they not a profession of clever hypocrites?

There is no denying that the bar appears to employ elaborate pretenses to foster the misguided notions of the populace. Lawyers do not merely sustain the vulgar notion that law is capable of being made entirely stable and unvarying; they seem bent on creating the impression that, on the whole, it is already established and certain. When a client indignantly exclaims, "A pretty state of affairs when I can't learn exactly what my rights are!" how does the lawyer usually respond? With assurances that the situation is exceptional, that generally speaking the law is clear enough, but that in this particular instance, for some reason or other the applicable rules cannot be definitely ascertained. Often the facts are the scapegoat: "If," says the lawyer, "the facts of your case were established and undisputed, the law could be categorically stated." When this explanation won't wash, because the pertinent facts do not happen to be in doubt, the client is told that the rules affecting his problem have become but temporarily unsettled:

"Congress has just passed a badly worded statute," or "The judges who have recently tampered with the law of the subject are exceptionally stupid, or thoughtless, or weak, or radical, or what not." Implicit in these rejoinders is the view that, for the most part, legal rights and obligations are clear and indubitable, and that such small portion of the law as is not already certain can easily be made so.

Of course, such assurances are unwarranted. Each week the courts decide hundreds of cases which purport to turn not on disputed "questions of fact" but solely on "points of law."[18] If the law is unambiguous and predictable, what excuses can be made by the lawyers who lose these cases? They should know in advance of the decisions that the rules of law are adverse to their contentions. Why, then, are these suits brought or defended? In some few instances, doubtless, because of ignorance or cupidity or an effort to procure delay, or because a stubbornly litigious client insists. But in many cases, honest and intelligent counsel on both sides of such controversies can conscientiously advise their respective clients to engage in the contest; they can do so because, prior to the decision, the law is sufficiently in doubt to justify such advice.

It would seem, then, that the legal practitioners must be aware of the unsettled condition of the law. Yet observe the arguments of counsel in addressing the courts, or the very opinions of the courts themselves: they are worded as if correct decisions were arrived at by logical deduction from a precise and pre-existing body of legal rules. Seldom do judges disclose any contingent elements in their reasoning, any doubts or lack of whole-hearted conviction. The judicial vocabulary contains few phrases expressive of uncertainty. As Sir Henry Maine put it—

When a group of facts comes before a court for adjudication, "the whole course of the discussion between the judge and the advocate assumes that no question is, or can be, raised which will call for the application of any principles but old ones, or of any distinctions but such as have long since been allowed. It is taken absolutely for granted that there is somewhere a rule of known law which will cover the facts of the dispute now litigated, and that, if such a rule be not discovered, it is only that the necessary patience, knowledge or acumen, is not forth-coming to detect it. The uninformed listener would conclude that court and counsel unhesitatingly accept a doctrine that somewhere, *in nubibus,* or *in gremio magistratum,* there existed a complete, coherent, sym-metrical body of . . . law, of an amplitude sufficient to furnish principles which would apply to any con-ceivable combination of circumstances."

Why these pretenses, why this professional hypo-crisy? The answer is an arresting one: There is no hyprocrisy. The lawyers' pretenses are not *consciously* deceptive. The lawyers, themselves, like the laymen, fail to recognize fully the essentially plastic and mutable character of law.[19] Although it is the chiefest function of lawyers to make the legal rules viable and pliable, a large part of the profession believes, and therefore encourages the laity to believe, that those rules either are or can be made essentially im-mutable. And so you will find lawyers saying that "The judicial process in ascertaining or applying the law is essentially similar to the process by which we acquire our knowledge of geometry. . . . In the great majority of cases the solution of them [legal prob-lems] is as certain and exact as an answer to a prob-lem in mathematics."[20]

Now the true art of the lawyer is the art of legal modification, an art highly useful to the layman. For the layman's interests, although he does not realize it, would be poorly served by an immobile system of law. Especially is this so in the twentieth century. The emphasis of our era is on change. The present trend in law is, accordingly, away from static security — the preservation of old established rights — and towards dynamic security — the protection of men engaged in new enterprises.[21] Which means that the layman's ordinary practical needs would be seriously thwarted by an inelastic legal arrangement. A body of undeviating legal principles he would find unbearably procrustean. Yet paradoxically he and his lawyers, when they express their notions of a desirable legal system, usually state that they want the law to be everlastingly settled.

Here we arrive at a curious problem: Why do men crave an undesirable and indeed unrealizable permanence and fixity in law? Why in a modern world does the ancient dream persist of a comprehensive and unchanging body of law? Why do the generality of lawyers insist that law should and can be clearly knowable and precisely predictable although, by doing so, they justify a popular belief in an absurd standard of legal exactness? Why do lawyers, indeed, themselves recognize such an absurd standard, which makes their admirable and socially valuable achievement — keeping the law supple and flexible — seem bungling and harmful?[22] Why do men of our time repeat the complaint made by Francis Bacon several hundred years since, that "our laws, as they now stand, are subject to great incertainties" and adhere to his conviction that such "incertainties" are pernicious and altogether avoidable?

Why this unceasing quest of what is unobtainable and would often be undesirable?

One keen thinker, Wurzel[23] has directed his attention to this question. He, too, questions why there exists a longing for complete certainty in law and why a pretense that it can be attained. He finds the answer in what he terms a "social want" for a body of law which shall appear to be, what it can never be, an exhaustive list of commands, issued by the State, sufficient to settle every conceivable controversy which may arise. He maintains that the psychology of our administration of justice imperatively requires that this "social want" be satisfied by false appearances.

This is scarcely a sufficient answer.[24] It provokes the further questions, What is back of this "social want"? Why must law seem to be, what it is not, a virtually complete set of commands? Why do lawyers who seem to be keen-minded, hard-headed realists, use numerous devices, however unwittingly, to deceive themselves and the public? Why this desire to be fooled? What is the source of this curious "social want"?

We shall in this essay attempt a partial answer.

Let us first rephrase our problem. Only a limited degree of legal certainty can be attained. The current demand for exactness and predictability in law is incapable of satisfaction because a greater degree of legal finality is sought than is procurable, desirable or necessary. If it be true that greater legal certainty is sought than is practically required or attainable, then the demand for excessive legal stability does not arise from practical needs. It must have its roots not in reality but in a yearning for something unreal.[25] Which is to say that the widespread notion that law either is or can be made approximately stationary and certain is irrational and should be classed as an illusion or a myth.

What is the source of this basic legal myth?[26]

Thurman Arnold, Symbols of Government (1935) pp. 46-52; reprinted by permission of the author and the Yale University Press.

THE MYSTERY OF JURISPRUDENCE

It may seem odd to the reader that in a book which purports to select for analysis the more important symbols of government, a chapter should be given to jurisprudence. Here is a subject which not even lawyers read. Its content is vague; its literature abstruse and difficult. Nevertheless there is a general feeling that under this title are hidden the most sacred mysteries of the law. Even in popular nomenclature, ordinary men at law are called by the commonplace name of attorneys, or lawyers, and great names at the bar bear the title of "Jurists." It is considered undesirable to teach law efficiently as a trade, and socially important to omit the tricks of the trial lawyer in order to teach it as a philosophy.

Jurisprudence is the holy of holies of government,

the science of that great symmetrical body of principles which is supposed to constitute the law, the description of its deepest sources, and the unifying element of the law throughout history. Without a science of jurisprudence, law might be considered a collection of man-made rules for practical situations. With it the Law becomes the cornerstone of government. Therefore the literature of jurisprudence is a most important symbol of our rational moral attitude toward human institutions. By analyzing it we may begin to understand how similar the effects of that moral rational attitude are whether they appear in other great literatures such as economics, or in minor literatures such as common-law pleading.

The way of thinking that we are describing here as moral and rational must be distinguished from another way of thinking which may be described as practical, or benevolent, which produces entirely different social results. Where we take the latter attitude we do not philosophize at all. No complicated rational sciences arise out of conduct which we take as a matter of course, and which we do not seek to fit into a logical and symmetrical scheme. The difference between these two attitudes is difficult to define, but it is easy to illustrate. For example, there is no great logical structure of moral principles involved in the treatment of an insane man who has committed murder. We do not hang him, even though society might be better off if he were out of the way. We preserve him in an institution where he is better treated than he would be in a penitentiary. No logical reason can be given for so preserving him. We simply do not argue about the matter, and let it rest on general sentimental or humanitarian grounds. There is no jurisprudence concerning the proper treatment of insane criminals. Jurisprudence steps in only when we try to draw a logical line between the sane and the insane. Once we designate a man as "sick," whether mentally or physically, we proceed to cure him, and are shocked at any discussion as to whether he morally or logically deserves to be cured.

The difference between the two attitudes is well

illustrated by an incident which was reported in the *New York Times,* during the early years of the depression, when governmental relief was still regarded as the ruin of national character. On a cold winter day a shanty colony was being removed from a vacant lot in New York City to make way for the erection of a building. The newspaper report of poor hungry people driven from makeshift dwellings was pathetic. Yet nothing could be done about it. To give them a dole would establish a dangerous precedent and be contrary to the rational and moral ideals of rugged individualism. The eviction of these unfortunates was therefore a symbol of a faith that economic competence can only be developed by refusing to protect incompetence.

After the work of demolition began two unconscious men were found under one of the improvised dwellings. Immediately a whole new set of attitudes and symbols rose as if by magic. Rational moral government ended and pure benevolence took charge. The idea that it was wrong to protect men from the results of their incompetence vanished. Twenty thousand dollars' worth of ambulances, consuming an inordinate number of gallons of gasoline to the mile, clanged their way through crowded streets, manned by the most expensive nurses and internes that money could buy. The men were transferred to surroundings which in sanitation and equipment were beyond the reach of even the millionaire of fifty years ago. If a logically minded individual had asked why so much money should be expended on individuals who would never be anything but a burden on society, and who would have to be turned out to suffer again after their stay in the hospital, he would have been simply brushed aside. Humanitarian ideals are not defined by logic. It was the duty of the ambulance to get the men to the hospital, not to discuss jurisprudence.

Thus a practical or humanitarian attitude develops techniques, and not logical arguments. A rational moral attitude develops philosophies and priests, rather than technicians. The institution which is at the head of the hierarchy representing the rational moral attitude today is the law. A hundred years ago its place was shared by the church.

The treatment of jurisprudence as a symbol of government makes it unnecessary to go into the refinements of the various theories associated under that name. For the purposes of the social effectiveness of the symbol, such details are unimportant. It is significant here only to describe the way of thinking which has resulted in this voluminous and unread literature.

The reader is asked therefore to consider this chapter, not as a chapter on jurisprudence as a separate science, but as a chapter on the kind of literature which all rational thinking about government in general, or its details, inevitably produces. Considered as such he will find that the subject is not complicated, but simple, and that the ideas are simply the vague notions of the man on the street done into a great arabesque of words.

The Practical Function of Abstract Jurisprudence

As we have shown, the law consists of a large number of mutually contradictory symbols and ideals. Such contradictions are apparent to any man on the street who becomes involved in the judicial process. He must therefore believe, if he is to keep his faith that government is symmetrical and rational, that there exists somewhere, available to him if he only could get time to study it, a unified philosophy of science of law.

Therefore he believes that there exists a science of jurisprudence, and gives a place in the social scheme to a priesthood whose duty it is to expound that science, unmoved by the irrelevancies of practical day-to-day governmental action.

An official admission by a judicial institution that it was moving in all directions at once in order to satisfy the conflicting emotional values of the people which it served would be unthinkable. It would have the same effect as if an actor interrupted the most moving scene of a play in order to explain to the audience that his real name was John Jones. The success of the play requires that an idea be made real to the audience. The success of the law as a unifying force depends on making emotionally significant the idea of a government of law which is rational and scientific.

The unifying principles which are behind all of the various activities of admittedly legal institutions are the concern of jurisprudence. Its task is to prove that such principles exist, and to define them in general terms sufficiently broad so that all the little contradictory ideals appearing in the unending procession of particular cases will appear to be part of one great set of ideals. Functionally the primary purpose of the science of the law is to be a sounding board of both the prevalent hopes and the prevalent worries of those who believe in a government of law and not of men; to reconcile these hopes and worries somewhere in the mists of scholarship and learning; and never to admit that this is what it is doing.

Jurisprudence must necessarily be different for different times and for different people living in the same age. Its task is much simpler for an age which is willing to accept on faith that truth is revealed to judges from some mystical source beyond and above the light of reason. Perhaps, in some future time which accepts "Experimentation" as the source of knowledge and is willing to trust in the personal expertness of judges, as today we trust in the expertness of physicians, jurisprudence may again be simple. Yet neither faith in the notion that truth is revealed to judges, nor trust in the personal expertness of any individuals sitting as judges, is congenial to our ways of thinking today. We still think as Newton thought, as Blackstone thought, that our governmental institutions must be rational.

This way of thinking has its discomforts in a world which also reverences science. It compels us to assume that there is a separate faculty of the human mind called "reason," and another separate faculty called "will." This so-called "faculty theory" of psychology is no longer held by scientists. They, indeed, have a tendency to regard thought as only another form of behavior. Hence the rise of realists in juristic debate just as they used to rise in theological debate, equipped with arguments unanswerable and at the same time emotionally unacceptable because we have no formula to reconcile the attitude of the scientist with that of the theologian.

The scientific attitude is useful in order to study the folkways of the people and to determine what kind of formulas most appeal to them. However, this way of thinking violates the great idea that jurists must be "sincere." They must not be politicians, and they should not be permitted to advance theories for a purely practical purpose. Hence jurisprudence has been forced to supply the deficiencies of the rational process by applying more reason. Such conflicts always have the effect of producing an enormous amount of argumentative literature.

A practical result of this conflict, and one which affects even the most ignorant layman, is the fact that twenty-five thousand cases pour from our appellate courts every year. This great literature follows from the idea that the inconsistencies of the reasoning process can always be cured by applying more reason. If the law gets complicated, the only way to simplify it is to add more law to it. Therefore the American Law Institute spent millions in producing a restatement of the fundamental principles of this mass of cases. However, this restatement was not intended to be a substitute for the cases but only to clarify them. It therefore becomes only an additional source of argument.

Out of the confusion, elasticity is undeniably obtained, and at the same time the appearance of certainty, symmetry and order. This order is not observable in practice, and those who come in contact with the courts are constantly complaining about the lag between the law and social justice, or the law and efficiency. In answer to their complaints they are informed that great law schools are working day and night to eliminate these minor inconsistencies as fast as "politics" and "human nature" will permit. The better judges of the future are expected to come out of these law schools, equipped with the training to reconcile the contradictory behavior of the various legal institutions into a rational unity, and to weave into a syllogistic design of pure intellectual beauty all the contradictory ideas which people have about law and government.

Thus the law school has come to symbolize the unifying principles necessary to make the judicial institution with all its complexity appear to be a government of abstract law. It is a guaranty to the public that somewhere, professors, separated from the confusing irrelevancies of a moving world, are working out a rational system which the world may someday follow. The public of course does not read the works of the professors. If it did, doubts might arise as to the efficiency of their efforts. It is enough for the public to have faith in institutions of legal learning as guaranties that principles, forgotten in the wickedness of a political world, are being constantly refined and made more useful for the world of tomorrow.

Edwin N. Garlan, Legal Realism and Justice (1941) pp. 3-14; reprinted by permission of the Columbia University Press.

Law is by nature conservative. It crystallizes loose institutional and group habits into permanent principles of action; it forges the ways of men into stable structures which are highly resistant to change. The power of words to fix patterns of action has few better illustrations than are to be found in law. Law is considered, and not without cause, as the chief symbol and the closest embodiment of the ideals of certainty, security, and permanence, and, true to its conserving function, law responds to new forces only after the consequences of these new forces in ideas, methods, and objectives have become well articulated in other institutions and the sciences concerned with these institutions.

So it is that today men in law are still struggling against a frame of reference predicated upon premises, principles, and methods characteristic of eighteenth-century rationalism and nineteenth-century evolutionism and utilitarianism, attitudes which have already been seriously questioned and modified in other social disciplines. The shift in attitude is in the direction of a pragmatic philosophy of law. Though anticipated by many individuals and by the development of a sociological jurisprudence, the effective struggle against traditional attitudes has arisen in the United States with the emergence of a realistic jurisprudence.[27] Today the realists in contemporary American jurisprudence are providing a more concrete and practical approach to law than was afforded by a more abstract and formal jurisprudence. The center of interest for the realist is twofold: in devising an experimental and fact-controlled method and in a functional interpretation of law as an institutional process operating in the larger social matrix and tested by its contributions to the larger whole.[28]

The Revolt Against Conceptualism

Though American legal realism is heavily influenced by contemporary intellectual currents, the pragmatic and realistic approach to law has some of its deepest roots in the practices, the insights, and the practical art of the lawyer. This is especially true in respect to the realists' primary interest in more adequate predictions and descriptions of what courts do in fact, an interest which is one phase of the larger interest in the criticism and reform of both the methods and the content of the existing system of law. The constant critical scrutiny of laws in respect of their descriptive adequacy has always been an essential part of the method of the good lawyer, whether as an advocate he prepared to argue cases or as a counselor he advised clients. As an advocate he must predict the effectiveness of legal arguments to evoke from the court the decision which he seeks; as a counselor he must predict the outcome of the course of action which he advises his client to take. Essentially, the realists have taken seriously the practical techniques of the lawyer and have transformed them into generalized and critical methods of research, thereby opening avenues of insight hitherto virtually untouched by an analytical and formal jurisprudence and affecting profoundly our settled convictions about law.[29]

The lawyer is interested in accurate knowledge of the operating factors that govern a given situation, on the basis of which he hopes to be better able to predict the outcome of specific future cases. What is significant in this procedure is that recourse to much more than the formulated statements in lawbooks is needed for this prediction. The attention of the lawyer is not infrequently directed to the question of whether a rule ought or ought not to be the rule for decision, but this attention is given because the correct answer will be one of the factors which enables a prediction to be made respecting what will be the rule for a given decision. The extent to which rules of law do in fact describe what courts will actually do and the extent to which reliance may or may not be placed on stated doctrine are of primary interest. The meaning of a rule is determined by its effects upon the operations of judges or other officials.[30] Rules, then, for the lawyer are instruments; for him they are primarily instruments of prediction. Rules, if they are to be considered meaningful, must have an empirical relevance to actual procedures of courts.

The Austinian conception of law[31] as acts of command offers an insufficient theoretical and practical basis for all that the lawyer finds important in his work. The working formulae of the lawyer contain too much that is either ignored or unintelligible in the Austinian framework. Rules for the lawyer are comments in the sense of being shorthand expressions of much that is not understandable merely as acts of command or illustrations of sovereignty. A lawyer's interest in the problem of prediction is one which carries even a cursory investigation beyond the conventional legal formulae of statute, judicial opinion or treatise. The reason is that in predictions one is interested in the future actions of courts, and future actions, while indisputably grounded in a legal tradition, are equally rooted in present social practices and in what a critical evaluation of foreseen consequences implies for these present practices and the legal forms in which they are or will be crystallized.

In transforming the practicing lawyer's empirical procedures into a refined and thoroughgoing experimental approach and into a thoroughly functional and instrumental conception of law, the American legal realists have in effect broken down a contradiction between the prevailing beliefs men had about law and the methods exemplified in the practice of law. For while the practice of law had its own implicit principles, reflective thinking about law had explicit formulations which took little account of these working principles. Men borrowed their thought about law not from the principles of practice but from traditional philosophies of law. These philosophies of law, with some exceptions as in the case of historical and sociological jurisprudence, operated with conceptions of the nature and method of law far removed from, if not irrelevant to, the *de facto* law with which the practicing lawyer and judge had an empirical acquaintance. Consequently, from the beginning the realists have directed their attention to a criticism of the prevailing philosophies of law and have made a concerted effort to meet the need for reconstructing our most general conceptions of law and its methods.[32]

This general interest in formulating more accurately the working principles of law was given significance, meaning, content, and direction by empirical, functional, and institutional investigations into specific bodies of law, specific court practices, and into the specific inter-relations of laws and social practices. Today there are few branches of law where the influence of an instrumentalist approach has not been felt. In every direction, the attempt to understand laws in terms of what they do and in terms of how they operate is altering the actual structures

and operations of law, as well as our understanding
of that law.[33] Whether the field be that of torts, procedure, contracts, legislation, constitutional law, business, or administrative law, the results of such activity
are apparent. The general effect of these studies has
been to clarify the need for, and the importance of,
fundamental revisions of the concepts of law, and
even where revision is not imperative, there is yet a
different conception of the specific role of concepts.
Only a few of the larger concepts which have received
attention need to be mentioned: in the law of contract, the idea of contract itself, the conventional
analysis into offer and acceptance, the doctrine of
consideration, the theory of reasonable expectation,
and the relation of contract to quasi contract; in tort
law, the doctrines of reasonableness, proximate cause,
and negligence; in the law of property, the idea of
property[34] and the doctrine of nuisance; in criminal
law, the conceptions of accessory, malice, *mens rea*,
and attempt; in constitutional law, the conceptions of
due process, states' rights, freedom of contract, and
delegation of powers. The number of studies of more
particularized concepts is legion.

Realistic Negations

Throughout these various investigations and especially in the various initial efforts to formulate the
theoretical foundations of realism, the burden of
criticism was negative in its emphasis, consisting for
the most part of destructive criticism of prevailing
concepts and vigorous denunciations of previous
theories about or formulations of law that had emphasized the formal and systematic organization of
the existing principles. Furthermore, the realists found
that an empirical approach to law led to emphasis on
the relationships existing between law and its content on the one hand and such other disciplines as
anthropology, psychology, economics, and sociology
and their respective subject matters on the other and
to a study of the operation of what courts do in these
various contests.[35] This combined emphasis on the
need to understand law in terms of all that enters

into and affects its operation and the critical attitude that realists assume toward an excessive logical emphasis have had the general effect of convincing many that legal realism takes an irrational approach to law, denying to law any significant logical or systematic character.

What realism has attacked is, however, not logic but the tendency to use logic alone with insufficient concern for any but the formal character of the premises.[36] Its own aim is an adequate, though thus far unobtainable, logical structure. It attacks not consistency but inadequately based rationalization, not the syllogism but the misdirected use of the syllogism and the content of particular syllogisms. It is critical of the power of logic exclusively to control law: first, because logic has been, and probably will be, unable to do so; and, second, because to improve law more than logic is necessary unless logic operates from premises-to-be-formed as readily as from premises-in-stock. Descriptively, it denies that logic in fact controls law. Even as an ideal, the value of logical form is limited in that techniques require a flexibility to adapt law to new interests, especially in a dynamic culture. Realism demands not less logic but more intelligence in regard to the methods and premises involved in the use of logic. The tendency to use a deductive logic mechanically and the tendency to use ancient formulae exclusively as premises are the greatest obstacles which realism finds to better understanding and effective control of law.[37] Basically, the realistic criticisms are not of concepts but of what happens to concepts when they are uncritically used and when their role as instruments is insufficiently emphasized. A most casual survey of realistic legal studies would indicate that the realists' objective is not the elimination of concepts but, on the contrary, an emphasis upon the multiplication of concepts and working categories.[38] But the emphasis includes a realization that rules are instruments as well as ends of judgments and that as instruments and as ends they have a social relevance and dimension to which they are initially sensitive and to which they must be kept sensitive. Nor have the realists reduced law to something else — to economics, to psychology, or to physics. The realists have asserted, however, that law is not something isolated and separate from society; for them law is completely understood only as the ways of law are seen as part of the very fabric of social ways.[39]

Unfortunately, the fruitful results attained by the realists have been somewhat obscured. The realists, in recognizing the underlying bias of the characteristic traditional emphasis in law, often overreached in seeking arguments and illustrations which would bring into the sharpest focus possible the weakness of the more usual approach. Not always content with a factual and operational approach to their own problems, nor satisfied with providing evidence of the irrelevance of most of the prevailing philosophies to the pressing needs of law, and proceeding cautiously to state the realists' own method and perspective, some realists brought confusion into their arguments by attitudes and analyses which are misleading if not erroneous. This has brought about the opposition and misunderstanding of such men as Morris R. Cohen, Kantorowicz, Kocourek, Pound, Dickinson, and others.[40] The criticisms of these men were, in part at least, justified by the positions taken by some of the extreme realists. Thus, J. W. Bingham, one of the first and most extreme of the realists, weakened an otherwise incisive argument by resorting to an extreme nominalism which was quite unnecessary to the argument and made unrealistic assumptions as to the nature of rules and of generalizations.[41] Jerome Frank rested much of his analysis upon psychoanalytic interpretations of the traditional emphasis on the ideal of certainty and logical form, which even he later recognized to be built of straw.[42] Thurman Arnold criticized theories in law in terms of a series of incisive caricatures which, if taken strictly, appear to necessitate the view that all reflective analyses and ideal projections are but the rantings of lunatics.[43]

The effect of such writing has been to play into the hands of those who feel that an understanding of law is better realized through other means and by a more conservative approach. Nevertheless, the results of a realistic approach to the problem of describing existing laws far outweigh the excesses its more enthusiastic adherents may have committed. As a program of action and as a method of analysis, it remains inescapably fixed as an extremely important and fruitful contribution to the better appreciation of the present content of law, the full effects of which method we have yet to see.

Realism and Justice

If the emphasis of American legal realism upon the interrelations of law and life and upon empirical methods of investigation has been fruitful of better predictability, this emphasis has as well a special relevance to problems of justice. The concern of realism with laws as predictions, with the methods, techniques, assumptions, content, and meaning of existing laws, leads to a concern for both the general theory and the particular problems of justice. It leads to these problems in the sense that they are implied in a consideration of laws which are viewed as predictions and in the sense that these problems are the contexts which make prediction itself a moral concern. It leads to a reconsideration of the general theory of justice, because the introduction of empirical methods in law affects seriously many of the reigning assumptions of existing theories — assumptions which are not compatible with empirical methods as applied to problems of justice.

One who reads the literature of American legal realism will discover many indications of the presence of an altered conception of the character of the quest for justice. The literature exhibits a more empirical, pragmatic emphasis in the approach to normative problems than has hitherto been generally found in practice or given due recognition in theory. Yet an empirical approach to the problems of justice has appeared to many to be insidious if not, in fact, a rejection of all concern for justice.[44] It has been interpreted as a denial of the possibility of serious consideration of what ought to be, a substitution of the individual prejudice in the judge for impartial judgment in accordance with principle, or as a complacency with the actual as it is. W. B. Kennedy writes: "There is grave danger that functionalism [legal realism] having turned to the study of facts, things, and tangibles may end by shutting itself up in that reality and closing the mind to the consideration, analysis, and evaluation of the facts."[45] A functional or empirical approach, it is argued, is to take the short range view, to make standards either impossible, irrelevant, or a matter primarily of subjective selection.[46]

D. Legal Experimentalism

This movement has for its inspiration the idea that law and the social disciplines can be combined in an exeprimental science. This is an attempt at a radical implementation of a central aspect of sociological jurisprudence and the realist revolt against "legal fundamentalism." It is necessarily visionary at present, since no social science is truly experimental as yet. An additional obstacle to the program is the enormous complexity of legal materials. In the first place there is no agreement as to what aspects of law properly lend themselves to experimental treatment; and secondly, there is a substantial body of opinion against the notion that law can ever have anything to do with experimental science. Naturally the legal experimentalists are opposed to the second point of view although they would have to admit that the first objection is well taken.

Underhill Moore, My Philosophy of Law (1941) pp. 218-225; reprinted by permission of the Julius Rosenthal Foundation of Northwestern University and the Boston Law Book Company.

The following is the fragment of a theory applicable in life situations in which there is present the behavior of a large enough number of persons to make a frequency distribution of their responses statistically significant.

As stated at the beginning of this paper behavior and artifacts which are signs are distinguished on the basis of the degree of the pain or humiliation or the degree of satisfaction derived from the reward by which responses to those signs have been learned. It is hypothesized that the difference between the behavior which occurs in the presence of a given sign a response to which has been reinforced and the behavior which occurs in the absence of that sign, which difference is the learned response to the sign, varies directly with the degree of pain or reward by which the response to that sign has been learned.

Two obvious problems confront the person who desires to verify this proposition by observation and experiment. The first is the definition of the behavior to be observed in the presence and absence of a given sign. The second is the construction of an operational scale for the measurement of degrees of pain or the satisfaction derived from rewards.

In attempting to solve the first problem, one of the peculiarities of word signs mentioned above— namely that the non-verbal responses to such signs which have been *reinforced* are almost always responses the verbal definition of which corresponds to the dictionary meaning of the words in the signs— is a fortunate accident. This accident makes it possible to define, in the case of word signs, the behavior to be observed in the presence and absence of the sign. Since the response which has been *reinforced* is the response defined by the words in the sign, the change which will *occur* will be a change "toward" that response, that is, it will be a change in the frequencies of that behavior which may be distinguished as corresponding or not corresponding, or as corresponding in some degree, to the behavior defined by the words in the sign.

The second problem, the construction of a scale for measuring pains and rewards, is approached as follows: It is hypothesized that, in any case of learning in life situations, the degree of pain or reward by which responses to signs are reinforced varies directly with the ratio, which obtains before the reinforcing agent is applied, between the frequency of the behavior which does not correspond to the words in the sign and the frequency of the behavior which does so correspond. It will be recalled that the cases with which this analysis is concerned are all cases in which the pain or reward, by which a response to a sign is reinforced, is applied, and its weight controlled, by some person or persons. Those persons have in view the changing of behavior, as it exists before the application of the reinforcing agent, to behavior which, in the presence of the sign, will correspond to the words in the sign. The greater the reward or punishment, the greater the change is likely to be. Therefore, the greater the difference between the responses being given before the reward or the pain is applied and the responses a description of which would correspond with the words in the sign, the greater will be the reward awarded or the pain inflicted. For example, if, on rainy days, all of the children always come into the house with mud on their shoes, the punishment inflicted on each, if any is inflicted at all, will be greater than the punishment inflicted if the offense seldom occurs. Or if all the boys in the neighborhood frequently commit burglary the punishment inflicted by a parent, if any is inflicted at all, will be greater than if the commission of burglary were rare.

From the two hypotheses just stated there may be deduced a third which, as formulated, is operational in cases in which a sign, to which a response already has been learned, is introduced into a situation for the first time. In order to be operational in cases in which a sign, to which a response has not been learned, is introduced, the hypothesis would require certain elaboration. This third hypothesis is that the change which is the learned response to a sign varies directly with that part of the sign which is the ratio, observed to obtain before the words of the sign were introduced, between the frequency of behavior not

corresponding to the words in the sign ("failures")
and the frequency of behavior corresponding to the
words in the sign ("successes"). In life situations in
which an individual is being conditioned to give a
reinforced response to a sign, the learned responses
of others to that sign are part of the stimulus situation.
By the second hypothesis the degree of pain or reward by which the response of the individual is
reinforced varies with the relative frequency of failures to successes in the responses of those others.
Accordingly there is a relation, throughout the learning periods in which responses to a large number of
signs are learned, between the relative frequency
of failures to successes in the behavior of others and
the degree of pain or reward by which the response
of the particular individual is conditioned. Since this
behavior of others is present to the senses of the
individual during the learning process and since the
degree of pain or reward varies with it, the behavior
of others becomes a part of the sign and differing
ratios of failures to successes become parts of different
signs to which different responses are learned because
differing degrees of pain or reward have been applied
in the process of teaching those responses.

The last hypothesis satisfies the requirements for
an operational hypothesis and may be verified or
disproved by a contrived experiment or by observation of a process. The observation of each of a number of behavior situations before a sign including
words is introduced and the observation of each of
those situations after the sign is introduced should,
by the hypothesis, disclose that, in each situation,
there is the same relation between the relative frequency of successes to failures before the sign is
introduced, on the one hand, and, on the other, the
change which follows the introduction of the sign.
The relative frequency of successes to failures in
each situation may be stated quantitatively by stating
the total number of occurrences of successes (or failures) in each situation as a percentage of the total
number of occurrences of both successes and failures.
The change which follows the introduction of the

sign may be stated quantitatively by stating the difference between a quantitative value on a scale of success (correspondence) assigned to the total of the occurrences of the behavior in each situation before the sign is introduced and the value, on the same scale, assigned to the total occurrences after the sign is introduced. Such a scale of success (correspondence) may be no more than a scale of the ratios of total successes to total failures; or it may be a more detailed scale which distinguishes, quantitatively, between degrees of success or failure. Thus, for example, in an experiment in which a sign is to be introduced, which sign includes the word series "30 Minute Parking," the change following the introduction of the sign may be measured by the difference between the percentages of total parkings which were successes, i.e., had a duration of thirty minutes or less, or by the difference between the percentages which were failures, i.e., had a duration of more than thirty minutes, before and after the introduction of the sign; or the change may be measured by a quantitative difference between two distributions, which, respectively, record the observed occurrences of parking before and after the introduction of the sign, and which distinguish durations of parking in one, or five, or ten-minute categories and state the percentage of the total occurrences in each category.

Illustrative of this procedure for the verification of the operational hypothesis is a series of experiments made by the writers, with Miss Emma Corstvet and others, as part of the work of the Yale University Institute of Human Relations. The briefest mention of some of them will serve the purpose. In ten of the experiments notices, including words purporting to limit the duration of parking, were posted by the police. In each experiment observations were made both before and after the posting of the notice. In some of the experiments the limitation stated by the words on the posted notices was 60 minutes, in others 30 minutes, in others 15 minutes and in others "No Parking." There was no tagging, or other administrative action, by the police at the sites of any of the experiments during the time of observation. The changes were measured by the differences between before and after distributions of parking durations in one, five, and ten-minute categories. From these experiments it appears (1) that there is the same relation in each experiment between the ratio of successes to failures before the introduction of the notice and the difference between the before and after distributions and (2) that the relation is expressed by the formula $y = a - ab^{xp}$. In this formula y is the cumulative percentage of the total up to any category of the after distribution; x is the cumulative percentage of the total up to the same category in the before distribution; a is a constant with a value 102; b is a value which varies with the ratio of success to failures before the introduction of the notice according to the formula $b = 1 - \dfrac{1}{8.52^{z.3}}$, when z is the ratio of successes to failures, expressed by stating the number of observed parkings having a duration less than the time stated in the notice as a percentage of the total observed parkings; and p is a value which varies with the ratio of successes to failures before the introduction of the notice according to the formula $p = 1.235 + .01209z$, when z is the ratio of successes to failures, expressed as above.

Whether this relation would appear in other parking experiments in the same or any other geographical area, or in the case of legal regulations other than parking restrictions, can be determined, of course, only by further experiments.

Frederick K. Beutel,[1a] Some Implications of Experimental Jurisprudence, 48 Harvard Law Review pp. 169-179 (1934); reprinted by permission of the author and the Harvard Law Review.

Characteristic of the economic and political life of the world, but lagging far behind it, there has been

considerable unrest in the field of American jurisprudential thought, not the least of which has come
from the realists.[1] This group, if it be safe to classify,[2] seems to represent a branch of the school of
sociological jurisprudence, which is chiefly interested
in the "facts" and social behavior clustering about the
legal system rather than its fictions, concepts, and
traditions. Probably their greatest service has been
the final debunking of the profession, by calling
attention to some of the actualities in the legal order
and insisting upon "grubbing for facts."

Facts, however, are extremely elusive concepts
which the ancient philosophers suggested were mere
figments of the mind. Modern physics in the new
quantum theory has recently recognized that in this,
the most concrete of all sciences, the researcher must
work only with shadows of shadows, and reality is
beyond the realm of human attainment.[3] In the light
of these ancient and modern truths it is not surprising
that some of the most earnest disciples of the realists
seem to have come to the end of the search for facts,
surrendering to the conservatives, and returning to
"rational analysis which finds and orders abstractions
which can be organized into systems" under which
law becomes "a body of principles and rules developed in the light of the rational science of Ethics
and Politics."[4]

It is even more significant that, almost simultaneously with these utterances, another leading realist
who is taking an active part in the New Deal, threw
out a challenge to the jurists in the term "experimental jurisprudence."[5] As he explained it, this seemed
to be a rationalization of the empirical process of the
so-called pragmatic method now alleged to be changing the whole political, legal, economic, and social
structure of our nation. Although Mr. Frank con-
fessed that he had not thought the matter through,
and although the idea of applying the technique of
experimental science to jurisprudence is not new,[6]
the term experimental jurisprudence is a happy one.
Its implication should be examined with care.

1. *The Elements of an Experimental Science*

Before considering the possibility of jurisprudence becoming an experimental science, it might be useful, at the risk of being trite, to reexamine hastily the fundamental postulates and concepts underlying the scientific method. The scientists like the philosophers will readily admit that the only knowable truth in the strict sense is Descartes's famous dictum *cogito ergo sum;* all else in the field of scientific knowledge springs from a group of basic postulates, tentatively adopted in the hope that they may prove useful in explaining the myriads of sensations which come into the consciousness of the "I am." These basic postulates may be roughly classified as: (1) the existence of phenomena in an external universe; (2) the possibility of observation of such phenomena; (3) the validity of memory, or the possibility of recording the observation; and (4) the postulate of uniformity, that is, the assumption that under identical conditions exterior phenomena will act the same.[7]

Starting with these basic postulates, the scientist observes his sensory impression of the phenomena about him in his chosen field of investigation, records his observations, and attempts an explanation of his findings. This explanation or hypothesis becomes the basis for prediction of future action and reaction of the observed phenomena. Controlling the materials before him, the scientist reports his observations or makes new ones and thus checks the validity of his hypothesis, proceeding to verify and extend it, or, if it fails to correspond with the results of his experiment, to reject it and devise a new hypothesis which in turn is subjected to further testings, checking, observation, and variations.[8] Under this method the physical sciences have achieved vast quantities of knowledge, in the form of working hypotheses. Inventors and engineers, relying upon this knowledge, have been able so completely to change human society that rapid advances in the mechanical equipment of industry sometimes cause new laws and political innovations to become obsolete before they can be set in motion.

Until recently the so-called social scientists have lagged far behind their colleagues in the physical fields. Problems of observation, recording of data, and control of the experiments are far more complicated but not entirely insurmountable. The other social scientists are beginning to make progress in the right direction. Jurisprudence, however, has consistently fallen farther behind.[9] We are told that the methods of experimental science cannot be applied to jurisprudence,[10] that human actions are beyond observation, control, and predictability,[11] that the science of law must depend upon rationalization,[12] ethics,[13] politics,[14] sociology,[15] psychology, religion, the judicial hunch,[16] the traditions of a trained bar,[17] and the like. It is submitted that these and similar discouraging statements are mere rationalizations of the jurists' failure to come to grips with the real problems of legal science.

II. Practicality of Adopting in Jurisprudence the Fundamental Postulates of Experimental Science

A careful observation should show that there are many reasons to support a belief that the fundamental postulates and methods which underlie experimental physical sciences are capable of application in the field of juristic science. There is little reason to question the first postulate, the existence of phenomena to be studied. Certainly it may be assumed that in the society about us there are various types of social adjustment which are usually called laws. There are also governmental organizations, courts, legislatures, and administrative officers creating and enforcing these laws. To some degree these activities affect the individuals and groups which go to make up organized societies and nations. Myriads of actions and reactions cluster about the social phenomena which we call law.

The second postulate is also easy to reach. These numerous activities clustering about the phenomena called law are capable of observation. It is true that the reactions of individuals or a social group to a rule of law, whatever that may be, are not as easily discerned as are the microscopic shadows of physical matter on a sensitive photographic plate. Although objects reflected are more distant and the outlines are seen through a thicker haze, the technique of statistics and other sociological means of recording human reactions show great possibilities. The Cleveland Survey,[18] the Harvard Law School Survey of Crime in Boston,[19] the report of the National Commission on Law Observance and Enforcement, the results of the study at Johns Hopkins Institute of Law, and works of like nature[20] indicate that social reactions to legal phenomena can be observed. The lines of the reports may not be so fine as are those of the physicist or chemist, but the gross results are clear enough to be capable of scientific observation.

The accuracy of such observations may still be far from what has been achieved in the physical sciences. The variation in the human element of recording is strikingly illustrated by the dissenting opinions in the report of the National Commission on Law Observance and Enforcement,[21] and the various points of view which appear in accounts of current or past history; but conflicting evidence has never deterred the lawyer in his search for facts. It is even less conceivable that it should frighten a jurist. The number of observers used and the scientific nature of their training can go far to minimize or entirely eliminate the personal bias from statistical reports on social and legal phenomena.

The laboratory apparatus is still to be developed; but even here the lie detector and similar instruments of scientific crime detection, which is still in its infancy, point the way to other mechanical means of recording observations with accuracy far beyond human apprehension.

The fourth postulate, that of uniformity of action, is the one which gives to the experimental jurist the most difficulty. It may be objected at once that there is no evidence or reason for supposing that human beings will react uniformly to the same stimuli; or that, even if they would, the complexity of factors involved in the social structure is such that accurate generalizations, in the form of scientific laws describing the reaction of that group of social phenomena which we term law or legal, are beyond human attainment.

Turning to the last objection first, it is true that the factors involved in studying the reactions of a body politic to a law or system of laws are exceedingly various and complex. Still, complexity has not prevented the advance of biology, organic chemistry, and the science of social hygiene. The problem of maintaining a given system of law and studying its results is scarcely less complex than that of devising plans to protect the health of the same group. Complication of factors has not stopped the scientists from cleaning up such pest holes of the world as the Isthmus of Panama. The lessons learned from observation of such experiments have suggested the scientific laws which make possible, to a large degree, predictability of the success of future ventures of like nature.[22] Given the proper equipment, there seems no reason why complication of factors should deter the experimental jurist from making similar searches for the scientific laws governing the social activities surrounding the phenomena called law.[23]

The first objection to the postulate of uniformity in the social sciences founded upon the old dictum of free will is more serious, and constitutes the most formidable citadel which has repeatedly turned back the attacks of the protagonists of experimental social science. Although the doctrine of the free-willing individual appears throughout literature, religion, philosophy, and legal dogma, it is surprising to note that it has very little experimental support. Almost all researches in the field have tended to cast grave doubts upon the universal application of the doctrine even when it is directed to the single individual. The recent development of child psychology and the work of the behaviorists have given the devotees of free will some rude shocks,[24] and today there are many scientists of standing who will support the proposition that by controlling the individual's environment you can control his character and predict his future actions.[25] Granting that heredity plays a part, the biologists have gone a long ways toward working out the science of inherited characteristics, so even here there is evidence that free will of the individual is on shaky ground.[26] Outside of the field of heredity and environment, experiments with the lie detector and other psychological apparatus have indicated that under certain given situations it is possible to predict that most all individuals will react in the same manner.[27]

But the postulate of uniformity in experimental jurisprudence need not rest on the predictability of the actions of single individuals. Jurisprudence is interested in mass reactions. The verdict of a particular jury, or the decision of a single court, while of great importance to the practicing lawyer,[28] is of little significance to the experimental jurist. If he can observe and predict the reactions of juries in general, of hundreds of judges and appellate courts, of thousands of legislators, and of the population of cities, states, and nations, he will have created an experimental science of inestimable value.[29]

Viewed in this light the postulate of uniformity is on as solid ground in jurisprudence as it is in other modern sciences. The physicist cannot predict the action of a single molecule, or state the laws governing its particular actions; but the laws as to mass actions of physical objects are still sound.[30] Even as physics has been reduced to a statistical science, so also it is not too much to assume that jurisprudence may likewise be molded into an experimental science based upon statistical data and using the postulate of uniformity to study mass actions. Modern economists and students of business statistics are rapidly demonstrating that most economic actions are controlled by definite knowable laws.[31] Mortality tables, criminal statistics, and the like show the possibility of predicting actions of large numbers of people and suggest the opportunity of studying the underlying laws behind them.[32] A nation which fought to make the world safe for democracy, believed that German soldiers were bloody barbarians organized to rape women,[33] fears athletes' foot and pink tooth brush,[34] knows that communism is against the will of God,[35] and is satisfied that public ownership of utilities is a greater source of corruption than private ownership,[36] offers little solace to one who wishes to argue that mass human actions are neither controllable nor predictable. There is no reason why the arts[37] of propaganda, applied economics, and advertising, can rest on scientific data[38] while the art of the lawyer must forever be founded on the occult mysteries of judicial hunch and professional dogma.

III. *Materials and Objectives of Experimental Jurisprudence*

If it is possible to adopt the fundamental postulates of experimental science for a new jurisprudence, what would be its material, the nature of its objectives, its technique, and the results which it might be expected to attain?

The sociological jurists have made a great contribution to the advancement of jurisprudence by calling attention to the fact that the law is a conscious or unconscious adjustment of human interests[39] instead of the will of a sovereign, the inevitable working of history, or the natural development of an ideal justice. Dean Pound has attempted to classify these interests and to call attention to some of the legal devices for securing them.[40] Unfortunately, however, such systems are little more than rational speculation based on the legal *status quo* and supported by little or no experimental evidence.

The term interests needs further scrutiny. It obviously subdivides itself into the interests of individuals, of groups, and of society as a whole,[41] each of which may correspond or clash with the interests of its own and of the other classifications. What is more important, there are conscious and unconscious interests; that is, what the individual, group, or society wants, and what is good for it regardless of its wants. While speculation and rationalization may be useful in this field, it can never discover the real interests involved by examining or analyzing the results achieved by laws or legal systems. Experimental jurisprudence demands an experimental factual examination of these interests regardless of the particular form in which they seem to appear in the positive law or the decisions of the courts.

After the interest is discovered by the jurist it is, perhaps, his problem to evaluate it, but the lawyer, statesman or judge must give, or refuse to give, it an amount of recognition and put it in its place in the whole system of law[42] by passing statutes, advising clients, or deciding particular cases. At present every law, every court decision, every ruling of a commission, policeman, or administrative officer represents such an adjustment upon an impressionistic basis. These adjustments create a situation where the methods of trial and error must prevail; the result is an experiment whether one likes it or not.

The problem of experimental jurisprudence is (1) to study these results, (2) to state the jurisprudential laws which govern the phenomena surrounding the attempts of the legal system to make such adjustments,[43] and (3) by observation and experiment to test the sufficiency and efficiency of the legal system, to accomplish its purpose.

Whether or not the adjustments of any particular system are proper ones may be determined by a pragmatic test of their actual workings in everyday life. The ultimate good need not be known. It may be a hedonistic one of the greatest good for the greatest number, good being measured by physical, material, or cultural standards attained. Again it may be one of race power, national aggrandizement, or spiritual or intellectual advancement; on the other hand, it may be an attempt to create outstanding individuals at the expense of the masses.[44]

Experimental jurisprudence properly applied can test the efficiency of the legal system in attaining its particular end, and in turn can state the results which follow attempts to reach such ends. The data thus accumulated may throw great light on the value of the objectives and the effectiveness of the means used to attain them. The ethical problem of what is the ultimate good, although it may eventually become one of the problems of jurisprudence, is today too far removed to require consideration.[45] While questions of this nature must await the perfection of the technique of scientific jurisprudence, yet, when that is achieved, such problems will be capable of much plainer answers than have ever been deemed possible.

Julius Cohen, Reginald A. H. Robson, Alan Bates Ascertaining the Moral Sense of the Community: A Preliminary Report on An Experiment in Interdisciplinary Research, 8 Journal of Legal Education pp. 137-142 (1955); reprinted by permission of the authors and the Journal of Legal Education.

THE BACKGROUND

If one were asked to name one of the most recurrent themes in legal literature, both old and new, he would be inviting little disagreement if he were to suggest: The relationship of law to morals. From this common theme have sprung the variations that characterize and distinguish many different modern approaches to the nature and function of law. John Chipman Gray, for example, would treat morals as "one of the main sources from which the law is drawn."[46] Were he a judge "in a case where there is nothing to guide him but the notion of right and wrong," he would take note of the moral sentiment of the community, but would not feel bound to follow it.[47] Cardozo, on the other hand, would, in such a situation, feel himself "under a duty to conform to the accepted standards of the community, the *mores* of the times."[48] To Morris R. Cohen, the moral sense of the community — the community's sense of justice — would serve as one of the norms for controlling or guiding law itself. Without conformity "in large measure" to such a norm, "the body of the law could not long maintain itself."[49] To Ehrlich, law should have its source and support in the moral principles inherent in the "living law," the rules of law emerging, as it were, from the early ordering of social groups.[50] Pound would utilize the moral ideals of "the time and place" for the purpose of "shaping and developing legal materials."[51] To Kantorowicz, principles of morality would be "nascent implicit law," which courts would be free to use when "formal law" is unavailing for a solution.[52] Justice Frankfurter writes of those judges[53] whose whole training and proved performance substantially insure that their conclusions reflect understanding of, and due regard for, law as the expression of the views and feelings that may fairly be deemed representative of the community as a continuing society.

These examples are merely illustrative (they are by no means exhaustive) of the diversity of views concerning the relation of morals to law. For the moment, however, what is important is not that there are variations, but that there are variations upon a common theme. Of the views mentioned, all of them would, at the very least, posit the need to identify and measure the moral ingredient — no matter how or to what extent it would be utilized in any particular formulation of what law ought to be. A closer look would reveal that all of them would utilize the moral ingredient either as a norm to consider or as a norm to follow.[54] But how ascertain it? How measure it? The authors of the philosophical and jurisprudential formulations concerning the relationship of law to morals have, with rare exception,[55] been silent or vague about such problems. Indeed, the variety of terms that are used and the levels of abstraction that are employed in these formulations— "moral sense," "mores of the time," "positive morality,"[56] "the moral ideal of time and place," "the common conscience,"[57] etc. — suggests the absence of a common core of understanding concerning the very meaning of the moral ingredient itself. Does the term "morals" comprise the notions of good and bad that are implicit in customary behavior, as perhaps Ehrlich would view it? Or are they notions which themselves

And what of the term "community"? If the moral sense of the "community" is sought, is it the views of the "ethical leaders" of the community, as Judge Frank insisted in his dissenting opinion in the *Repouille* case,[58] or is it, as Justice Cardozo suggested, "the views of the men and women of the community whom the social mind would rank as intelligent and virtuous"?[59] Or would it be the men and women of all walks of life? When "community" morals are referred to, is complete homogeneity assumed? If heterogeneity is assumed, at what point do diverse moral views become "community" morals? These and many other similar problems have, in the main, not been dealt with too critically by the theoreticians. Nor has any great attention been given to them by the more practical minded, who have neither the time nor the patience for such fine-spun analysis. The account of the recent proceedings of the American Law Institute in its deliberations on the Modern Penal Code is a case in point.[60] The issue of whether sodomy should be enjoined by law was debated by Judge Parker and Judge Learned Hand. Judge Parker urged that private homosexuality should be prohibited by law because such conduct flies "in the face of public opinion as evidenced by the code of every state in the union." Judge Hand supported the opposite view on the ground that "criminal law which is not enforced practically is much worse than if it was not on the books at all," and that sodomy "is a matter very largely of taste, and is not a matter that people should be put in prison about." How was the issue resolved? By consulting the community concerning its own moral sense? Not at all. According to the report, the Institute settled it by *voting* "35 to 24 to uphold Judge Hand's . . . view" that sodomy be recommended for removal from the list of crimes.

And what of the lawmakers themselves? Legislative lawmakers, in the main, rely on pressure groups for their estimate of the moral sense of the community— a method inherently defective in that all groups in a community are not organized, and all that are not organized cannot exert enough pressure to make their views known or felt in the proper places. Judicial law-makers, seeking to utilize this moral sense as a guide for their policy-making activities (this includes the process of molding the common law, the interpretation of statutes, and the nullification of statutes on constitutional grounds), rely, in the main, upon intuitive hunch, on the vagaries of "judicial notice," on the predilections of the groups identified with the social origin of the lawmakers, on crude personal observations, on a "best guess," or by some such other esoteric method of divining the *Zeitgeist*. Indeed, there are those who would rely on "hunch" or the "best guess" simply because of the belief that no other methods are feasible. This was pointed up rather sharply by Judge Learned Hand in a series of cases involving the "good moral character" standard in naturalization proceedings. In *United States* v. *Francioso,* Judge Hand stated that in applying the statutory standard of "good moral character" he felt obliged to consult "the moral feelings now prevalent generally in this country" or "the generally accepted moral conventions current at the time".[61] In *Repouille* v. *United States,* the test of "good moral character" was not his own belief, but whether "the moral feelings now generally prevalent in this country would be outraged."[62] In *Johnson* v. *United States,* he again stated:[63]

"Our duty in such cases, as we understand it, is to divine what the 'common conscience' prevalent at the time demands; and it is impossible in practice to ascertain what in a given instance it does demand. . . . Nor is it possible to make use of general principles, for almost every moral situation is unique. . . . Theoretically, perhaps, we might take as the test whether those who would approve the specific conduct would outnumber those who would disapprove; but it would be fantastically absurd to try to apply it. So it seems to us that we are confined to the best guess we can make of how such a poll would result."

But Judge Hand goes much too far. First of all, the quality of uniqueness is not unique to moral situations. Each physical phenomenon, in this sense, is likewise unique. To deny the utility of general principles to the physical realm because of this would deny the legitimacy of the very method of the physical sciences. Likewise, to deny general principles to the moral realm would deny feasibility to the organizing and systematizing function of ethics. Actually, what often appears, at first blush, to be unique may turn out, upon closer inspection, to contain elements of similarity with other so-called unique phenomena. It is the very purpose of science to search out these common elements and organize them into larger, more general categories. Indeed, if it be true that much of judicial law itself grows by inductive case-by-case generalization by analogical reasoning,[64] how can it be done without assuming the very existence of those common elements which are extracted from uniquely dissimilar cases? Now, granted that such a "poll" as suggested by Judge Hand would not yield any general principles covering *all* moral situations; granted, also, that it would be impracticable to poll the community concerning *each* specific moral issue raised in litigious controversies — would it not be more reliable to develop analogically from a poll of sentiment of *several* concrete moral issues, concerning which the views of the community are relevant, than it is to develop analogically from a surmise or "guess" by a judge as to the nature of the community sentiment regarding those issues?[65] Take the situation in the *Johnson* case. Johnson had failed to support his legal wife; for years he had been living with a paramour. Was he of "good moral character" within the meaning of the naturalization statute? Judge Hand held in the negative because of his belief that it conformed to his "best guess" of what the "common conscience" would be on the facts of the case. Now, suppose that Judge Hand were confronted with another case, the facts of which varied slightly from the *Johnson* case. Would he not be on firmer ground in the second case if he had at his disposal an accurate "poll" of the community's reaction to the situation in the *Johnson* case than he would be upon his "guess" of what the moral sense of the community would be with respect to it? We think he would be. For if he erred in his judgment in the first case, the error would be pyramided in the second, in the third, and in the other analogical extensions that would follow.

II

THE EXPERIMENT[66]

The Aims

If the ascertainment of the moral sense of the community is relevant to the lawmaking process, either as a norm for the lawmaker to consider or as a norm to follow, it is our view that it need not be left to conjecture, to hunch, or to intuition, and that modern social science techniques could more reliably be utilized for the task. With financial support from the University of Nebraska, we undertook a pilot project to demonstrate this concretely. It was our purpose (1) to develop a more reliable method than is now used by lawmakers for measuring the moral sense of the community; (2) with this method, to test empirically the assumption often made by lawmakers that the legal norms that they establish are in harmony with the moral sense of the community; (3) to test empirically the oft-expressed view that the community has *a* moral sense, rather than *many* moral senses; (4) if, and where, there is heterogeneity of values in the community, to ascertain whether groups of people holding roughly the same sets of values could broadly be identified by reference to such other independent criteria as age, religion, income, etc.; and (5) if it is possible to distinguish such groups, to ascertain whether the law coincides with any of the values held by such groups in the community, and also whether the law generally tends to coincide more consistently with the values of one group than with those of others.

It is fairly obvious that, with limited resources, it

would not be possible for us to achieve these aims with respect to *all* laws, or with respect to *some* laws encompassing the *entire* United States. The scope of the study was therefore confined to the laws and community of Nebraska. The focus of the study was further narrowed by successive stages: first, to the area of family law; then, within that area, to law as it concerns the relations between parent and child; and finally, from this segment of family law, a number of specific issues were chosen. There were several reasons for demarcating the parent-child area for our study: (1) Some of the law in this area seemed, in part at least, to be in a state of flux, lawmakers evidencing disagreement concerning the directional lines that should be taken. (2) Sociological and other literature suggested broadly that changing community attitudes towards many aspects of child-parent relationships were not reflected in law. (3) The area of child-parent relationships has, for some time, been a common hunting ground for both lawyers and sociologists. Although each group heretofore has been looking for different game, it was thought that familiarity with the terrain would make a joint hunting party more attractive, would encourage greater communication between specialists in different disciplines, and thereby extend the scope of mutual interest. (4) It is an area in which there is virtually little reliable scientific knowledge concerning the consequences of alternative proposals that could serve the lawmaker as a norm for guiding the directional lines of legal policy. (5) And because some lawmakers have, accordingly, chosen as their norm what they believe to represent the moral sense or feelings of the community.

Although our particular study is, of necessity, confined to a very small area of law and also only to one state, we believe that the hypotheses, research procedures, and type of analysis used in our project could readily be applied to the study of other areas of law in other communities. In this sense, we suggest that in so far as the present research is successful, it could be used as a model for future studies concerned with similar problems.

[Thereafter follows a consideration of Hypotheses, Research Procedures, Selection of Specific Issues, The Interview Schedule, concluding with a brief summary of the progress of the study to date. T. A. C.]

Thomas A. Cowan, Postulates for Experimental Jurisprudence,[67] 9 Rutgers Law Review pp. 404-417; 424 (1954); reprinted by permission of the Rutgers Law Review.

I. *Introduction*

The art of stating a philosophical position in the form of a set of postulates, while not unknown to jurisprudence, is nevertheless sufficiently new in its modern form to justify a preliminary account of the process for the benefit of law-trained readers.

At one time human thought took axioms and postulates for avowals of unalterable truth, but the nineteenth century made common the practice of speculating with alternative pre-suppositional systems,[68] so that deeper insight into the nature of this scientific device revealed it as merely one among many for clarifying and fecundating thought.

The older tradition was founded in the main upon the deep reverence, amounting almost to worship, which the Renaissance felt for Aristotelian logic and Euclidean geometry. The revival of Greek learning in the late middle ages, reinforced by the extremely high regard which Greek geometry occupied in the minds of the humanists, combined to make popular among intellectuals the conviction that the axioms, postulates and definitions of this mathematical system not only represented eternal truth, but served also to elevate human reason to a pinnacle approaching godhead, since these truths made no claim to religion as their immediate basis but were the avowed products of the human mind.

There is no evidence that the Greek mathematicians claimed anything so spectacular for their science. For Euclid, apparently, axioms were mere "common notions"; ideas of so general a character that no one would wish to waste time disputing them. Nevertheless, it lay with the deepest interests of the rationalists of the sixteenth and seventeenth centuries, those men who were opposing to religious revelation the claim that human reason alone is the source of eternal truth, to exploit to the utmost the best example at hand of an eternally true product of the human mind, Euclidean geometry.

They did their work well. So well, indeed, that geometry with its unalterably true propositions following necessarily as a matter of syllogistic logic from self-evidently true premises (axioms, postulates, definitions) became the very type and example of all scientific truth-seeking.

Descartes, father of rationalism, laid the groundwork for a universal scientific method of deduction. Spinoza, carrying forward the work into the forbidding realm of secular morality, devised a mathematical ethics, an *Ethics Demonstrated After the Manner of a Geometry*, one of whose most noteworthy theorems was the deductive proof that God exists! This was the age of rationalistic natural law. If morality could be found to have an unexceptionable foundation in human reason, could not the law, its twin sister, avail itself of equal certitude? The job was undertaken by Christian Wolff, confrére of Leibniz. Wolff published an enormous eight-volume work entitled *Jus Naturae*[69] wherein the whole body of the law was deduced by inexorable logic from eternally true first principles derived from an analysis of human reason itself.

This feat was never duplicated. Indeed Wolff's more famous colleague Leibniz was even then laying the foundations for a revolution in logic and mathematics in attempting to develop universal logic to put an end once and for all to the weary processes of scientific trial and error investigations. The implications of Leibniz' theories as leading to a complete shattering of older scientific methods, rather than to the consolidation and extension of them as Leibniz fondly thought, had to await the nineteenth century to be clearly visible.

So little was the nineteenth century revolution in deductive methodology anticipated even in the eighteenth, that the immortal Kant was able to regard the principles of Euclidean geometry as so intimately a part of the structure of the human mind that if their absence be conceived then human experience itself would be inconceivable. Though we have no right to consider such principles as eternal, yet they would endure as long as human reason itself existed. Thus Kant at the end of the eighteenth century.

The story of how nineteenth-century logicians and mathematicians began to undermine the eternal principles of Aristotelian logic and Euclidean geometry has been told in many places. Perhaps the best reference for our purposes would be to Professor C. I. Lewis' *Survey of Symbolic Logic* (1918).

The twentieth century witnessed a clear-cut division of the presuppositional field into two opposing groups and their numerous progeny. This division corresponded with the age-old division of the sources of human knowledge into (a) the world of nonhuman existence and (b) the human mind itself. The first is generally known as the empirical bias or emphasis; the second, the rationalistic or (sometimes) the idealistic bias or emphasis. Common sense unceremoniously lumps these two sources together; professional philosophy strives to divide, differentiate, synthesize them, thus giving rise to the primary philosophical systems.

Until the nineteenth century most postulational systems were rationalistic in character. Their claim to eternal validity rested on intuitions of reason. Unfortunately, experience caught up with and outmoded them all except Aristotelian logic and Euclidean geometry. When these two bastions fell, the rationalistic postulational systems fell with them. Thereafter, empirical postulates became a possibility. These of

course purport to be no more than empirical generalizations, good only so long as the events or objects
they summarize remain relatively unchanged. In law,
for instance, they purport to express the long range
claims, demands, policies, and interests or ideals of
the culture.

Modern postulational systems show the strains of
all the main modern varieties of rationalism and empiricism, i.e., what part the human mind and what
part nature contribute to human knowledge. Modern
Kantians still think of a postulational system as having
aprioric validity, that is, validity quite apart from
human experience. The postulates are "pure," not
mixed with "impure" experience. This position is a
counterpart of logical positivism, a philosophy which
resolutely keeps its pure and its impure elements
from being mixed. The "logical" part of the dualism
regards postulation in its widest sense as the product
of the human mind functioning as a reasoning mechanism only. The "positivistic" aspect of the system
deals with experience apart from "logic." The connection between the two is a series of miracles.

Modern idealists treat postulation as the basis of
hypothetico-deductive systems. This is modern idealism's offer of compromise to empiricism. The hypotheses may be arrived at on the basis of experience.
But they must be purified and disciplined by reason
using the criteria of logic. This rapport, or attempted
rapport, gives modern idealism its air of common-
sense practicality. It must be admitted, however,
that modern idealism has not been very successful
in inducing empiricists to submit their empirical
generalizations for the purifying bath of logic.

The school which breaks violently with the rationalistic ideal of postulation is the pragmatic philosophy.
Logic is not an organon or mere instrument for testing the validity of premises whose truth-value is
indifferent to it. Logic, for the pragmatists, is scientific inquiry itself, not one of inquiry's inanimate tools.
Logic for the pragmatists became what one nowadays
would call "scientific methodology." Let John Dewey,

the great pragmatist, tell us about this point in his own words:

> Inquiry in order to be inquiry in the complete sense has to satisfy certain demands that are capable of formal statement. . . . The position here taken holds that (postulates) are intrinsically postulates of and for inquiry, being formulations of conditions, discovered in the course of inquiry itself, which further inquiries must satisfy if they are to yield warranted assertability as a consequence. . . . The postulate is also a stipulation. To engage in inquiry is like entering into a contract. It commits the inquirer to observance of certain conditions. A stipulation is a statement of conditions that are agreed to in the conduct of some affair. The stipulations involved are at first implicit in the undertaking of inquiry. As they are formally acknowledged (formulated), they become logical forms of various degrees of generality. They make definite what is involved in a demand. . . .[70]

It is interesting to note how Dewey uses the language of the law to explain what he means by scientific inquiry.

Postulation today still preserves a certain allegiance to the fundamental divisions of philosophy into rationalism and empiricism. Although it is quite unusual for either school to regard postulation as partaking of "eternal truth," yet it is still possible to see the main lines of rationalism as against empiricism being roughly adhered to. The rationalists today occupy the fields of symbolic logic, foundation mathematics and formal physics. For the empiricists postulates are nothing more than long range hypotheses. Perhaps the nearest to a genuine amalgam of the two "motifs" is the scientific methodology of the Experimentalists, followers of John Dewey and Edgar A. Singer, Jr.[71]

The attempt to introduce the pure postulational method into law never got very far. Wolff's *Jus Naturae*, mentioned above, is about the only classical example of the method known to the author. This work purported actually to be a complete deductive system, with axioms, postulates, and definitions all discovered by the pure light of reason. The theorems of the system, the positive law, were derived by application of syllogistic logic to the self-evidently true postulated principles.

Despite the fact that Wolff's system was unique in its alleged logical rigor and in its comprehensiveness, it was nevertheless just a proto-type for practically all the writers of the rationalistic period of natural law. Jurists in this period used the phraseology of the eternal, the inexorable, and the inevitable. But none of them except Wolff undertook the labor of constructing a rigid deductive system. They merely used its terminology and fell into the habit of announcing that their legal propositions were based on eternally fixed principles of the law of nature.

The influence of the rhetorical device was pervasive. In this country it was very popular until the end of the last century. Chief Justice Marshall was a master of it. Judge Story used it to telling effect. Indeed, Walter Wheeler Cook took great pains in Chapter II of *Logical and Legal Bases of the Conflict of Law* to show how Story offended against modern principles of postulation by calling certain of his own notions in the conflict of laws "axioms," "natural principles," etc. Professor Cook, by taking Story's rhetoric seriously, had no difficulty showing that Story failed to live up to the rigor of a modern deductive system, that his "axioms" were partisan, and his "natural principles" were natural or necessary only on the basis of Story's own biased assumptions. Of course, Professor Cook knew well enough that Story was not attempting to pass off his treatise as a work of strict logical deduction.

Roscoe Pound's postulates for law in a civilized society are familiar.[72] They are empirical generalizations which endeavor to frame the legal demands of civilized society's members against one another. Pound claims nothing more from them. Yet, Professor Stone, in *Province and Function of Law,* notes with astonishment that an idealistic philosopher regarded these postulates as "not only stating the characteristic ideals of American civilization at the time but as having done so *sub specie aeternitatis*."[13] Similar to the above is the call for a general postulate set to express the cultural demands of modern society issued by F. S. C. Northrop in *Logic of the Sciences and the Humanities* (1947).

The postulates set forth in this paper are like Pound's in certain respects only. They are similar in that they are not designed to serve as a presuppositional base for a deductive system. Like his they are *material* postulates, not *formal* ones.

Unlike Pound's postulates, however, which are supposed to sum up in condensed form part of the positive law itself or at least certain of the ideal elements in positive law, the writer's aim is to lay the foundation for a scientific methodology for law. Now "science of law" is only a small part of law. Furthermore, the writer is interested in this article in only a small part of general "science of law," namely experimental legal science.

The law reader will, I am sure, be struck by the fact that although postulate makers try to pretend that no one in his right mind could challenge the validity of their postulates, nevertheless in fact such fundamental statements are highly controversial and argumentative. For instance, when Story calls his fundamental assumptions in the Conflict of Law "axioms," he is arguing, and arguing about controversial matters. By the same token, Walter Wheeler Cook is also arguing when he purports to show up "logical" weaknesses in Story's alleged deductive system.

Still, not even modern postulational sets argue their case *directly*. What they attempt to do is to state as clearly as possible fundamental presuppositions on a speculative area of human thought. Postulates serve to differentiate the basic assumptions of one system from those of its competitors. They let us see where our basic acceptances and rejections tend to lead us; and tell us roughly the cost of our loves and loyalties. In calling for the acceptance of basic prin-

ciples they point out that if these principles are rejected, lesser principles, precepts, trends, biases and
influences must also be surrendered. Therefore,
although the method of postulation is not very familiar to law-trained readers, it should be easy for
them to recognize and uncover its inherent though
disguised argumentative character.

II. *Philosophy and Law*

The writer's philosophical bias in science is Experimentalism. In jurisprudence, then, so far as science of law is concerned, I am an experimentalist. It
is my hope that the present paper will lay the philosophical foundation for legal experimental science.
The procedure in this paper, then, is to set out general postulates for the philosophy of science known
as experimentalism. A brief "argument" will explain
what each postulate entails philosophically. At the
end of each argument a jurisprudential postulate will
be framed corresponding to the philosophical postulate. At the end of the paper the jurisprudential postulates will be gathered up and briefly considered for
their relevance to the experimental science of law.

It will be readily noted that our proposed postulate
sets possess a certain philosophical bias. This is not
only inevitable; it is also desirable. It is the writer's
hope that they will set the stage for the continuation
of sociological jurisprudence which in this country
rests mainly on the philosophical doctrine of pragmatism. Pragmatism, he believes, leads to relativism,
relativism leads to scepticism, and scepticism leads
to frustration. These postulates or "demands" attempt
to take pragmatism safely past the pitfalls of scepticism into the territory of scientific experimentalism
They also aim to avoid the snares of scientism. Perhaps the term scientific humanism best fits the attempt here made. The extent to which the effort is
successful remains to be seen.

III. *The Philosophical Postulate Set*

I. *A mechanical conception of nature is meaning-*

> *less without teleology or purpose; teleology is impotent without mechanism.*
> II. *There are no pure a priori elements in science; neither are there any basic unalterable facts.*
> III. *There is no difference between experience and experiment except degree of precision.*
> IV. *Every experiment involves a question of control.*
> V. *Every question of control involves a moral choice.*

Even a cursory examination of the above postulate set shows that it presupposes the inextricable relatedness of morality and science. Now, to say that morality and science are closely woven together surprises no one trained in the law. But the above postulates set forth a theory of science that appears to go much farther. It is one thing to speak about the relation of law to science, but what about the relation of law to *experimental science?* Does any such relation exist?

Had the question been the broader one, namely, is law related to science in general, a respectable line of authority from Roman times on would have answered with emphasis: Law *is* a science.[74] But inasmuch as the last three centuries have come more and more to regard experiment as an indispensable mark of science, the opinion has grown that neither law nor sociology nor indeed psychology, save in certain inoffensive respects in which it resembles physiology can lay claim to the name science since all of them deal with the subject-matter least adapting itself to the methods of experiment: human conduct.

That human nature is difficult material for the scientist to deal with may be readily admitted. And the difficulty, because of its profoundly important character, finds itself expressed in contrasting philosophical doctrines whose net effect has heretofore been not to solve the problem but to perpetuate it in the form of unshakeable dogmas.

For example, if one should go so far as to insist that only the laboratory sciences and their adjuncts can properly be called science, then it is evident that social psychology, sociology and law have really nothing to do with science. Their subject-matter either cannot or will not be controlled in this sense. On this basis the best claim these disciplines can make to the name science is descriptive science, that is, not science at all but mere taxonomy. The philosophy known as positivism, together with all its modern variants, sums up this methodological creed. The ultimatum that positivism delivers to the social scientist is this: find a way to subject human conduct to laboratory control or its equivalent, and, pending the success of this venture, admit that your activity is not science at all.

Those who take the first part of this ultimatum to be chimerical, that is, those who on faith believe that human conduct can never be scientifically controlled, divide scientific method into two basic parts. For the study of non-human objects they admit that laboratory control or something like it is adequate. For human conduct they insist that laboratory control is simply an irrelevancy. Here they think the proper scientific method is *speculation.* Thus, scientific dualism emerges, based on division of subject-matter and leading to two mutually exclusive scientific methods: experiment and speculation.

Positivists are apt to call such a philosophical attitude *mysticism.* The "mystics" reply that any philosophical position which refuses to see the inherent inadaptability of human behavior to laboratory control (because of the free, moral or teleological character of human action) is philosophical mechanism or determinism. As such, on the subject of human nature it is simply vacuous because it fails to concern itself with what is the distinctive mark of human behavior: its freedom.

These are ancient and well-known issues, worn bare by more than two millenia of philosophical controversy. But although the dispute is over two thousand years old, there is no good reason why it should be allowed to grow still older. Against the mystics let it be firmly insisted that scientific method is one, namely experiement, with speculation an adjunct and not an independent method. Against the positivists let it be resolved that the whole meaning of experiment must be renovated and enlarged to encompass free purposeful human conduct.[75]

These resolutions set the stage for the basic problem of all who are interested in making a science of the study of human conduct. The problem can best be stated in the form of a short question: How is social experiment possible? Otherwise put, the question is: How is "control" possible in the study of human conduct? For without "control," social science can at best be descriptive. But with control of the laboratory variety, the subject-matter immediately loses its distinctive character, its freedom.

How then is it possible to obtain scientific control of human behavior without destroying its freedom in the process? At precisely this point jurisprudence enters with the reflection that legal philosophy has always taken its central task to be the matter of "controlling" human behavior consistently with freedom. Whether you think well or ill of the law and its processes, it alone has a vast experience in "controlling" human beings in ways that social science can use, i.e., by secular political power. Unlike the Church, law coerces the body; unlike the military, it coerces men to peace-ways in accordance with the culture's notions of freedom.

Partial insights of nineteenth-century positivism led many Anglo-American jurists to assert that the essence of law is force. No one, I suppose, can hold this opinion today without most serious qualification. To characterize law in terms of what theoretically happens when it is flouted is as bad as to describe human life in terms only of its pathology. Law is not force, as the hand is not a fist. Still, law does mean what it says. It insists that it be obeyed. Shall we go far wrong if we say that the law *controls* a large part of human behavior? Is not "control" the term we are after? Especially if we keep in mind that the most effective means of controlling human behavior may be to accord it a maximum degree of freedom. If we say that law controls human behavior best by exerting a minimum of force we will not be far wrong. To paraphrase Jefferson, "that government is best which coerces least." And in order *not* to coerce human behavior and to let people freely manage their complicated affairs in modern society law may well have to grow to a vast enterprise.

This has its direct analogue in modern scientific methodology. Scientific control is not force, certainly not brute force. Control in science is essentially flexible. The scientist varies his controls with the purpose of his investigations. Legal control on the other hand seems to many to connote "inexorable" imputation. Force (a physical concept), it is claimed, and not experimental control is the scientific analogy to legal control. Unquestioning obedience to an unaccountable sovereign will on the one hand, or undeviating compliance with the dictates of a law of nature or of God on the other is thought to be the "sovereign" mark of law. How then can one reasonably use the term legal control as analogous to experimental control?

The theoretical answer to this objection could be framed as follows: to anyone who objects to a teleological or purposeful conception of the nature of law, legal control is and must be force and nothing more. The model is the physical laws of nature whose operation is "inexorable" or "immutable," terms themselves borrowed from the vocabulary of jurisprudence. But if law should be recognized as a *means* of social control, not as an end in itself, then the control it exercises would be governed by the ends law takes to be worth pursuit. And as means law is and throughout its history in fact has been flexible. Each element of flexibility in law (equity;[76] individualization, discretion, delegation) makes legal control in an important way analogous to scientific control. And as a practical matter, "discretion" is precisely the generic term for the right (and the duty) of the law enforcer to "experiment" as best he can that the ends law serves and not the means prevail. If we bear in mind problems raised by the massive economic structures our culture has reared to effectuate its purposes, can we say that there is at present any system of control of human behavior consistent with freedom conceivable save through law? Not law as we now know it, to be sure. For many radical improvements in our present legal systems are not only conceivable but obviously long overdue. Still, however much improved, the system of compulsory control of human behavior must remain law. *For law is now the predominant moral means by which human beings may force one another to act in a given way.* Hence, if the social scientist disregards law in his search for scientific control, he runs the risk of confining himself either to mere description, to chance uniformities in human behavior, or to those systems of human control of extralegal character which modern culture has relegated to the ranks of the relatively trivial. The conclusion is that the social scientist is forced to go to the jurisprudent, and the jurisprudent is forced to seek out and accept the social scientist if either is to fulfill his present-day function. It remains to show how a philosophy of experimental science may serve as a foundation for this necessary rapport.

We turn then to a brief consideration of each of the philosophical postulates set forth above. It must be borne in mind that the postulational method of "argumentation" states its conclusions very boldly at the outset; attempts to enlist sympathy and support on the basis of such forthright statement; and leaves to loyal supporters the task of devising ways and means of implementing the principles. As such, it is the reverse of the method which purports to set out first to gather evidence impartially; and then to arrive at its conclusions (often reluctantly if one can believe its adherents) only because the "objective" facts, events, data permit no other outcome.

Philosophical Postulate I. *A mechanical conception of nature is meaningless without teleology or purpose: teleology is impotent without mechanism.*

The control of nature (including human nature) is here taken to be the sum of all human aspirations. Mechanism, or the insistence on the recognition that inexorable rule or uniformity operate without regard to human will, is the principle of coercion. There is

some evidence that historically philosophical mechanism arose out of law, that is, out of the legal demand
that justice be impartial.[77] The laws of nature are to
be relied upon to exact retribution regardless of the
all-too-human propensity to leave the scales unbal-
anced. Projecting the power and the duty to exact
retribution to non-human deities or to the impersonal
order of nature is taken to guarantee even-handed
justice. The unexceptionable character of mechanical
law introduces order and certainty into the course of
nature and into human affairs, it is felt.

Teleology on the other hand represents the demand
that nature conform to human purpose. Without
teleology, humanity becomes the victim of its own
creature, mechanical law, which is then conceived of
as subordinating mankind to its "dominant purpose,"
inescapable uniformity. Thus man's primary device
for controlling nature ends by controlling him. The
way out of this dilemma is to recognize that "mechanical necessity" is a human invention and that human
purpose is primary. At this point it is well to remember that while "mechanical necessity" is a human
product, nature is not man's creation. The world is
not the free product of human imagination. The task
of philosophy is to make mechanism and teleology,
the two necessary conditions for the control of nature,
consistent with each other.[78]

Turning to law, we note at once that the history
of law does not lack systems based on pure mechanism whether physical or biological. The theme of
inexorable necessity is generally taken up in law in
the form of the conviction that the "sovereign" will
must be obeyed regardless of its effect, that is, no
matter what its results or as we might say without
respect to its "real" purpose. This notion is of course
one of the main tenets of analytical jurisprudence.
Historical accident assigned to the British Parliament
the role of the completely unaccountable sovereign.
In competition with the claims of the executive to unaccountability as a divine right, Parliament was able
to get accepted for itself the power of plenary unaccountability *under law*. The law proved to be a

powerful ally. And the unspoken compact between court and legislature was never broken. The Judicial Committee of the House of Lords does not find it necessary to invalidate the legislation of the whole Parliament of which it is a part. Conversely, the parent body has always been careful not to make things too uncomfortable for the Law Lords: a neat arrangement for perpetuating "sovereign" power.

For the purposes of analytical jurisprudence with its mechanistic conception of the nature of political power, the sovereign may be an individual divinely appointed or one freely or irrevocably chosen by its subjects. Or the sovereign may be the whole people binding itself by commands directed against itself. Whatever form the sovereign takes, it is recognized that its commands must be obeyed "mechanically." That is, it is regarded as a contradiction in terms to imagine a law-giver whose pronouncements may be examined in the light of the purposes of those to whom the commands are directed. Legal mechanism imagines the existence of a supra-individual entity which somehow or other has acquired the right and power to coerce unchallengeably the conduct of the individuals which compose it.

Teleology in law does challenge sovereignty's title to unaccountability. It insists that sovereignty state its "purposes" and justify them. It forces distinctions among these uncovered sovereign purposes. We can think of a theory of interests, such as Pound's, emerging at this point and precipitating out individual, social and public interests. The problem of legal teleology stated in its broadest term is the problem of freedom. The task of legal philosophy is to make the legal mechanism (order) consistent with freedom. The ideals of order and freedom are encompassed in the term justice.

By the first part of Postulate I, namely that mechanism by itself is meaningless, experimental philosophy announces a principled objection to all mechanical systems of jurisprudence.

The motifs of mechanism may run through the whole law, not merely in the conception of sovereign power. Particularly has its influence been felt in the theory of judicial decision. The notion that the judge is a "logic machine" whose task is the mechanical comparison of the facts of a given case with the principles of law set by legislation or custom, that the judge in other words, does not make but merely interprets the law has had a profound effect on the theory of judicial administration. It has been thought necessary to suppress or to deny outright the creative aspects of adjudication. Yet, to deny that judges make law is as unrealistic as to deny that the sculptor makes a statue because he does not create the marble upon which he works.

Another aspect of mechanical jurisprudence is the process known as the "jurisprudence of conceptions." Here the assumption is that a jural conception retains its content unaltered no matter what context it enters into. The substance-procedure dichotomy is a familiar example. We have seen what Walter Wheeler Cook was able to do with the analysis of this conception in chapter VI of *The Logical and Legal Bases of the Conflict of Laws.* Although the jurisprudence of conceptions has been under merciless attack from continental writers for three-quarters of a century, and from Pound and most notably the "realists" in this country, it is too much to say that it is altogether dead. In fact, a revival of the jurisprudence of conceptions took place in Conflict of Laws. This is the doctrine of characterization, which follows the traditional practice of conceptualism by assuming that the decision in choice of law is mechanically determined by the process of conceptualizing or characterizing the fact situation in the domestic law. Indeed, the characterizers go further. They make the explicit assumption, nowhere justified on juristic grounds, *that characterization must precede choice of law.* The conception is primary to and determines the decision of choice of law.

Therefore the first part of Postulate I condemns mechanical jurisprudence because it ignores the purposes law is designed to achieve. But it must be remembered that this condemnation does not throw out the good in a mechanistic philosophy. In fact, such philosophy states certain of the indispensable aspects of every system of law, namely, order, uniformity, and certainty. Mechanical jurisprudence claims that these principles are a *sufficient* basis for a complete system of law. We claim that they are merely a *necessary* part of it.

By the second part of Postulate I, namely that teleology alone is helpless, this system of philosophy states its opposition to non-principled demands for individualization, free law, Kadi justice, absolute discretion, the unique case and the like. It admits, however, that the call for freedom wherever it may arise is not to be disregarded with safety.

The realist's preoccupation with the "unique case" illustrates the difficulty of insisting that the purpose of every legal event be considered to the exclusion of its proper place in an orderly system of legal relations. The term "unique case" is itself paradoxical. For if a case is truly unique, no one can say what it is a "case of."

On the other hand, legal teleologists have done an inestimable service for modern law by breaking up the rigid assumptions of mechanical jurisprudence. Hence, legal teleology while not a *sufficient* basis for modern jurisprudence, is quite obviously a *necessary* part of it.

The first philosophical postulate can therefore be restated in the following jurisprudential terms:

Jurisprudential Postulate I. *The mechanical aspects of a legal system are empty until given concrete meaning by legal purposes; the purposes or ends of law are helpless without form, order, legal mechanism.*

Philosophical Postulate II. *There are no pure a priori elements in science; neither are there any basic unalterable facts.*

This postulate sums up the modern relativistic temper. In the history of philosophy the search for fixed unalterable starting points represents the attempt to place science on firm foundations. The endeavor was based on the conviction that science must start with some sort of unchallengeable and unalterable truth. Prior to the nineteenth century there was fundamental agreement on this point, the schools differing in the main only as to which of two forms this fixed fundamental sort of truth could take: (1) General truths of reason unmixed with experience (rationalism); or (2) some form of experience, in its origin independent of any mental element of the knower (empiricism). Kant combined the two as simultaneous constituents of all knowledge, independent of each other in some sense yet sources of certainty.

The nineteenth century made serious inroads on the doctrine that at least some of the elements of knowledge are fixed and certain and thus necessary starting points for science. Twentieth-century pragmatism completed the assault. For pragmatism, the unshakeable certainties of one person or one era become the acute points of doubt for other people and other times. The very search for certainty is regarded as neurotic.

Everyone of pragmatic or relativistic bent is in agreement that Kant's search for pure a priori elements of knowledge was bound to fail. But the attempt yielded modern postulational systems in place of the pure a priori. The same people are convinced that nothing compels the scientist to start with unchallengeable sensation, hard fact, unalterable event, or unique case. Facts are mere data, raw rata at that, and uninterpretable except in the light of basic assumptions (the old a priori) which give them meaning.

The affirmative side of this postulate can be stated as follows: Every scientific investigation requires presuppositions to serve as a suitable frame-work upon which to fit data, fact, case, event.

As applied to jurisprudence, the first part of this postulate leads us to reject all theories of "pure" law, and all norms taken to be fundamental in an absolute sense regardless of experience. Conversely, the second part of the postulate rejects empiricism's attempt to settle law on the sole basis of the decided case, the enacted law, the issued order or decree.

These legal "facts" are no more fundamental than "legal laws." It is a matter of the purposes of the investigator whether he concentrates his attention on the case, event, fact side of law or conversely on the principle, rule, axiom, postulate side. American jurists show a decided preference for the empirical elements of the law and therein undoubtedly lies our strength. But it accounts equally for our weakness in international and comparative law, conflict of laws, codification, legal philosophy and such like activities.

In short, neither legal theory nor legal practice is possible without the other. Neither is paramount. Each is an indispensable element in legal knowledge. Just where to place the emphasis, bias or preference is a matter of choice.

Hence we can frame the second postulate in the following jurisprudential terms:

Jurisprudential Postulate II. *There are no pure a priori elements in legal science; neither are there any basic unalterable legal facts.*

*   *   *   *   *

Postulates for Experimental Jurisprudence

   I. *The mechanical aspects of a legal system are meaningless without purpose; the purposes or ends of law are impotent without form, order, rule, mechanisms.*

  II. *There are no pure a priori elements in legal science; neither are there any basic unalterable legal facts.*

 III. *The science which law uses must be based on experience and experience must ultimately rest upon experiment.*

 IV. *Every social experiment involves ultimately a question of legal control.*

  V. *Every question of legal control involves a moral choice.*

The aim of the foregoing jurisprudential postulate set is to state part of a creed for scientific humanism in the law. The set shows first and above all that the term science which in recent years seems to have become the private property of certain investigators into the physical processes of nature must regain its ancient freedom. Science is as broad as the "knowing" part of human experience. Science is knowledge. The methods of the physical scientist will simply not do to handle the most pressing problems confronting the race: human behavior. Hence the methods of science must be renovated and enlarged. The temptation to retreat to irrationalism in human affairs must be resisted. Experience here, as in the handling of non-human nature, is our sure guide. And experience must be made more and more precise so that that which adequately will serve to describe the process is *experiment.* Experiment presupposes control if the social scientist is to be something more than a mere observer of chance patterns of human behavior. And control in social science means law since law is the name for the conscious effort of the race to *coerce* human behavior consistently with freedom.

FOOTNOTES TO SECTION III-B

1. Berolzheimer, System der Rechts und Wirthschaftsphilosophie, II, 385-386; Charmont, La renaissance du droit naturel, 122-127.
2. Del Vecchio, I presupposti filosofici della nozione del diritto, 86-93.
3. Pound, "Administrative Application of Legal Standards," Proceedings American Bar Association 1919, pp. 441, 449.
4. *Ibid.,* p. 451; *cf.* Pound, "Mechanical Jurisprudence," 8 *Columbia L. R.* 603.
5. "Sociological Method," transl., 9 Modern Legal Philosophy Series, p. 131.
6. Gmelin, *supra; cf.* Ehrlich, "Die juristische Logik," p. 187; Duguit, "Les Transformations du droit depuis le Code Napoléon," transl., Continental Legal Hist. Series, vol. XI, pp. 72, 79.
7. *Op. cit.,* vol. II, p. 92, sec. 159.
8. Vol. II, p. 91.
9. Pound, "Juristic Science and The Law," 31 *Harvard L. R.* 1047, 1048.
10. *Cf.* Duguit, *supra.*
11. Haines, "The Law of Nature in Federal Decisions," 25 *Yale L. J.* 617.
12. Hough, "Due Process of Law Today," 32 *Harvard L. R.* 218, 227.

13. *Cf.* Hough p. 232; also Frankfurter, "Const. Opinions of Holmes, J.," 29 *Harvard L. R.* 683, 687; Ehrlich, "Die juristische Logik," pp. 237, 239.

14. 198 U. S. 75.

15. P. 75.

16. P. 76.

17. Noble v. State Bank, 219 U. S. 104; Tanner v. Little, 240 U. S. 369; Hall v. Geiger Jones Co., 242 U. S. 539; Green v. Frazier, 253 U. S. 233; Frankfurter, *supra.*

18. Burgess, "Reconciliation of Government and Liberty."

19. Adams v. Tanner, 244 U. S. 590.

20. People v. Williams, 189 N. Y. 131.

21. People v. Schweinler Press, 214 N. Y. 395.

22. Muller v. Oregon, 208 U. S. 412; Pound, "Courts and Legislation," 9 Modern Legal Philosophy Series, p. 225; Pound, "Scope and Progress of Sociological Jurisprudence," 25 *Harvard L. R.* 513; cf. Brandeis, J., in Adams v. Tanner, 244 U. S. 590, 600.

23. U. S. Const., 14th Amendment.

24. Holmes, J., dissenting in Coppage v. Kansas, 236 U. S. 1, 27.

25. Montpellier, Coulet et fils, éditeurs, 1910.

26. "There is now a tendency to consider no contract worthy of respect unless the parties to it are in relations, not only of liberty, but of equality. If one of the parties be without defense or resources, compelled to comply with the demands of the other, the result is a suppression of true freedom."—Charmont, *supra*, p. 172; transl. in 7 Modern Legal Philosophy Series, p. 110, sec. 83.

27. Klein v. Maravelas, 219 N. Y. 383, 386.

28. *Cf.* Frankfurter, *supra;* McCulloch v. Maryland, 4 Wheat. 407.

29. Munroe Smith, "Jurisprudence," pp. 29, 30; *cf.* Vander Eycken, *supra*, pp. 383, 384; also Brütt, *supra*, p. 62.

30. Kohler. "Interpretation of Law," transl. in 9 Modern Legal Philosophy Series, 192; *cf.* the Report of Prof. Huber on the German Code, quoted by Gény, "Technic of Codes," 9 Modern Legal Philosophy Series, p. 548; also Gény, "Méthode et Sources en droit privé positif," vol. I, p. 273.

31. Munroe Smith, *supra.*

32. *Cf.* Eubank, *Concepts of Sociology* (1932) 220.

33. *Les Formes élémentaires de la vie religieuse* (1912) 593.

33a. *Crime and Custom in Savage Society* (1926) 58; *idem,* Introduction to Hogrin, *Law and Order in Pelynesia* (1934).

33b. *De Officiis,* i. 41.

33c. *Sociology of Law* (1936) 24, 169.

34. Pound, Outlines of Lectures on Jurisprudence (5th ed., 1943) 96 (cited below as "Outlines"). For a longer commentary, see Patterson, "Pound's Theory of Social Interests," in Interpretations of Modern Legal Philosophies (1947), 598.

35. Letter of Pound to Holmes, Feb. 22, 1913, in Sayre, The Life of Roscoe Pound (1948) 270.

36. Pound, "A Theory of Social Interests," (1921) 15 Proc. Amer. Sociological Soc. 16; Hall, pp. 238-246. However, the survey of interests appeared in the 1914 edition of his Outlines of Lectures in Jurisprudence (2d ed.) 56-59.

37. "A Survey of Social Interests," (1943) 57 Harv. L. Rev. 1-39 (cited below as "Survey" with page number).

38. See letter, *supra*, n. 35.

39. Dewey, Human Nature and Conduct (1922), esp. Pt. II, secs. V, VI, where he cogently argues that there are no separate instincts.

40. Hall, p. 243; 57 Harv. L. Rev. 13.

41. An Introduction to the Principles of Morals and Legislation (Oxford, 1892), 3. A thing promotes the individual's interest when it increases his happiness. *Ibid.* But James used it in a broader sense. *Supra*, §4.41, n. 20. "Value" has been defined as "the object of any interest." Perry, General Theory of Value (1926), c. V.

42. 57 Harv. L. Rev. 1.

43. Holmes, "The Path of the Law," in Collected Legal Papers (1920), 168.

44. Similarly, Bentham had to extend his simple conception of pain and pleasure to include potential and remote pains and pleasures. *Supra*, §§4.41, 4.42.

45. Dewey, Problems of Men (1946), 278-279 (first published 1944).

46. *I.e.*, not against anyone before the thief has gained possession.

47. "Interests of Personality," (1915) 28 Harv. L. Rev. 343; "Equitable Relief against Defamation and Injuries to Personality," (1916) 29 Harv. L. Rev. 640; "Individual Interests in the Domestic Relations," (1916) 14 Mich. L. Rev. 177.

48. "Individual Interests of Substance—Promised Advantages," (1945) 59 Harv. L. Rev. 1.

49. 57 Harv. L. Rev. 1.

50. Which referred to property open to use by people generally, such as roads, bridges and rivers. Ihering, The Law as a Means to an End (Husik trans., 1914), 348-9.

51. 57 Harv. L. Rev. 3.

52. Pound's examples include the dissent by McKenna, J., from a decision upholding the constitutional validity of an Arizona statute making an employer liable without fault for injuries to his employees in their employment. McKenna, J., viewed the decision with alarm as a menace to all rights, "subjecting them unreservedly to conceptions of public policy." Arizona Employers' Liability Cases, 250 U. S. 400, 439, 39 Sup. Ct. 553, 562, 563 (1919), 57 Harv. L. Rev. 2.

53. Taylor v. Georgia, 315 U. S. 25, 62 Sup. Ct. 415 (1942).

54. Outlines, 104-111; 57 Harv. L. Rev. 14 ff.

FOOTNOTES TO SECTION III-C

1. Jerome Frank refused me permission to sign his name as joint author to this paper, on the ground that it was my fist which pushed the pen. But his generosity does not alter the fact that the paper could not have been written without his help. I therefore write the first sections, in partial recognition, as "We," meaning thereby Frank and myself. In the description of the realists, I turn to the first person singular, partly because any alignment of such diverse work is individually colored; partly because any phrasing which would seem to suggest a non-existent school would be unfortunate.

2. Both Adler (*Law and the Modern Mind—Legal Certainty* (1931) 31 Col. L. Rev. 91) and Cohen (*Justice Holmes and the Nature of Law* (1931) 31 *id*. 352) have discussed "realism" adversely, Cohen addressing himself especially to Frank, Moore (uncited specifically), Bingham, and Oliphant; Adler to the same (except Moore), especially Frank, and to Cook, Yntema, and Green (all uncited) as well. Dickinson, *Legal Rules: Their Function in the Process of Decision* (1931) 79 U. of Pa. L. Rev. 833, bases his criticisms (especially of Cook, Frank, Llewellyn) largely on specific citations. Radin and Yntema publish admirable papers on the matter with which I concur almost *in toto*. Radin, *Legal Realism* (1931) 31 Col. L. Rev. 824; Yntema, *The Rational Basis of Legal Science* (1931) 31 *id*. 925. Citations of realists are lacking in their papers also: they speak not of or for a school, but for themselves. So far as the present paper purports to be descriptive, it sins in non-citation. (As did my controversial paper, *supra* note 18, in non-specificity as to where the views criticized might be found. *Mea maxima culpa!* and may whoever feels that he was caricatured forgive me. Preparing the present discussion has shown me that error of my ways.) I had hoped in this part to build a fair bibliography of the literature but time has not served. Felix Cohen has been kind enough to aid me in this and I include his references, marked "(C)."

3. Names for them vary. I call them realists (so do Frank, Radin, and often, Yntema; Bingham also recognizes the term. And I find it used in the same sense in the work of Cook, Douglas, Frankfurter)—stressing the interest in the actuality of what happens, and the distrust of formula. Cook prefers to speak of scientific approach to law, Oliphant of objective method—stressing much the same features. Clark speaks of fact-research, Corbin of what courts do. "Functional approach" stresses the interest in, and valuation by, effects. Dickinson speaks of the skeptical movement.

4. As to each of the following points I have attempted to check over not only the general tone of work but several specific writings of the twenty men named and a number of others—*e.g.*, Kidd, Maggs, Breckenridge, Morse, Durfee, Bohlen, Bryant, Smith and Goble—and to make sure that each point

was applicable to each. Errors may have crept in. Note how closely the description fits Holmes' work as early as 1871-72: "It commands the future, a valid but imperfectly realized ideal."

On the common points of departure see especially Corbin, *The Law and the Judges*, 3 Yale L. R. 234; Llewellyn, Cases and Materials on the Law of Sales, Introd., Oliphant, *A Return to Stare Decisis*, 14 A.B.A.J. 71, 159; Patterson, *Can Law Be Scientific?* 25 Ill. L. R. 121; all cited in Appendix I. See also Arnold, *Criminal Attempts—The Rise and Fall of an Abstraction* (1930) 40 Yale L. J. 53; Arnold, *The Restatement of the Law of Trusts* (1931) 31 Col. L. Rev. 800; Clark, Douglas and Thomas, *The Business Failures Project—A Problem in Methodology* (1930) 39 Yale L. J. 1013; Douglas and Thomas, *The Business Failures Project—II. An Analysis of Methods of Investigation* (1931) 40 *id.* 1034; Burch, *The Paradoxes of Legal Science: A Review* (1929) 27 Mich. L. Rv. 637; Radin, *The Permanent Problems of the Law* (1929) 15 Corn. L. Q. 1; Yntema and Jaffin, Preliminary Analysis of Concurrent Jurisdiction (1931) 79 U. of Pa. L. R. 869; Yntema, *supra* note 2. And see (C) Isaacs, *How Lawyers Think* (1923) 23 Col. L. Rev. 555; Laski, *Judicial Review of Social Policy in England* (1926) 39 Harv. L. Rev. 832.

On checking rules descriptive against the facts of the decisions, see especially Corbin, Douglas, Klaus, Tulin, *infra*, Appendix I; (C) Finkelstein, *Judicial Self-Limitation* (1924) 37 Harv. L. Rev. 338; Finkelstein, *Further Notes on Self-Limitation* (1925) 39 *id.* 221; Isaacs' more recent work in general, but especially *The Promoter: A Legislative Problem* (1925) 38 *id.* 887; Brown, *Due Process of Law, Police Power, and the Supreme Court* (1927) 40 *id.* 943; Hamilton, *Affectation with a Public Interest* (1930) 39 Yale L. J. 1089.

5. See note 6 of my article, *The Implications of Legal Science* (1933) 10 N. Y. U. L. Q. R. 279, 282.

6. This hypothesis will be found expounded, *more magistrali*, in the article by Professor Morris R. Cohen, *Justice Holmes and the Nature of Law* (1931) 31 Columbia Law Rev. 352, 357 ff. See the comment by the present writer in *The Rational Basis of Legal Science, id.* 925, 934 ff., and the response by Professor Cohen in an illuminating article, *Philosophy and Legal Science* (1932) 32 *id.* 1103 ff. [Both of Professor Cohen's articles are reprinted in Law and the Social Order, Essays in Legal Philosophy (1933).]

In a footnote, it is inappropriate and for present purposes, it seems unnecessary, to reopen this discussion, particularly since it seems to have resulted in a clarification of the main issue with which the writer was and is here concerned,—namely, the importance of detailed research as to the operation of law, the validity of which was definitely questioned in the article first cited above. From this point of view, Professor Cohen's more recent comments are more sympathetic, *viz.*: "Some of the 'empirical' or 'realistic' investigations in the field of law may succeed in bringing fruitful results. I ardently hope that they will. But a hopeful program does not justify arrogance or intolerance toward those who are not convinced of its perfect sufficiency. My own program may be a puny one but it has a right to live." *Id.*, 1118.

It would be perhaps a trifle captious to suggest that "the right" of programs to live, asserted in the last sentence, needs to be squared with the remark at page 1105 of the same article: "The untenable assumption remains untenable no matter what the profession of the one who makes it." Apart from this, the statement of mutual tolerance, which presumably cuts both ways, is one which will command general assent. The statement generously concedes as much as can be reasonably asked for a projected type of scientific investigation, empirical or theoretical,—the possibility of useful results.

It also deserves remark, that, on the corresponding question of the significance of theoretical speculation, the difference is far less than appears on the surface of the discussion. Fundamentally, what Professor Cohen and others of his school of thought have recently been urging is the extremely important consideration that an emphasis upon detailed specialization in legal research needs to be paralleled by emphasis upon theoretical and historical analysis. As the writer has been at pains to point out on various occasions, each is needed to supplement the other; both form essential parts of any scheme of legal science.

There remains only a theoretical issue, having indubitable practical implications, as to the relation between speculation and empirical research. In general the metaphysical division of knowledge into separate realms of existence, implicitly raising the spiritual over the physical, tends to drive a wedge between speculation and practical knowledge and, unless carefully explained, to seem to validate so-called pure theory by depreciating its specific application. In an applied science, such as law, this tendency appears to the writer at once illusory and unfortunate. It is not only inevitable, but it is desirable in the interests of sound legal scholarship that the various branches of scientific legal study should be explicitly related, while the question of priority between them is like determining the pre-existence of the egg or the chicken. In sum, the choice is between what the writer cannot but regard as an illogical distinction of ideas and facts relating to law and what Professor Cohen has appropriately termed their "logical confusion."

Discussion of this interesting and important, though from the present point of view incidental, problem and, more particularly, of what may be intended by the "normative" nature of law, must be postponed to some other occasion. Meanwhile, the central issues as to the desirability of proceeding with various types of legal study have presumably been suggested. In view of this, it seems the more reasonable to waive the question of metaphysical technique for the time being, in the hope that perhaps a *modus vivendi in mundo spirituali* may occur.

In the last analysis, the points of agreement are more important than those of difference.

7. "Gedanken ohne Inhalt sind leer, Anschauungen ohne Begriffe sind blind." Kritik der reinen Vernunft, 77. (Kehrbach.)

Incidentally, it may be noticed that Professor Cohen's paraphrase of the apothegm, as "Rules without cases are empty and cases without rules are blind," *supra* note 5, at 1110, diverts somewhat from the meaning of the original.

See the references cited *supra* note 5.

8. The commission has made a preliminary report, which has been published as Legislative Document (1932) no. 92. While this article has been going through the press, the commission has published its final report as Legislative Document (1934) no. 50, advocating a judicial council with investigative and advisory powers as to the administration of justice, and also a law revision commission to study "the amendment and correction" of the law not relating to judicial administration. It may be questioned whether the proposed division and limitation of functions contemplates an effective official organ for the improvement of the legal system.

9. Needless to add, what has been suggested with respect to New York City will apply, *mutatis mutandis,* to other large urban centers in this country.

10. 12 American Bar Association Journal, 153.

11. Pound's other writings indicate that he would admit as much. The explanation quoted in the text is perhaps what Llewellyn calls one of Pound's "bed-time stories for the tired bar."

12. Napoleon later modified these views somewhat; see below, Part One, Chapter VII.

13. Frederick Soddy, one of the world's great physicists, winner of the Nobel prize in 1921, views lawyers as "charlatans" who deal in legal necromancy and who aim to preserve legal secrets and "mystify the public" when they should make law "intelligible and predictable." "A clergyman or statesman or doctor are, as such, useful men," said the Marquis of Salisbury. "These professions do good. But the barrister is at best but a tolerated evil. He derives his living from the fact that law is unintelligible."

William Durran has recently written a book, "Bench and Bar," devoted entirely to portraying "the conflict of attitude between barrister and layman." The layman, he finds, "dreads uncertainty in law," whereas the lawyer "naturally loves opportunities for expatiating on the largest possible number of points. . . . It is not the certainty of the law but the uncertainty that pays the lawyer. . . . The multiplication of uncertainties, of lawlessness, and of advocates' incomes keep pace with each other. . . . A gross deception is being practiced upon the man in the street. Nor is it for his good; it is for the good of the profession of lawyers which admittedly prospers by piling one uncertainty on another. . . . A vested inter-

est, far and away the greatest trade union in the world, will
fight resolutely and with all the resources of wealth and
sophistry in support of guess-work in law. . . . [There is]
confusion and uncertainty in the legal standards deliberately
engineered and increased by the Bar." Durran writes of "the
common law with its evil train of uncertainties . . . uncertainties which pay the lawyer" and sees little likelihood that
"those who derive their income from the fact that law is
unintelligible will . . . be overcome by a desire to make it
intelligible, accessible and inexpensive."

14. Unheeded by most members of the Bar, a minority
group of brilliant critics of our legal system have demonstrated
that anything like complete legal certainty cannot be realized.
They have made clear that, in the very nature of things, not
nearly as much rigidity in law exists or can be procured as
laymen or most lawyers suppose. The law, they point out,
can make only relative and temporary compromises between
stability and indispensable adjustment to the constantly shifting
factors of social life. "All thinking about law has struggled
to reconcile the conflicting demands of the need of stability
and the need of change." And this struggle has been incessant.
Law, in attempting a harmony of these conflicting demands,
is at best governed by "the logic of probabilities." This point
the reader will find expounded by such writers as Maine,
Holmes, Pound, Cohen, Cardozo, Cook, Demogue, Gény,
Gmelin, Gray, Green, Coudert, Bingham, Yntema, Hutcheson,
Radin, Llewellyn and Lehman.

Evidence of the uncertain character of the law will appear
in the following chapters.

15. No approbation of *mere change* is intended; see pp.
250-252.

16. See Appendix III on "Science and Certainty: an Unscientific Use of Science."

17. Barry, "The Scientific Habit of Thought," 138; Whitehead, "Science and the Modern World," 166; Whyte, "Archi-
medes or The Future of Physics," 30-39; Burtt, "The Metaphysical Foundations of Physics"; Eddington, "Space, Time
and Gravitation," 198, 201, and "The Nature of the Physical
World"; Bridgman, "The Logic of Modern Physics"; Rueff,
"From the Physical to the Social Sciences"; Morris Cohen,
"The Social Sciences and the Natural Sciences," in "The Social
Sciences and Their Interrelations," 437.

See Bridgman, "The New Vision of Science," Harper's Magazine, March, 1929, 443, for a statement of Heisenberg's "Principle of Uncertainty," the essence of which is "that there are
certain inherent limitations to the accuracy with which a physical situation can be described," and that the ultimate possibility of exactness of measurements in physics is forever limited. See Eddington's account of the "Principle of Indeterminacy," in "The Nature of the Physical World," 306.

The postulate of complete ultimate scientific certainty may

still be useful if accepted on a purely fictional basis. See Appendix III, on "An Unscientific Use of Science."

18. In this country, in upper courts alone, approximately five hundred cases are decided each week, of which presumably one-half turn primarily on disputed "law points." If lower court cases are also considered, the number of weekly decisions of this type may safely be numbered in the thousands.

That questions of law and questions of fact are not really separable in many cases, see below, Part One, Chapters XII, XIII and XIV.

19. Except, that is, an astonishingly small minority who have heeded the critical writings noted above. The great majority of lawyers ignore these writings and accept views such as those expressed by Professor Beale that "Wherever there is a political society, there must be a complete body of law, which shall cover every event there happening."

Of course, even among the majority, there are varying degrees of awareness of the inherent uncertainty of law. Indeed, any one lawyer may vary from time to time in his apprehension of this truth.

20. Abbott, "Justice and the Modern Law."

21. See below, Part Two, Chapter III, for a discussion of these types of security.

22. At the very moment when they are doing their best work, when they are engaged in the indispensable task of skillfully renovating the law and adjusting it to meet new problems, the men of law seem to the public, and often to themselves, to be desecrating the ideals to which they have vowed allegiance. Inevitably, as a result, lawyers are attacked as incompetent or dishonest. Inevitably, too, the lawyers are baffled by their own apparently dual and inconsistent obligations. See further on this point, Part One, Chapter III.

23. "Methods of Juridical Thinking," printed as Chapter X of "The Science of Legal Method." Although the writer here and later criticizes Wurzel, he must acknowledge his immense debt to Wurzel's stimulating way of formulating many of the problems discussed in this book and particularly those considered in Chapters I and III.

24. For the writer's indebtedness to Wurzel, see pages 229 and 326.

25. There is no denying that, in part, the demand for exactly predictable law arises from practical needs, has its roots in reality. But the practical aspect of the demand is usually exaggerated. (See below, Part One, Chapter III.) Moreover, it often happens that the same man who today wants law to be inflexible, tomorrow wants it pliable; yet, significantly, when he comes to articulate his notion of desirable law he usually remembers only his demand for legal fixity and forgets the occasions when his practical aims were best served by fluid law. (See below, page 223.)

Finally, it must not be overlooked that although a demand

arises from practical needs, it may yet be incapable of satisfaction; such a demand any man, so far as he is objective-minded, therefore abandons. Jones may be in Tokio at the very moment when his practical needs require him to be physically present in New York. A wishing-rug would be handy. But although practical needs prompt his desire for instantaneous transportation across the globe, it can scarcely be said that, if Jones insists upon procuring his wishing-rug, his demand is therefore practical in its nature. (See below, Part One, Chapter XIV and page 361.)

26. This myth is an old one, although its form and expression have often changed. See pages 264-265 and 290-293.

27. See Llewellyn, *A Realistic Jurisprudence—the Next Step* (1930) 30 Columbia Law Review 431 and *Some Realism about Realism—Responding to Dean Pound* (1931) 44 Harvard Law Review 1222; Patterson, *Pragmatism as a Philosophy of Law* in The Philosopher of the Common Man (1940) 172-204; Cohen, *Transcendental Nonsense and the Functional Approach* (1935) 35 Columbia Law Review 809 and *Problems of Functional Jurisprudence* (1937) 1 Modern Law Review 15; Frank, *Realism in Jurisprudence* (1934) 7 American Law School Review 1057. These are probably the best statements of this interest of realism. See the Selective Bibliography for others.

28. The common center of contemporary American realistic jurisprudence is found in its critical temper and method. As in any movement, the emphasis of the realists is not entirely homogeneous, yet the variations are not of such a nature as to exclude a basic identity of interest. Llewellyn, *Some Realism about Realism* (1931) 44 Harvard Law Review 1222, surveys the different emphases to be found among realists, together with their common basis. The common grounds which Llewellyn emphasizes are: (1) a common point of departure; and (2) a cross relevance, a complementing and interlocking of their varied results, and a common faith in their methods. The common points of departure which Llewellyn notes may be summarized as: (1) a conception of law in flux; (2) a conception of law as a means to social ends; (3) a conception of society in flux; (4) the temporary divorce of *is* and *ought* for purposes of study; (5) a distrust of traditional legal rules and concepts; (6) a distrust of the importance given to prescriptive rules in reaching decisions; (7) a belief in the value of grouping cases in narrower categories; (8) an insistence on evaluation in terms of effects; and (9) insistence on "programmatic and sustained attacks along these lines."

29. The realists have, many of them, turned their attention directly to a frank statement of the lawyer's procedure. See Isaacs, *How Lawyers Think* (1923) 23 Columbia Law Review 555; Radin, *The Education of a Lawyer* (1937) 25 California Law Review 676; Moore and Sussman, *The Lawyer's Law* (1932) 41 Yale Law Journal 566, 567. "An endeavor to understand the field of law must begin with the activities and ways of thinking of the practitioner."

30. See especially Frank, *What the Courts Do in Fact* (1932) 24 Illinois Law Review 645 ff.

31. Austin, Jurisprudence (4th ed.) I, 182.

32. See, for example, one of the earlier realists, Bingham, *What is the Law?* (1912) 11 Michigan Law Review 1, 109. See also Hale, *Some Challenges to Conventional Legal Views* (1923) 9 American Bar Assoc. Journal 330; Isaacs, *The Law and the Facts* (1922) 22 Columbia Law Review 1. For the emphasis upon scientific method, see Yntema, *The Rational Basis of Legal Science* (1931) 31 Columbia Law Review 925; Patterson, *Can Law Be Scientific?* (1930) 25 Illinois Law Review 121; Llewellyn, *Legal Tradition and the Social Science Method* in Essays on Research in the Social Sciences (1931); Douglas and Thomas, *The Business Failure Project—a Study in Methodology* (1930) 39 Yale Law Journal 1013 (1931) 40 Yale Law Journal 1034; Oliphant, *Current Discussions of Legal Methodology* (1921) 7 American Bar Assoc. Journal 241; Radin, *Scientific Method and the Law* (1931) 19 California Law Review 164; Cook, *Scientific Method and the Law* (1927) 13 American Bar Assoc. Journal 303. See the bibliography of realism, "Realistic Jurisprudence," at the end and note the many studies concerned with this problem of an empirical methodology.

33. For an earlier selective bibliography of actual work done on law by realists, see Llewellyn, *Some Realism about Realism* (1931) 44 Harvard Law Review 1222.

34. Especially the connection of property with tax power and such questions as who "owned" what within a corporate structure.

35. For the economic emphasis, see Hale, Legal Factors in Economic Society (1937) and *Force and the State: a Comparison of "Political" and "Economic" Compulsion* (1935); 35 Columbia Law Review 149; Hall, Theft, Law and Society (1935); Llewellyn, *Through Title to Contract and a Bit Beyond* (1938) 15 New York University Law Quarterly Review 159; Pickett, *Nicknames and Unfair Competition* (1935) 35 Columbia Law Review 33.

For the sociological emphasis, see Moore, *The Rational Basis of Legal Institutions* (1923) 23 Columbia Law Review 609 and *An Institutional Approach to the Law of Commercial Banking* (1928) 38 Yale Law Journal 703; Frank, *Institutional Analysis of Law* (1924) 24 Columbia Law Review 480; Moore, Sussman, and Corstvet, *Drawing against Uncollected Checks* (1935) 45 Yale Law Journal 1, 260; Cairns, Law and the Social Sciences (1935) and *Law and Anthropology* (1931) 31 Columbia Law Review 32; Llewellyn. *On Warranty of Quality* (1936) 36 Columbia Law Review 699, (1937) 37 Columbia Law Review 341.

For the psychological emphasis, see Robinson, Law and the Lawyers (1935); especially Chapters IV-VIII; Frank, Law and the Modern Mind (1930); Cook, *Act Intention and Motive in the Criminal Law* (1916) 26 Yale Law Journal 645; Burtt, Legal Psychology (1931).

36. The best illustrations of this are in Llewellyn. *The Rule of Law in Our Case Law of Contract* (1938) 47 Yale Law Journal 1243 and *Our Case Law of Contract*: *Offer and Acceptance* (1938) 48 Yale Law Journal 1, 9 ff.

37. For a strong statement of this, see Nelles, *Toward Legal Understanding* (1934) 34 Columbia Law Review 862, 1041. On the other hand, that the realist is interested in logical analysis and symmetry is clearly evident in realists like Corbin and Goble. See, for example, Goble, *A Redefinition of Basic Legal Terms* (1935) 35 Columbia Law Review 535 and *Negative Legal Relations Reexamined* (1922) 6 Illinois Law Review 36; Corbin, *Rights and Duties* (1924) 33 Yale Law Journal 501 and *Legal Analysis and Terminology* (1919) 29 Yale Law Journal 163.

38. For a forceful statement of this, see Oliphant, *The Return to Stare Decisis* (1928) 14 American Bar Assoc. Journal 70. He puts the issue as a shift from *stare dicta* to *stare decisis*.

39. Robinson, Law and the Lawyers (1935) 327: "Obviously law is not identical with economics, sociology or psychology, but insistence on its *over-and-aboveness* has tended to insulate it from those very facts needed in the design of effective social control."

40. Cohen, *A Critical Review of the Last Hundred Years of American Jurisprudence* in Law, a Century of Progress, 1835-1935 (1937) II, 266; Kantorowicz, *Some Rationalism about Realism* (1934) 43 Yale Law Journal 1240; Kocourek (a criticism of Bingham), (1913) 9 Illinois Law Review 138; Pound, *The Call for a Realistic Jurisprudence* (1931) 44 Harvard Law Review 697; Dickinson, *Legal Rules and the Process of Decision* (1931) 79 University of Pennsylvania Law Review 833 and *Legal Rules: Their Application and Elaboration* (1931) 79 University of Pennsylvania Law Review 1052. Dickinson's criticisms of the realists' conception of rules, like most of the others, rested upon a misunderstanding; the realists for their part have heartily accepted his own fine analysis of rules and principles. Fuller, *American Legal Realism* (1934) 82 University of Pennsylvania Law Review 429, makes a fair evaluation of realism except that he wrongly insists that the realist is overemphasizing the rightness of the actual. Kennedy has been the most persistent critic of legal realism. See, for example, his *Realism, What Next?* (1938) 7 Fordham Law Review 203. See the bibliography, "Criticism and Evaluation of Legal Realism," at the end for a list of his articles criticizing realism. The fairest criticism is probably by Cordozo, who at the time of writing was not sure whether he was a realist or not. His sympathy, however, permitted him to go to the heart of realism and to avoid the obvious misunderstandings. See his address printed in (1932) 55 New York Bar Association

Reports 263. For other critical estimates of realism, see the Selective Bibliography.

41. Bingham, *What is the Law?* (1912) 11 Michigan Law Review 1; this was followed by *Science and the Law* (1913) 25 Green Bag 162, by *Legal Philosophy and the Law* (1914) 9 Illinois Law Review 98, and by *The Nature and Importance of Legal Possession* (1915) 13 Michigan Law Review 535. "Rules are not outside the mind and are not discovered; they are psychological. Ideas are not copies of the world; language is not a copy of either." There are no "first" realists in law, but Bingham came close to achieving the title by virtue of the very vigor of his writing. It should be noted that Bingham recognized the necessary role of generalizations in law. "The intelligent direction of human action," writes Bingham in 11 Michigan Law Review 35, "necessarily involves the use of generalizations. Generalizations therefore have a causative force in producing legal effects . . . but they are not the whole field."

42. Frank, Law and the Modern Mind (1930); see Appendix X to the 1931 reprint and his reference to the book in Save America First (1938).

43. Arnold is discussed below, pp. 15-17, 108-13.

44. See also Stone, *Pound's Theory of Justice, a Critique* (1935) 20 Iowa Law Review 531.

45. *Functional Nonsense and the Transcendental Approach* (1936) 5 Fordham Law Review 272, 276. See Hutchins, *Autobiography of an Ex-Law Student* (1934) 7 American Law School Review 1051.

46. Kennedy, *Pragmatism as a Philosophy of Law* (1924) 9 Marquette Law Review 63 and *Men or Laws* (1932) 2 Brooklyn Law Review 11.

FOOTNOTES TO III-D

1. Frank, Law and the Modern Mind (1930); Llewellyn, *A Realistic Jurisprudence: The Next Step* (1930) 30 Col. L. Rev. 430; Pound, *The Call for a Realist Jurisprudence* (1931) 44 Harv. L. Rev. 697; Llewellyn, *Some Realism about Realism —Responding to Dean Pound*, 44 id. 1222.

2. *Id* at 1256.

3. Bridgman, The Logic of Modern Physics (1927) 33; Planck, The Universe in the Light of Modern Physics (Johnston's trans. 1931) 14, 40. And the psychologists concur. See report of Dr. Pieron's address before American Ass'n for Advancement of Science (July 8, 1933) 116 Lit. Dig. 19.

4. Hutchins, *The Autobiography of an Ex-Law Student* (1934) 7 Am. L. School Rev. 1051, 1055. Whereupon Dean Pound was heard to remark: "That's where the conservatives have been for thirty years. . . ." But see remarks of Llewellyn, in Handbook of Ass'n of Am. Law Schools (1933) 119.

5. Frank, *Realism in Jurisprudence* (1934) 7 Am. L. School Rev. 1063.

6. See, *e. g.*, Oliphant and Hewitt, Introduction to Rueff, From the Physical to the Social Sciences (1929) (but experimental jurisprudence need not be limited to the methods there suggested); Holmes, *Law in Science and Science in Law*, in Collected Legal Papers (1920) 210, 225, 226; *The Path of the Law*, id. 167, 187; Frankfurter, Llewellyn, Sunderland, *The Conditions for, and the Aims and Methods of Legal Research*, in Handbook of Ass'n of Am. Law Schools (1929) 26; Pound, *The Scope and Purpose of Sociological Jurisprudence* (1912) 25 Harv. L. Rev. 489, 514. See also Vacca, Diritto Sperimentale (1923).

7. The new physics seems to have thrown much doubt on this postulate insofar as it applies to particular molecules or atoms; but as a statistical law describing the actions of grosser matter it still seems to hold. *Planck, Where is Science Going?* (Murphy's trans. 1932).

8. See Swann, *What is Science?*, in Essays on Research in the Social Science (1931) 11.

9. 2 Beard and Beard, The Rise of the American Civilization (1930) 761-803.

10. See Pound, *Law and the Science of Law in Recent Theories* (1934) 7 Am. L. School Rev. 1057, 1060 (1934) 43 Yale L. J. 525, 532; Lauterpacht, *Kelsen's Pure Science of Law*, in Modern Theories of Law (1933) 105.

11. Spengler, *Social Science Becomes Exact* (June, 1930) Am. Mercury 202; Beard, *Method in the Study of Political Science as an Aspect of Social Science*, in Essays on Research in the Social Science (1931) 51, 59; Oliphant, *Facts, Opinions, and Value—Judgments* (1932) 10 Tex. L. Rev. 127.

12. Yntema, *The Rational Basis of Legal Science* (1931) 31 Col. L. Rev. 925.

13. *Cf.* Morris R. Cohen, *Philosophy and Legal Science* (1932) 32 Col. L. Rev. 1103; Felix Cohen, *The Ethical Basis of Legal Criticism* (1931) 41 Yale L. J. 201.

14. Hutchins, *loc. cit. supra* note 4.

15. See Angell, *The Value of Sociology to Law* (1933) 31 Mich. L. Rev. 512.

16. Hutcheson, *The Judgment Intuitive: The Functions of the "Hunch" in Judicial Decision* (1929) 14 Corn. L. Q. 274; *Lawyer's Law, and the Little, Small Dice* (1932) 7 Tulane L. Rev. 1.

17. Harno, *Theory, Experience, Experimentation and the Logical Method* (1931) 17 A. B. A. J. 659, 663.

18. Survey of Criminal Justice in Cleveland (1921-1922).

19. The first two volumes by Sheldon and Eleanor T. Glueck and by Warner are now available. Glueck and Glueck, One Thousand Juvenile Delinquents (1934); Warner, Crime and Criminal Statistics in Boston (1934).

20. Some of this material may be found by reference to

Current Research in Law (Johns Hopkins Institute of Law 1929, 1930).

21. Report on the Enforcement of Prohibition (1931) 85 *et seq.*, and see especially Mr. Lemann's dissent, at 139 *et seq.*

22. See, *e.g.*, Sedgwick, Principles of Sanitary Science and the Public Health (1920).

23. For interesting evidence of this nature in the field of sanitary laws, see Rosenau, Preventive Medicine and Hygiene (1917) 35, 43.

24. Watson, Psychological Care of Infant and Child (1928); and note the experiments cited by Thomas, *The Relation of Research to the Social Progress,* in Essays on Research in the Social Sciences (1931) 175 *et seq.*

25. Bechterev, General Principles of Human Reflexology (Murphy's trans. 1932) 63 *et seq.;* Heidbreder, Seven Psychologies (1933) 247 *et seq.*

26. See Holmes, The Trend of the Race (1921) cc. II-V; Conklin, *Mechanism, Vitalism, and Teleology* (1921) 8 Rice Institute Pamphlet 351. The legislatures of this country have not been unmindful of the biological principles involved. See Landman, *The History of Human Sterilization in the United States—Theory, Statute, Adjudication* (1929) 23 Ill. L. Rev. 462.

27. Inbau, *Scientific Evidence in Criminal Courts* (1934) 24 J. Crim. L. 1140; (1933) *id.* 440, 441; Keeler, *Debunking the "Lie-Detector"* (1934) 25 *id.* 153. See also Luria, The Nature of Human Conflicts (Gantt's trans. 1932), and numerous experiments there cited.

28. Much of the confusion which has arisen about the realist point of view has developed around the attitude of the practitioner. Predictability in this sense is, of course, far beyond the scope of any present-day science, and if it could be perfected would entirely eliminate the practice of law before courts, if not the courts themselves.

29. We are dealing here with the science of law and not its administration. The problem of adjusting a rule of law to an individual case is one of administration only; but even here, careful observations by the jurist might prove exceedingly valuable to the judge or practitioner engaged in individualizing the law.

30. See Planck, *op. cit., supra* note 7.

31. For example, Gresham's law of the circulation of money, the business cycle, the law of supply and demand, and the like.

32. The possibilities of work along the line of criminal statistics, together with numerous citations to material now in print, are set out by Robinson, *History of Criminal Statistics* (1908-1933) (1933) 24 J. Crim. L. 125.

33. Lasswell, Propaganda Technique in the World War (1927) 81, 87, 131, 214 *et seq.;* Ponsonby, Falsehood in War-Time (1928).

34. Chase and Schlink, Your Money's Worth (1927).

35. Seldes, You Can't Print That (1929) 194-212.

36. See Thompson, Confessions of the Power Trust (1932) pts. VI-VII.

37. Art here is used in the sense of applied science as distinguished from pure science; thus, physics is a science, engineering the art; chemistry the science and chemical engineering an art.

38. See Lumley, The Propaganda Menace (1933) 363 *et seq.;* Moore and Sussman, *The Lawyer's Law* (1932) 41 Yale L. J. 566.

39. See Llewellyn's excellent comment, *supra* note 1, 30 Col. L. Rev. at 445.

40. Outlines of Lectures on Jurisprudence (4th ed. 1928) 60 *et seq.*

41. It may be that there is no such thing as an interest of society in the sense that society demands or even needs something; perhaps the whole thing should be viewed as individual interests of members of a larger unit known as society. This is a philosophical and psychological problem not capable of immediate answer, but it offers interesting experimental possibilities.

42. Note here the important distinction between "Is and Ought", Llewellyn, *Legal Tradition and Social Science Method —A Realist's Critique,* in Essays on Research in the Social Sciences (1931) 89, 101. This difficulty is forcefully brought out in Dickinson, *The Law Behind Law* (1929) 29 Col. L. Rev. 113, 285, 289 *et seq.*

43. A sharp distinction must be drawn between jurisprudential laws as used here and the many uses which the term has. (1) Law in its usual sense is a means of social control, *i. e.,* the statute, ordinance, court decision, traffic light, *etc.;* it is in no sense scientific. It may or may not be the result of a scientific process of experimentation but it is seldom called jural law. (2) Then there is the so-called "Law Behind Law", *i. e.,* the ideal "Natural Law" rule which all law as a means of social control should approximate. The existence of such a law is ably refuted by Dickinson, *supra* note 42. (3) There is the so-called scientific law which merely states that under given circumstances there will be a given sequence of events, *e. g.,* an unsupported object will fall to the ground, or, perhaps a highly unpopular law cannot be enforced against the will of an actual majority. The term jurisprudential laws is used here in the third sense. See, *e. g.,* Rueff, From the Physical to the Social Sciences 68 *et seq.* But it is not at all clear that such laws are subject to the limitations asserted there. See *id.* at 70 *et seq.*

44. Note Mr. McDougal's very pertinent questions on this point. Handbook of Ass'n of Am. Law Schools (1933) 119-20.

45. Jurisprudence as a science of ethical values, norms, and the like, can have no value in the present state of research equipment beyond philosophical speculation. Such speculation may be exceedingly interesting and may result in highly sug-

gestive working hypotheses, but it can never have any true
scientific value until it is put to the acid test of practical application in the form of social control applied under the careful
observation of scientists. Here pragmatic ethics may become a
living reality through the development of the technique of
experimental jurisprudence.

46. John Chipman Gray, The Nature and Sources of Law
305 (1921).

47. *Id.* at 287-88.

48. Benjamin N. Cardozo, The Nature of the Judicial
Process 108 (1925).

49. Cohen, *Jus Naturale Revividum,* 25 Philosophical Rev.
761, 766 (1916).

50. Eugen Ehrlich, Fundamental Principles of the Sociology
of Law 38, 52-53 (Moll transl. 1936).

51. Roscoe Pound, Law and Morals 113 (1923).

52. Kantorowicz, *Legal Science: A Summary of Its Methodology,* 28 Colum. L. Rev. 679, 696 (1928).

53. Frankfurter, *The Job of a Supreme Court Justice,* N. Y.
Times Magazine, Nov. 28, 1954, p. 14.

54. This, of course, is consistent with the broader teleological view of law, *i. e.,* that it should conform to human purpose. See Cowan, *Postulates for Experimental Jurisprudence,*
9 Rutgers L. Rev. 404, 414 (1955).

55. A notable exception is the work of Eugen Ehrlich. See
Professor Page's account of it, *Professor Ehrlich's Czernowitz
Seminar of Living Law,* Ass'n of American Law Schools, Pro-
ceedings of the Fourteenth Annual Meeting 46 (1914).

56. This term is utilized by John Austin. See his Jurisprudence Lecture V, at 187 (4th ed. 1873).

57. This term was employed by Judge Learned Hand. See
Johnson v. United States, 186 F. 2d 588, 590 (2d Cir. 1951).

58. Repouille v. United States, 165 F. 2d 152 (2d Cir.
1947).

59. Benjamin N. Cardozo, The Paradoxes of Legal Science
37 (1928).

60. The account appeared in Time, May 30, 1955, p. 13,
col. 1.

61. 164 F. 2d 163 (2d Cir. 1947).

62. 165 F. 2d at 153 (2d Cir. 1947).

63. 186 F. 2d 588, 590 (2d Cir. 1951).

64. On the role of analogy generally, see Edward H. Levi,
An introduction to Legal Reasoning (1949). See also Pound,
op. cit. supra note 5 at 65.

65. We shall be able to demonstrate later (in our final
report) that it would not be economically or otherwise infeas-
ible to undertake such a poll of sentiment in key areas of
policy where the views of the community are crucial to the
decisional process.

66. The interdisciplinary research team which conducted
the experiment combined the experience and skills of lawmen

and sociologists, among others, and utilized a staff of rigorously trained interviewers.

67. A pilot study of these postulates was published as *A Postulate Set for Experimental Jurisprudence* in Philosophy of Science Vol. 18, No. 1 (1951) to test the reaction of scientific methodologists to the form of the postulates, though not to their jurisprudential content. Certain philosophical references contained there are omitted here.

68. Beginning with the Non-Aristotelian logics and the Non-Euclidean geometries. Consult C. I. Lewis, Survey of Symbolic Logic (1918).

69. Wolff, Jus Naturae (1740-48).

70. John Dewey, Logic, the Theory of Inquiry 16 (1938).

71. See E. A. Singer, Jr., *Philosophy of Experiment,* Symposium Vol. 1, No. 2 (1930); H. B. Smith, *Postulates of Empirical Thought,* in Philosophical Essays in Honor of Edgar Arthur Singer, Jr. 24 (1942); E. A. Singer, Jr., Mind as Behavior (1924); C. W. Churchman, Theory of Experimental Inference (1948); R. L. Ackoff, Design of Social Research (1953).

72. Outlines of Lectures on Jurisprudence 168-186 (5th ed. 1943).

73. Stone, Province and Function of Law 367 (1946).

74. On the question of what is happening to the historic relation between jurisprudence on the one hand and science and philosophy on the other see Huntington Cairns, *Philosophy as Jurisprudence* in Interpretations of Modern Legal Philosophies 52 (1947).

75. C. W. Churchman argues these matters at length in Theory of Experimental Inference (1948) especially in cc. X to XIII.

76. The right of the chancellor to "experiment" with the operation of the decree illustrates the point. H. L. McClintock, Handbook of the Principles of Equity 32 (2d ed. 1948).

77. Hans Kelsen, Society and Nature (1943). On the point generally see Werner Jaeger, Paideia, The Ideals of Greek Culture (1939-44).

78. The theoretical resolution of the paradox of mechanism and purpose is worked out with exactness by E. A. Singer, Jr. in *Logico-Historical Study of Mechanism*, in Studies in the History of Science, Univ. of Penn. Bicentennial Conference (1941).

INDEX

INDEX

DOCKET SERIES

No. 1—THE HOLMES READER—Opinions, speeches, biographical study of the great American Jurist, collected and edited with illuminating commentary by Julius J. Marke, Librarian, New York University School of Law.

No. 2—THE FREEDOM READER—A collection of historic decisions on momentous questions in the development of our constitutional and administrative law, collected and edited by Edwin S. Newman, attorney and authority on civil rights and civil liberties.

No. 3—THE MARSHALL READER—A collection of the decisions, writings, speeches and other pertinent works by and about the Father of American Constitutional Law, John Marshall, collected and edited by Erwin C. Surrency, Librarian, Temple University Law School, in the Marshall Bicentennial year.

No. 4—THE WILSON READER—A collection of writings by and about the former President of the United States, Woodrow Wilson, with emphasis on his contribution to international law and political science. Compiled by Frances Farmer, Librarian, University of Virginia Law School.

No. 5—THE DANIEL WEBSTER READER—A collection of writings by and about one of the fascinating characters in American politics. Compiled by Bertha Rothe, Librarian, George Washington University Law School.

No. 6—THE MEDICO-LEGAL READER—A collection of readings on the areas of joint concern to the medical and legal professions. Compiled by Samuel Polsky, Director of the Philadelphia Medico-Legal Institute, and Associate Professor of Law, Temple University. Sponsored by Temple University Schools of Law and Medicine.

No. 7—THE BRANDEIS READER—A collection of writings by and about the eminent Supreme Court Justice. Compiled with editorial comment by Ervin Pollack, Librarian, Ohio State University Law School, and author of a number of legal treatises.

No. 8—THE AMERICAN JURISPRUDENCE READER— Edited by T. A. Cowan. Ready October, 1956.

Available individually or on standing order.
No. 1-3, published 1955   No. 4-8, published 1956
Library edition, cloth, $3.50 each   Paper, $1.00 each